THE PIONEERS OF
WEST HAM UNITED
1895-1960

THE PIONEERS OF
WEST HAM UNITED
1895-1960

PHILIP STEVENS

DB PUBLISHING

Acknowledgements

I acknowledge the generous help given by so many friends and colleagues in the production of this book, particularly Steve Marsh and Stuart Allen for access to their extensive collection of everything claret and blue. I am especially grateful to Steve Marsh for providing the foreword. My thanks go to Jenni Munro-Collins at the Newham Local Studies Unit for guiding me through old newspapers and council minutes. Debbie Silver at West Ham United has been a great source of encouragement and I must thank my great friend Mark Cripps for indulging me as usual and for his honest criticism.

Very special thanks go to Jean, David and Martin Musgrove, Susan Dick and Yvonne Lyall for their time and allowing me access to the archives of Malcolm Musgrove, John Dick and John Lyall.

The book is dedicated to the memory of these three great West Ham pioneers.

First published in Great Britain in 2012 by The Derby Books Publishing Company Limited,
3 The Parker Centre, Derby, DE21 4SZ.

This paperback edition published in Great Britain in 2013 by DB Publishing,
an imprint of JMD Media Ltd

ISBN 978-1-78091-159-5

Printed and bound in the UK by Copytech (UK) Ltd Peterborough

Contents

Foreword

I have supported West Ham United since the age of 15, for most fans the team you support is bred in you from an early age, but for me I came from a family line that had no interest in the game whatsoever. It took a school friend to persuade me to attend my first ever football match. Thankfully for me he was a Hammers fan although it could have been far worse as I grew up in the St George area of east London which is nearer to The Den than Upton Park.

I can still recall the team that day in August 1968: Ferguson, Bonds, Charles, Peters, Stephenson, Moore, Redknapp, Boyce, Dear, Hurst and Sissons. A Geoff Hurst goal sealed a 1–0 victory over Nottingham Forest. Even a 1–4 home reversal against the Toffee Men of Everton two days later did not dampen my enthusiasm for my new-found passion. Those magical days and nights on the North Bank stayed in the recesses of my mind forever. I did not know it at the time but those events would ultimately shape my life and catapult me into the historical field of collecting and recording West Ham United memorabilia.

I may have been a late starter but I have more than made up for it in the last 43 years. Firstly, I am a founder member of the West Ham United Autograph Society, whose aim is to obtain a signature of the Brylcreem footballers back to the formation of the club. Secondly, I have created two websites dedicated to recording memorabilia associated with the Hammers. With the help of fellow programme collector Stuart Allen, I aim to establish a pictorial history of the club using the Hammers programmes of the day.

Night matches at fortress Upton Park were something special in the 1970s and 80s. The European Cup-Winners' Cup games against Den Haag and especially the Eintracht Frankfurt semi-final second leg will never be beaten for sheer football, noise and electrifying atmosphere. The Hammers also experimented with a Friday night game against Cambridge United in the lead-up to Christmas 1979, although only 11,721 were there on that snowy 'Jingle Bells' night. But they were privileged to witness the legendary Hammers DJ Bill Remfry get everybody dancing and bouncing by playing some memorable tunes to entertain the faithful, including, I remember, Mike Oldfield's 'In Dulci Jubilo' – I can see you all dancing now – an unforgettable night. If only we could have played all our home games under the Upton Park floodlights we would surely have been champions in 1986.

Those nights were lost forever with the redevelopment of the Boleyn Ground in the early 1990s, after Lord Justice Taylor's report into the Hillsborough disaster. The report recommended that football grounds in England and Scotland should rip out their old concrete terraces and replace them with smart, all-seater stadiums – the atmosphere at the Boleyn has never been quite the same since. A new chapter in the West Ham United story will start to unfold in 2013 with the move to the Olympic Park in Stratford. The stadium is unlikely to replicate the atmosphere that those heady nights at the Boleyn produced. New venue, new heroes, new hope…

To be a Hammers supporter is not about how many pieces of silverware there are in the trophy cabinet; you will need to support the likes of the Reds or the Blues for that. For me and many thousands like me we have been brought up on a diet of claret and blue.

It's more than a game – it's a way of life…

Steve Marsh

www.theyflysohigh.co.uk (Memorabilia associated with the Hammers)
www.whu-programmes.co.uk (A pictorial history from the West Ham United programmes of the day)

Introduction

West Ham United is a football club rich in tradition and history. Located deep in London's East End, the Hammers' Boleyn Ground has become the beating heart of this complex and often troubled part of the capital. Down the years the club has gained a well-deserved reputation for tactical innovation and an attacking, free-flowing style of football. Throughout the 1960s the Hammers enchanted football lovers across Europe. West Ham's own passionate supporters adore their team's purist approach and are capable of creating an electric atmosphere that is unique to Upton Park. The club is a product of the social and industrial landscape of East London. The origins of West Ham United are to be found in the heavy industry of the London docks on the north side of the River Thames. When Arnold Hills, owner of the Thames Ironworks and Shipbuilding Company, formed a works football team in 1895 to improve his firm's failing industrial relations, he would never have believed that one day his team would win a major European trophy and provide three players for England's only World Cup win in 1966.

In the early days of the club all players were employees of the firm. This rule was gradually relaxed as the club's fortunes improved, but to this day local players have formed the heart of the team. This has helped to generate support in densely populated areas like Stratford, Canning Town, Plaistow, Silverton, East Ham and West Ham. A combination of local players and fanatical support is the key to the passionate intensity of the North Bank on match days at the Boleyn.

It will be interesting to Hammers supporters today that Thames Ironworks folded due to financial difficulties, when the club's founder no longer felt able to support the club through his company. The founder's money had helped establish the club and when he pulled the plug, West Ham United arose out of the ashes. Mr Hills' Thames Ironworks FC played with distinction in the Southern League, the London League and the FA Cup. In the late 19th century the scene was set – with a few mishaps on the way – for a proud history of professional football in East London which will reach its rich peak in the Olympic Stadium in 2013.

The Essential History of West Ham United by Blows and Hogg (2000) provides the most reliable general history of the club. John Powles has written the definitive account of the Thames Ironworks FC. His book, *Irons in the Blood* (2005), is a detailed study of the early years of professional football in East London and compelling reading for all Hammers fans with an eye for the club's great traditions. Powles' book also includes brief sketches of the careers of the early pioneers. Tony Hogg's sumptuous *Who's Who of West Ham United* (2006) provides short, illustrated histories of all the club's players up to 2005. The aim of this book is to provide readers with more extended versions of the lives and playing careers of the characters who shaped the fortunes of West Ham United.

West Ham United has always been a blue-collar club, set in a strong working-class area. The fans are proud of being East Enders, proud of their club, its history and achievements. Of course, in many respects West Ham is no different from any other major English football club with roots in working-class culture. However, there is something special about the Hammers and their historic commitment to football's highest ideals. The emergence of such wonderful players as Bobby Moore, Martin Peters, Geoff Hurst and Trevor Brooking at West Ham can be attributed to the club's faith in exciting, attacking football.

Unfortunately for its proud supporters, the club's adherence to attacking football has brought as much heartache and frustration as joy and celebration. Joyous moments in European competitions and the FA Cup have been tempered by too many losing relegation battles and early Cup exits to lower League sides. It is not for nothing that a key line in the club anthem 'Bubbles' is the phrase 'fortunes always hiding'. Life for West Ham United simply echoes the lives of thousands of people in one of the poorest parts of the capital…'just like my dreams they fade and die'.

Despite the extremes of fortune over the past 120 years the story of West Ham United has been one of accomplishment and success. From its hard-edged industrial roots in East London at the end of the 19th century, the club has progressed to become an important member of the top flight of English football and, on one occasion, was triumphant in Europe. The club's history is a romantic story of a works team from one of the toughest industrial areas of Europe winning the West Ham Charity Cup in the first ever season and conquering Europe 100 years later.

West Ham has changed with the changing times. The Chicken Run of blessed memory, the hot Bovril and shabby tea bars are all gone and the Boleyn is now a smart modern stadium in keeping with the glitzy image of the Premier League. Today the club pays its modern players wages that are beyond the wildest dreams of the loyal fans, but their new-found riches have not brought success on the field in recent years.

East London itself has changed. The vintage Hammers and their fans would never have dreamed that their neighbourhoods around Whitechapel and Shoreditch would attract affluent artists, bankers and media types who have transformed this previously depressing part of the capital. But the core of West Hams fans has never been drawn from the now trendy Silicon Roundabout in Tower Hamlets, but further east in multi-cultural Newham. So it is entirely right that the club should move to the new Olympic Stadium in Stratford following the 2012 Olympic Games. The dreams of the pioneers would have been fully realised, their beloved club playing its home games at the nation's premier sporting arena. The world is coming to East London and part of the Olympic legacy will be that its football club will have a brand new 60,000-capacity arena as its home ground. The future is bright, although it would be typical West Ham if they spent the first season in Stratford outside the top flight of English football, following an all-too-familiar losing relegation battle in 2010–11.

The book might have carried the title *Before Bobby Moore*. One of the greatest players in world football and the captain of England's sole World Cup winning team remains, for most football lovers, the iconic image of West Ham United. Moore's influence on the club and its supporters is as strong today as it was in his playing days. But as the move to the new Olympic Stadium approaches, it is time to remember the great players before Bobby Moore, those who took the club to the point where it was able to produce one of the best footballers of all time.

Let us meet some of the people who made it all possible…

Charlie Dove: the Irons' first star footballer

The definition of an early pioneer of West Ham United is a player or manager who represents the best elements of the club's football philosophy. He was most likely to have been born in the East End and to have made a significant contribution to the club's development either on or off the field. Such characters were local heroes during their career and left an indelible mark on Hammers' history. Such a figure was our first pioneer, the irrepressible Charles 'Charlie' Dove.

Dove was born in Millwall (then in Essex) in 1877 and as a schoolboy captained Park School, leading his team to victory in two

local competitions. On leaving school at the age of 13, Dove signed for Forest Swift Juniors before moving to Plaistow Melville in 1892, where he was quickly named club captain. He later made several appearances for South West Ham and was widely regarded as one of the best East London players of his generation.

The Hammers enjoyed a long and productive relationship with Park School from Dove's time right up to the start of World War Two. West Ham historian John Helliar's careful research shows that the school's Saturday morning matches regularly attracted crowds of over 1,000 to the Ham Park Road ground in West Ham. In the 1921 Final of the English Schools Championship, over 10,000 watched West Ham schools beat Liverpool 3–2 at the

Boleyn. One of the goalscorers for the home side that day was Jimmy Barrett, who went on to enjoy a successful career with the club. It is clear from the local response to these games that school football was extremely popular in the East End in the early 20th century.

In the 1890s Trinity School was used by the Hammers for training purposes and for receptions after important matches. Park School produced Dove, Jimmy Barrett and the great Syd Puddefoot, while the club's current ground was leased from a local public school in 1904. There is a further interesting school link in the close friendship between Charlie Paynter and the Park School head teacher, Cornelius Beal. There is a myth that Beal, who was a great Hammers supporter, wrote the club's famous club song, *I'm forever Blowing Bubbles*. However, thanks to John Helliar, we know that the song was a big hit in America and later became a popular song in the British music halls. There are numerous recordings of the song dated around the 1920s, including one by the jazz singer, Dorothy Ward.

What is true is that Cornelius Beal adapted the words of the song so it could be used as the club anthem. Of course, *Bubbles* was a famous painting by the pre-Raphaelite artist Millais, and the picture became nationally famous when it was used to advertise Pears soap. Our Hammers-supporting headmaster had a boy in the same team as Jim Barrett who was known, because of his curly hair, as Billy 'Bubbles' Murray. From there the song began to seep into the consciousness of the Chicken Run in particular and soon the whole ground was singing 'Bubbles' in the final minutes before kick-off.

The Beckton Gas Works Silver Band picked up the crowd's adoption of the song in the 1920s and began to play 'Bubbles' in their pre-match spot. The bandleader said at the time: 'We played 'Bubbles' and it quickly became a favourite with the crowd. If we did not play the song the crowd would sing it – we always played it before kick-off.'

Successive brass and silver bands have continued this tradition until the British Legion band played their last warm-up session in the 1970s. Later versions have been jazzed up, but the essential song remains unaltered from the Park School days. Even today young Mark Noble, who was born round the corner from the ground, can be heard to sing 'Bubbles' in the tunnel before home matches – much to the delight of his bemused foreign teammates.

Although Charlie Dove would not have heard supporters singing 'Bubbles' in his days as a player, his school had a major influence on the club's heritage. Soon after leaving school, young Charlie joined the Thames Ironworks and Shipbuilding Company as an apprentice riveter and was thrilled to be selected for the firm's newly-formed men's football club. Not even the half a crown subscription, a significant part of his weekly wage, could deter the enthusiastic youngster from the chance to play men's football. His enthusiasm rubbed off on the senior players as the new club, much to the delight of founder Arnold Hills, went from strength to strength over the next five years.

The Thames Ironworks shipbuilding company occupied two sites at Blackwall and West Ham and at the height of its prosperity the family firm employed 6,000 people in the area.

The company was highly successful in the mid-19th century and built the country's first iron battleship, the *Warrior*, in 1860. Arnold Hills, a devout Christian, took over the company from his father and made himself a fortune before the firm's outdated technology and the shallow water of the River Thames forced shipbuilding out of the London docks. HMS *Thunderer* was the last ship to be built by Hills' men before the closure of the yard in 1912.

Concerned about the effects on production of industrial disputes and remembering the nearby Bryant and May's Match Girls strike 10 years earlier, Hills introduced a works football team as part of an attempt to improve the morale of his staff. He was aware that the two other major employers in the area, Bryant & May and Tate & Lyle, had introduced sports and social clubs in a similar attempt to develop good industrial relations. The company newsletter, the *Ironworks Gazette*, provides us with a flavour of the activities available to Hills' employees in the late 19th century. In addition to a full sports programme, there was a full range of classes, including Trigonometry, Calculus and Science. There were numerous clubs like the Operatic Society, Choral Group and String Band. Annual Sports Days were an enormous success and made, in Hills' words, 'a jolly good show'. The level and quality of these activities helps to destroy the popular myth perpetuated at the time and since about the so-called feckless, deserving poor of London's East End.

Hills' sporting initiative was an instant success as his football team quickly prospered. The new club entered the London League, the West Ham Charity Cup and even, cheekily, the FA Cup. Charlie Dove was at the heart of the side's success. In the June 1895 edition of the *Gazette* the editor wrote with an air of excitement that 'the first team has been entered for the English Cup, and I hope they make a good show'.

The Irons' first match was a friendly against Royal Ordnance on 7 September 1895 and ended in a 1–1 draw. This was followed by victories against Dartford, Manor Park, Streatham and Old St Stephens. Members of the side included Dove (apprentice riveter), Thomas Freeman (ship's fireman), Johnny Stewart (boilermaker), Walter Parks (clerk), Walter Tranter (boilermaker), James Lindsay (boilermaker), William Chapman (mechanical engineer), George Sage (boilermaker), George Gresham (ship's plater) and William Chamberlain (foreman blacksmith). In the early days of the club it was an absolute condition that all players were employed by the firm.

The new club's young hero was a highly effective and courageous midfielder and the best player in the short, five-year existence of Arnold Hills' team. Dove's buccaneering qualities might remind Hammers fans of their great hero of the 1970s, the incomparable Billy Bonds. Like Bonds, Dove could tackle, was good in the air and regularly covered every blade of grass on the pitch and he could really play. All these qualities mark Charlie Dove out as a prime candidate for elevation to pioneer status.

At 16, the likeable Dove was at home in the rough and tumble of men's senior football. Like many East End men right up until the 1960s, Charlie was always neatly turned out,

Tranter   Monteith   Craig

Lew Bowen   Allen   Dove   McEachrane   Grassam
Hunt   Corbett   Reid   Kaye   Fenton

WEST HAM UNITED FOOTBALL CLUB 1900 - 1901

Team group photograph from 1900–01.

with his trim moustache and slick hair. At six feet tall and weighing in at 12 stone the youngster was superbly fit, physically strong and a born leader. A genuine all-round talent, he played in most positions as a young player, including an appearance in goal for the Irons when, naturally, he kept a clean sheet. He later settled as a formidable old-fashioned right-half, a position where he could have the greatest impact on his team's performance and where he was to excel for Thames and later West Ham United. He was the only player to have appeared in all five seasons of the life of Thames Ironworks as a football club.

At a time when London League and Southern League players were beginning to receive payment, it is important to remember that Charlie Dove remained a genuine amateur footballer. He was a manager's dream. Strong and fearless, young Charlie had a heart as big as the pitch. In his first season for Thames he made 18 appearances and scored six goals – not bad for a young teenager playing with and against grown men. Billy Bonds scored a few important goals for the Hammers, but in his addition to great physical strength and undoubted skill Dove's surges into the opposition penalty area made him the more prolific goalscorer.

One occasion which reinforces Dove's status as an East End football legend was his performance in one of several floodlit matches played by the Irons in 1895. The club had erected a crude set of floodlights at the Old Castle Swifts ground in Hermit Road. Ten 2,000-candlepower bulbs were suspended on poles spaced around the pitch, all powered by an unreliable generator. Three thousand locals attended the game, showing the crowd potential of evening kick-offs. Barking Woodville were the visitors on that damp and cold January evening. To make it more visible in the semi-darkness, the match ball was regularly dipped in buckets of whitewash distributed around the touchline. Young Dove certainly saw the ball well that night as he powered through the Barking defence to score a hat-trick in the Irons' 6–2 victory.

John Powles refers to a report of the Barking match in the *West Ham Herald* in which an amused football correspondent wrote, 'Boys were swarming up over the fences for a free view when I put in an appearance. And what a smart man the Irons had at the gate. He seemed to think my ticket was a fraud...he turned it upside down, smelled it...but graciously passed me at last.' A little different from today's swipe card admission system adopted by most Premier League clubs.

With regular games against arch-rivals Millwall and London League champions the Grenadier Guards, gatemen needed to be vigilant if the matches were to make a profit, which fortunately they did. Arnold Hills' astute and far-sighted investment in a set of embryonic floodlights was rewarded.

As the Irons gained in confidence their results began to improve. In 1897–98 Hills' club won the London League Championship with Charlie Dove driving the team forward to victory after victory. The East Enders won their final game of the season against the 2nd Grenadier Guards to secure the title, edging out fellow challengers Brentford. The Irons had lost 0–1 to the West London side in the penultimate game of the season, a result which meant the title was undecided until the final match. The Brentford match at Shooters Field aroused a good deal of interest and one player in particular was singled out for attention. Charlie Dove was emerging as a real local hero, if not a full-blooded celebrity. Our young idol was the subject of a newspaper article in the *East Ham Echo* on 23 April 1898 which heaped praise on the young star: 'If not absolutely the finest right half-back in Essex, the subject of our sketch is undoubtedly one of the most brilliant men in the county in that position...He played centre-forward and full-back and it was not until he occupied every place...that his worth as a right-half was demonstrated.'

Combining exhausting full-time work with playing senior amateur football was bound to take its toll even on a super-fit youngster like Dove. Work in the London docks was physically exhausting with long hours and appalling conditions. Mr Hills at Thames was one of the more enlightened employers and actually lived in the East India Dock Road. But for young Charlie work as an apprentice in the Orchard Yard – and later as a fully-fledged shipwright – would have been extremely arduous. At home the Dove family lived in a cramped, back-to-back house often shared with his grandparents. By today's standards sanitary conditions were appalling, with a shared outdoor toilet and just one cold water standpipe for the whole street.

As Blows and Hogg (2000) confirm, 60 per cent of the population of Limehouse and Canning Town, in the heart of the docklands, lived below the poverty line. When it was available work was hard. London smog-type pollution was a constant winter hazard and sickness and unemployment were never far away. In difficult times work became tough to find and the call-on system for casual labourers did not help. As soon as the dock gates opened in the morning, men rushed to be first in line for work that day, with many disappointed.

In his study of poverty in London in the 19th century, Charles Booth wrote about the lives and home of one East End family which is in stark contrast to some of today's inhabitants of the trendier parts of the area.

> The man, Michael, is a casual dock labourer aged 38, in poor health, fresh from the infirmary. His wife of 43 is consumptive. A son of 18, who earns 8 shillings (40p) regular wages as a carman's boy, and two girls of 8 and 6, complete the family.
>
> Their house has four rooms, but they let two. Father and son dine from home. The Clergy send soup 2 or 3 days a week, and practically no meat is bought. It figures on the Sunday only. The food consists principally of bread, margarine, tea and sugar.

It is clear that the Doves were rather better off than this unfortunate family, with dad a skilled worker and Charlie learning the trade. But with wages of skilled dockers only around 20 to 30 shillings a week (£1–£1.50) and rent about eight shillings a month, life was very difficult and often harsh in the time of the Great Depression at the end of the 19th century. The Dock Strike of 1889 raised hourly earnings to the famous 'Dockers' Tanner', but we know that working hours were long and usually involved going in on Saturday mornings.

Despite the often appalling living and working conditions of the time, life for most East Enders, including the Dove family, was improving. Trade unions were becoming stronger and more confident. Music halls, libraries, swimming pools and leisure facilities were introduced by local authorities, although most people continued to use the public baths for their laundry. Later, cinemas and dance halls appeared all over the East End. Indoor swimming baths were boarded over in the winter months and used for concerts and dancing. Life was difficult, but often colourful as one modern writer describes: 'Men walked about with parrots on their shoulders, magnificent birds, pure scarlet, egg-yolk yellow, bright blue sky...The air on the corner of Martha Street hung sultry with the perfume of Arabian sherbet, and women in silks as bright as the parrots leaned out from doorways.' (Birch, 2011)

The introduction of a cheap rail service gave locals the opportunity for days out to Southend and Brighton. Despite the unforgiving efforts of trying to earn a living and the threat of the ever-present workhouse, a rich and varied culture was beginning to emerge in the East End, with football at its heart.

The growth of football has been the most enduring cultural development of the late 19th century in East London, with Thames Ironworks leading the way. The Irons were beginning to attract crowds of up to 5,000 people as new housing estates sprang up in Canning Town and the surrounding area. On Wanstead Flats, West Ham Park and Hackney Marshes, hundreds of park teams were involved in dozens of local leagues on Saturday afternoons and Sunday mornings.

Young Dove lived through these social developments as a young man and his five years at Thames, both as an employee and a footballer, make him a true claret and blue pioneer. In West Ham United's first season in 1900–01, the year the Irons club folded, Charlie played every game up to Christmas before his young frame failed him again. Dove was the Steven Gerrard of his day. His sheer physicality exposed his body to injury. The intensity of his game came at a price.

After missing much of 1901–02, Dove was sold to bitter rivals Millwall at the tender age of 22, much to the anger and disappointment of the club's growing number of fans. Charlie was a local hero and adored by football lovers in the East End. Even at the beginning of the 20th century professional football was a tough business and managers were forced to make hard and unsentimental decisions.

It is not surprising that the fans idolised Charlie Dove. The fact that he continued his apprenticeship at the Ironworks while committing himself wholeheartedly to his football endeared him even more to the club's supporters. Like his father before him, Dove was a conscientious worker and rose to the rank of shipwright. The combination of a physically demanding job and his wholehearted approach to his football finally ended his short career and he retired from the game in 1903 at the age of 24. He played 120 first-team matches for the Irons and was arguably the greatest influence on the team in those formative years.

The whole Dove family were committed to the success of the Irons. Charlie's father George was a ship's carpenter at Thames Ironworks – a tough but high-status job. But he still had the energy and enthusiasm to train the players in the evenings, while pursuing his own career as a professional sprinter at weekends. Local wisdom has it that George Dove was responsible for the Irons and later the Hammers, acquiring the famous claret and blue kit. In the summer of 1899 he took part in an athletics meeting in Birmingham close to Villa Park. For a side wager George took on a group of Villa players in a 100 yards sprint which the Londoner won with ease. Having no money to pay the bet, the Villa players gave Dove a set of their club's claret and blue strip and as they say, the rest is history. Charlie's dad set his son a wonderful example – what a role model!

Our first pioneer was a true hero and an example to the excessively well-paid players of the modern era. I like to think young Charlie was an engaging character, popular with his teammates and his family. The East End should be proud of Dove for his contribution to the sudden emergence of Thames Ironworks as a major force in London amateur and professional football. In many ways a more appropriate modern comparison is Mark Noble, rather than Billy Bonds. Noble is a local East End boy known to walk to the ground on match days. Like his predecessor, he is a highly committed, wholehearted player who loves his club. There, of course, the comparison ends. Unlike the young Dove, Noble does not have to work an exhausting 45 hours a week as a shipwright in the docks, train in the evenings and play on Saturdays after a morning's work. The modern young Hammer earns wages that, in the late 19th century, would keep half the East End in food for 12 months. Despite the stark differences in their lives these two youngsters are key characters in the intriguing story of West Ham United. Charlie Dove…come on my son.

William 'Billy the Kid' Barnes

Billy Barnes, our second pioneer, was the hero of the 1896 Cup win over Barking. Young Billy, like his teammate Charlie Dove, played regularly for West Ham when the Irons folded in 1900. Billy Barnes was born in East London on 20 May 1879. The Barnes' were an interesting family. Like the Doves, they were industrious and had a strong work ethic. His parents were keen to improve their standard of living and desperate to provide a good home for their children. The family were relatively comfortable. Billy's dad was a foreman in the Victoria Dock, while his mother ran a tea shop in nearby Silverton.

Young Billy left school at 13 and it was quickly apparent that he was a highly promising young footballer with an exceptional left foot. He joined Thames when he was just 16 years old and made five appearances in the club's very first season of 1895–96. Competition for places in the first team was fierce and Billy, lacking the physical strength of the young Dove, left to join South West Ham down at the Tidal Basin where he was guaranteed regular League and Cup football. However, the Irons had not forgotten the youngster and in 1896, when injury problems left the club with a weakened side, they included Barnes as a guest player in the West Ham Charity Cup Final. The Irons were well within the rules as Billy had played for them in the earlier part of the season. Their trust in the youngster was well rewarded.

The Thames Ironworks team for the second replay of the West Ham Charity Cup against Barking in 1896 included several outstanding players. Sadly, Charlie Dove's growing injury problems ruled him out of the match, although he did play a major part in the early rounds. The team on that sunny April evening at St Lukes was: Graham, Stevenson, French, Woods, Chapman, Hickman, Chamberlain, Sage, Freeman, Barnes, Stewart.

In the final match Barnes went close to scoring on a couple of occasions early in the game, but neither side was able to break the deadlock in the first period. Just after the restart Barking were reduced to 10 men, although a late injury to Freeman meant that both sides finished the match one man short. With the Irons dominant for much of the second half, the breakthrough finally came when Barnes, one month short of his 17th birthday, rifled home Sage's accurate corner. It is not known whether the youngster joined in the lively post-match celebrations at the nearby Trinity School. He certainly deserved a beer or two for scoring the winning goal, but his manager may have had other ideas.

Barnes was the youngest player ever to appear in the first team, making his debut at the tender age of 16 years and 166 days. Young Billy was a very quick, left-sided player with delightful ball skills. He may have struggled a little on heavy pitches with the old leather ball, but Billy impressed his teammates and coaches to the extent that he was selected for all three matches in the Charity Cup Final. The club's faith was repaid in full as young Billy turned out to be the hero of the hour. Barnes deserves his pioneer status just for scoring the only goal in the third match of the tie, giving his team an historic victory.

Barnes' heroic display in the 1896 Cup Final impressed everyone on the ground that day as the young winger grew in confidence. Over the next two seasons, he produced some breathtaking displays from his favoured outside-left position. Word began to spread that the Irons had discovered a special player and in 1898 Barnes decided to sign professional forms for Leyton in the South Essex League. By the time Billy had signed for Leyton he was 18 years old and stronger both mentally and physically. Playing professional football held no fears for the talented youngster. He shone at Leyton and produced a number of outstanding performances for his new club, but his goal in the Barking Cup Final must have stayed long in his memory.

All members of the Irons' team on that sunny evening at St Lukes should be remembered for playing their part in the historic victory, but a few deserve special mention. Skipper Robert Stevenson led his team admirably. The Irons' first captain joined the club from Arsenal in 1898 and the Scot quickly found a job at Arnold Hills' shipyard. He was an outstanding full-back, slight of frame, but quick in the tackle. He was popular with the Hermit Road crowd who loved his attacking style which, in his first season, earned him eight goals in 24 games. As we shall see, Stevenson was a proper pioneer.

Half-back Johnny Stewart was a Newcastle boy who, on leaving school, joined Thames Ironworks as an apprentice boilermaker. His football skills were quickly recognised and he grabbed the chance to play for the firm's side. As a result of injuries to key players, Stewart played as a forward in all the club's West Ham Charity Cup matches in 1895–96 and was outstanding in all three games.

Unlike Charlie Dove, both Stevenson and Stewart were professionals, which is an indication of the direction senior amateur football was heading towards the end of the 19th century. In their second season the Irons began to attract players from across London, and eventually the whole country, as a crude transfer system was introduced. This inevitable trend towards professionalisation, contrary to the Corinthian instincts of the patrician Arnold Hills, led to Thames, and later West Ham, ceasing to be entirely local clubs. Mr Hills reluctantly bowed to the pressure and agreed to drop his early insistence that his club be comprised exclusively of players who worked at the yard.

Local boys Charlie Dove, Dickie Pudan, George Webb and William Barnes all learnt their football with the Irons and West Ham. In 1905 the club's commitment to developing local talent was recognised by the Football Association who wrote in their journal, 'It is the proud boast of West Ham that they turn out more local players than any other team in the South. The district has been described as a hot-bed of local football, and it is so.'

The Hammers' emphasis on developing local talent has continued up to the present day. But, despite attracting players from outside the area, over the years West Ham has emerged as essentially a selling club. This policy has resulted in a considerable dip in the club's fortunes both on and off the field. As early as the end of the 19th century young professionals from the East End were sold by the Irons to rival clubs. Prolific goalscorer George Webb, the first West Ham player to win an England cap, was transferred to Manchester City in 1912, although it has to be said that Webb remained a staunch amateur throughout his career.

Inevitably, in the new world of highly competitive professional football, Barnes was bound to be spotted by a Football League club who would happily pay decent money for a fast and skilful winger with a devastating left foot. In 1899 Barnes signed full professional terms for Sheffield United, who had been watching the youngster for some time. He stayed in Sheffield for three seasons, but his career never really progressed at Bramall Lane, as is often the case when young players change clubs to play at a higher level. In Yorkshire Billy was what we call today a squad player, making just 23 first-team appearances and scoring six goals. There was one special moment for Barnes at Bramall Lane, however. Cup Finals had a special place in Barnes' career and just as he did for the Irons against Barking in 1896, Billy scored the winning goal for his new club in the 1902 FA Cup Final against Southampton, securing a place in the history of Sheffield United as well as Thames Ironworks.

After such a promising start for Thames, Barnes' career stalled at Sheffield where he had few opportunities to display his undoubted skills. Moving north would have been quite a culture shock to the young East Ender and he returned to London the following season, joining West Ham at the Memorial Grounds. The Hammers were beginning their third season in the Southern League following the demise of Thames Ironworks in 1900. Back in his home town environment, Billy made 48 appearances in the next two seasons, scoring a modest six goals. His career was back on track and over the next few years football took the young winger to places he could never have imagined when he made his debut for the Irons back in 1896.

Barnes arrived for the 1902–03 season with the club in good spirits. The Hammers were established in the Southern League and could beat anybody on their day. Manager Syd King signed Barnes to provide a regular supply of accurate crosses to his centre-forward Billy Grassam. The Scot was the club's top scorer in the previous two seasons and the pair immediately struck up an effective partnership, in the manner of the Sissons and Hurst pairing 60 years later.

In the first two months of the season both Grassam and Barnes scored regularly, although neither managed a goal in the Millwall derby match which the Hammers lost 0–3 in front of 10,000 disappointed home fans. Their form fell away in the November and December mud – a customary West Ham failing. In the second half of the season, they recovered after a disappointing Boxing Day defeat at home to a strong Portsmouth in front of 18,000 festive fans, the new Manor Park railway helping to boost the attendance. A 10th place League finish would have frustrated manager King, but young Barnes had a decent first season and established his place in the side with 24 appearances in which he scored four goals. The local youngster was clearly pleased to be back where he belonged and his tricky wing play endeared him to his growing band of devoted fans.

In their first few seasons the Hammers found it difficult to break into the top four Southern League clubs – Southampton, Portsmouth, Reading and Tottenham. Despite the heroics and goals of Billy Grassam the club failed to improve on its sixth place in that first season of 1900–01. At the end of 1902–03 Grassam was sold to Manchester United, but Barnes quickly found a new partner in centre-forward Charlie Satterthwaite, formerly of New Brompton and Liverpool. The centre-forward scored 18 goals in 36 games that season and struck up a good rapport with his outside-left. The winger himself scored just once, in the 1–2 League defeat away at Portsmouth. Despite Satterthwaite's goals, West Ham ended the season in a disappointing 12th place and lost to Fulham in the FA Cup.

On his return to East London Barnes made 48 appearances in two seasons. He was a huge talent and the growing band of Hammers fans loved his attacking wing play. But much like the wingers of the 1960s (Redknapp, Johnny Ayris and John Sissons), Billy never really fulfilled the potential he showed as a teenager. His career at the Memorial Grounds did not develop as his manager would have wished. Barnes was eventually sold to Luton in 1904 where he stayed for three years, scoring 12 goals in 101 appearances. His career did eventually take off when he returned to London – this time with QPR – where he enjoyed a few successful years, scoring 37 times in 216 matches and helping the West London outfit to a Southern League Championship in 1908.

Towards the end of his long career Barnes joined Southend United for a couple of seasons before retiring in 1914. He had enjoyed a long and largely successful time in football which began with his match-winning debut for Thames Ironworks as a raw 16-year-old in the West Ham Charity Cup Final. It is ironic that he played his best football away from his home club, but Barnes was a true Hammers pioneer and one of the first to become a full-time professional. One of the most interesting things about Billy was that, like many future ex-Hammers, he took up a career in management when he finally gave up playing.

Barnes had clearly absorbed a great deal about the professional game in nearly 20 years as a top-class player with three major clubs. He was keen to use his experience in a coaching capacity, a true indication of his love for the game. Interestingly, rather than begin his coaching career with one of the less fashionable London clubs, as he could easily have done, Barnes chose a more exotic location. At the end of World War One he joined the coaching staff at Athletic Bilbao. When West Ham undertook a pre-season tour to Spain in 1921, Barnes' new club entertained the Hammers, but this time the Londoners proved too strong for the Spanish side and ran out 2–1 winners.

Billy Barnes fully deserves his place in the pantheon of vintage Hammers. He was the youngest player ever to play for Thames, scored the winning goal in the Cup Final at the age of 16, hugely entertained the home crowd with his dazzling skills, was one of the very first professionals at the club where he made his debut and became one of the first ex-professionals in Britain to coach abroad. Billy had two other claims to fame. He was the brother of Alfred Barnes, the MP for East Ham, who served as transport minister in Clement Atlee's Labour government of 1945–51. It is a pleasing symmetry that the great Labour prime minister was MP for Poplar, a short tram ride away from the Hammers' Memorial Grounds.

Barnes' other claim to fame was a little more modest. He was a handsome young man as early photographs show us, although he never favoured the fashionable clipped moustache preferred by his teammates. At the beginning of the 20th century tobacco companies began producing cigarette cards of famous footballers. In 1903, Fosters, the cigarette card company based in Brighton, issued 74 postcards of West Ham footballers, including one featuring young Barnes. The picture of our hero shows a strong, determined and handsome face – clearly the face of a modern young professional destined to go a very long way in his profession.

Stevenson, MacEachrane and Bradshaw: factory footballers

Both Charlie Dove and Billy Barnes were stand-out players of their time. But there are others from the Thames Ironworks era, who because of their contribution to the early history of West Ham, deserve to be included in the list of early pioneers. Three players deserve special mention.

Robert Stevenson began his football career playing for Third Lanark in his native Scotland. He joined the increasing number of Scottish players to play for London clubs at this time. Seeking to develop his career, the hard-tackling defender came south and signed for Woolwich Arsenal in 1895. After a brief spell with the emerging Gunners at Plumstead, Stevenson signed for Castle Swifts, before becoming the first ever captain of Thames Ironworks in 1898. He settled into the Thames side at full-back and enjoyed nearly two seasons with the dockside club. He is generally recognised as one of the best players ever to wear the Oxford blue of the Hermit Road side.

Stevenson's greatest contribution to Thames was without question his superb marshalling of the Irons defence in the Final of the 1896 West Ham Charity Cup at the Old Spotted Dog ground in Clapton. In the second replay, Stevenson held the Barking forwards at bay and found time to join the attack with several penetrating surges down the right wing. The genial Scot was a real character and born leader. We cannot be sure how many appearances he made for Thames, but we do know he scored eight goals in his first season for the club he led with such distinction. Much in the manner of his 20th century counterpart, Bobby Moore, captain Bob led by strength of personality and example. There can be no greater compliment.

Much to the disappointment of Thames fans, Stevenson returned to his native Scotland in 1898 where he joined the little-known Arthurlie FC. His contribution to London football was recognised at the time: 'Robert Stevenson, a full-back of merit…was among those who helped to build warships when the suggestion of a football club was made at the Thames Iron Works, and he was the first captain of the team…He was a wonderfully good player and invaluable as an advisor to the fathers of the club.' (Dickford and Gibson, 1905)

Team group photograph from 1895–86.

Proud, upright and sporting an extravagant moustache fashionable among footballers of the period, Bob Stevenson's proudest moment was to lift the Charity Cup. He was unquestionably a key figure as he led the Irons to Cup victory, entry to the London League, the English FA Cup and the London Senior Cup. Stevenson was a real club man and a great help to the chairman as he steered the club through the difficult early years. One of the best-loved players of his time, Bob Stevenson was a genuine pioneer and despite being a Scot, had real 'Iron' in his soul.

Rod MacEachrane qualified to play for Arnold Hills' Thames Ironworks because he had a day job in the shipbuilder's yard in Canning Town. Also a Scot, MacEachrane was considered to be one of the best players to play for Thames in its five-year history. Despite his short stature, Roddy was a tough-tackling but skilful inside-forward in the manner of Hammers' post-war midfield stars like Ronnie Boyce and Geoff Pike. His crunching tackles, darting runs and perceptive passing brought approval from his teammates and the club management.

MacEachrane made his debut for Thames against Shepherd's Bush in September 1898. The talented young Scot was an ever present in 1898–99, helping the Irons to win the Southern League Division Two title by an impressive nine points. He was a key member of the team who made the transition from Thames to West Ham United in 1900–01, playing in every game of the Hammers' first season. The youngster endeared himself to the fans at the Memorial Grounds, who appreciated the Scot's commitment and big-hearted approach to the game. Roddy was imposing in defence and attack, his wonderful physicality and superb fitness levels ensuring that he hardly missed a game.

In some ways MacEachrane represented all the qualities Arnold Hills looked for in his employees. He moved to London at the age of 20, secured a job in the docks and quickly joined the football team. He was the model employee and a good example to his

younger colleagues. Despite his tough tackling, MacEachrane was an ever present in all three seasons he played for Thames. Roddy's no-nonsense style was the perfect foil for Syd King, Charlie Dove and forwards Billy Grassam and James Reid. He made an immense contribution to the success of Thames in the late 19th century and was one of the first players on Charlie Paynter's Hammers team sheet. In total he made 113 appearances for Thames and West Ham, scoring a modest six goals.

Old Arnold Hills would not have approved of MacEachrane's decision to turn professional, but probably supported his transfer to Woolwich Arsenal in May 1902. In truth Roddy, despite his contribution to the Hammers' early days, really made his name in South London. In his four seasons for the Division Two outfit he hardly missed a match and his stay coincided with the most successful period in Woolwich's history. MacEachrane's impressive displays in midfield helped the Gunners reach the FA Cup semi-final on two occasions. Scoring goals was not his greatest strength. He played 346 games for Woolwich and never scored a single goal. Despite this he was one of the best Scottish players never to win a full cap. He played his last game before retirement on 22 November 1913. Roddy MacEachrane died in 1952 aged 74. As a worker at the shipyard and a regular with both Thames and the embryonic West Ham, he was a genuine pioneer.

Born in 1873, **Thomas H. 'Harry' Bradshaw** was an itinerant footballer who began his career in 1892 with Northwich Victoria before joining his native Liverpool. During his time at his home club Bradshaw made 118 appearances scoring an impressive 46 goals – quite a haul for an outside-left. Young Harry's exciting wing-play was a decisive factor in the Reds' Division Two Championship triumphs in 1894 and 1896. While in the North West Bradshaw was selected for the Football League representative XI on two occasions and was awarded an England cap against Ireland in 1897.

Following his spell on Merseyside, Bradshaw moved south and joined Tottenham where he continued to accumulate representative honours. At that time Thames owner Arnold Hills, aware of the necessity to compete on equal terms with the top clubs, provided secretary George Hills with £1,000 to acquire new players. Hills bought three players from Tottenham – Bradshaw, Bill Joyce and Kenny McKay and, in a masterstroke, Syd King from New Brompton. Bradshaw was a major coup for Thames given his growing national profile. He made just 12 appearances for Thames, scoring only two goals. The second of these was at the Memorial Grounds in the 2–1 defeat by local rivals Millwall, played in front of a record gate of 13,000 people. His ability to dribble with the old leather ball, often caked in mud, excited the home supporters. The supremely talented young winger appeared to have the football world at his feet. Sadly, this was not to be. Bradshaw died on Christmas Day 1900, just 16 days after the derby match against Millwall. Blows and Hogg (2000) inform us that his death was attributed to an injury he sustained in a match against Bedminster early in the season. Bradshaw's career was tragically cut short just as he was beginning to realise his rich promise. Syd King later paid tribute to his young teammate: 'The record of 1899–1900…would not be complete without reference to Tom Bradshaw…How well I remember that match with QPR during the Christmas holidays, when Joyce brought over the sad message to the Memorial Grounds that our comrade had passed away. Poor Tom was one of the cleverest wing-forwards I have ever known and was immensely popular with everybody.' (Blows and Hogg, 2000)

King's reference to Bradshaw as his comrade is interesting, respectful and reminiscent of the time.

Combining goals and wickets was a Bradshaw trademark and he was an outstanding cricketer, spending his summers playing for one of Liverpool's leading clubs. John Powles (2005) reveals that the winger was offered a place on the Lord's ground staff for the summer of 1899, an indication of the depth of his all-round sporting talent. We can only speculate what Henry Thomas Bradshaw might have achieved had today's medical expertise been available to save his career and his life. All we can do is pay our respects to his memory and remember his place in the history of Thames Ironworks and West Ham United. For a very short time young Tom's star burned brightly in East London as he wove his magic in the Hammers forward line.

Syd King: founding father

Syd King is West Ham and West Ham is Syd King

If Bobby Moore is the defining character in the history of West Ham United FC, Syd King is the founding father. As secretary and manager of the club from 1902–32, King led the Hammers from the Division Two of the Southern League to the top flight of English football in just 20 years. In addition to achieving a prolonged spell in the Football League Division One, King's team reached the FA Cup Final in 1923. Later in the 20th century, West Ham won a major European competition, the FA Cup three times and provided the England captain and England's top scorer in the 1966 World Cup. None of this would have happened without King's inspired and unwavering role in the formation of the Hammers. King is synonymous with the early Hammers history and its earlier incarnation Thames Ironworks. As a player and later manager, he left an indelible impression on the history of the club and nobody connected with West Ham, before or since, better deserves the status of pioneer. As the first manager, King brought a real sense of pride to the area with his outstanding leadership of the East End's first professional football club. In contrast to modern managers King was a strong disciplinarian, who the players always greeted as Mr King. But the players respected rather than feared their esteemed manager. How the East End needed King's direction and guidance as local people faced the privations of war to add to their everyday hardships.

The average lifespan of someone living in East London at the end of the 19th century was 23 years, many were lucky to make it beyond 10 and the area had a disastrous public health record right up to the 1930s. Despite this grim background, it would be wrong to stereotype the East End as downtrodden and despairing at this time. In many ways life was improving, particularly for skilled workers. The 1891 census reveals that all kinds of skilled men lived around Poplar and Silvertown. Sailmakers, boilermakers, foundrymen, carpenters and glassblowers lived alongside tailors, butchers, bakers, cartmen and all kinds of river tradesmen.

At the beginning of the 20th century professional footballers can be added to this glittering array of skilled artisans. As we have seen, Thames Ironworks was a major employer in the docks and its football team quickly established a loyal following. When

West Ham moved to the Boleyn Castle ground in 1904, the club began to attract tens of thousands of East Enders. The bond between East End folk and West Ham United was established at this time and the iron hammers which echoed out from the shipyard to the streets around became the symbol for the inextricable link between the club and its supporters. This attachment remains as strong as ever, despite being tested to the limit over the past 30 years. Into this exciting, often dangerous mix of industry, extremes of poverty and growing local pride in their football club stepped Syd King.

Ernest Sydney King was not from the East End. He was born in Chatham in Kent in 1873 into a lower middle-class family. An intelligent boy, Syd attended Watford Grammar School before beginning his working life modestly as a clerk in an ordnance depot. Young Sydney showed early promise as a footballer and joined his local club Northfleet United where he quickly gained a reputation as an outstanding full-back. Legend has it that King scored three own-goals in a match against Swindon Town, but this unwelcome feat remains more myth than reality. But we do know that King was suspended for four weeks by the FA disciplinary committee following an offensive remark to the referee during the Swindon game. His colourful career had begun in earnest.

The following season, at the age of 24, King was transferred to Southern League club New Brompton in Gillingham where he stayed for two seasons making a total of 37 appearances. In 1899 his career took a fortunate turn when he left Kent and took the short journey up the river to join Arnold Hills' emerging ironworks side. At the Hermit Road club King quickly established himself as a useful full-back and more importantly, an intelligent and perceptive club man. At Thames he struck up an effective partnership with his full-back partner Tommy Dunn and later at West Ham with Charlie Craig. In his final season for the club he suffered a broken leg in a match against Spurs, an injury which would have ended the careers of most players in the late 19th century. However, King was made of strong stuff and recovered sufficiently to continue his career with the newly formed West Ham, enjoying three successful seasons as the Hammers right-back.

Syd King did not score a single goal in his career and was in reality no more than a decent full-back. His claim to pioneer status comes not from his 89 appearances, his solid defending and frequent surges up the right wing in front of the Chicken Run, but from the enormous contribution he made to the progress of West Ham United, firstly as a club administrator and subsequently as manager. Thames' secretary Francis Payne quickly recognised the ex-grammar schoolboy's managerial potential that marked him out from his teammates. Payne observed the young full-back's development with great interest and concluded that King had real leadership potential.

Francis Payne was a formidable personality and well aware of the task that lay ahead for his new young manager, both on and off the field. Just a couple of years before King's appointment, Thames Ironworks became effectively homeless when they were accused of violating the terms of their contract for the Hermit Road ground. The club were aware they had to improve their facilities in line with clubs of a similar standard and, quite reasonably, built changing rooms and a perimeter fence around the pitch. In addition, Payne introduced entrance fees on match days, further infringing the terms of their lease. The loss of Hermit Road did not discourage Payne and with the help of Thames' owner Arnold Hills, he eventually found a site in Canning Town to develop as a multi-sports athletic ground. The Memorial Grounds, now the home of East Ham Rugby Club, was built at a cost of £20,000 and opened on Jubilee Day in June 1897. The ground was ideally situated close to West Ham station (opened in 1901) and a short distance from Hills' factory. The new arena contained a cycle and running track and an outdoor swimming pool of over 30m in length – a sort of prototype to the new Olympic Stadium.

It is an interesting thought that if West Ham's ambitions to move to Stratford in 2014 are realised, the club will return to a multi-sports arena of the type created by the club's founders. But unlike the new Olympic Stadium, the new ground was completed within six months and was ready for the start of the club's second season in the London League. Settled in their new home, Payne could concentrate fully on his players. He would have been delighted to see them beat Brentford 1–0 in the inaugural match at the Memorial in September 1897, in front of around 2,000 paying spectators. Thames finished the season as London League champions and Payne could do no wrong in East London. These were happy days for Francis Payne and Thames Ironworks. Despite Thames' success Payne knew the club needed a professional manager if progress was to be maintained. He had the ideal candidate in his bright young full-back Syd King.

Payne steered Thames through this difficult period with great skill. But when the club achieved promotion to the Southern League in 1899 and became a fully professional operation, things began to go wrong both on and off the field. Many of the top clubs at the time employed several Scottish players to strengthen their squad. This influx of foreign players came at a price. The team began to struggle at the higher level and attendances dwindled. Hills might have been a patrician employer, but he was a hard businessman and was not prepared to give Francis Payne a blank cheque for new players. After five successful seasons the inevitable occurred and Hills' experiment in factory football was over.

Arnold Hills was a man of strong principle and never wanted to see the legacy of Thames Ironworks go to waste. Hills engineered a share issue to raise funds to support a new club to replace Thames in the Southern League – that club was West Ham United. In late spring 1890, in a carefully orchestrated operation, the club resigned from the Southern League and was officially wound up. Thames reappeared a week later under a new name – the long and distinguished history of West Ham United was about to begin.

Hills remained heavily involved for a few years and granted the new club a lease at the Memorial. He was there to see West Ham play their first ever match at the beginning of the following season at home to Gravesend. Blows and Hogg (2000) present the scene.

'All were present as the Memorial Grounds bade farewell to the new Hammers who could hardly have wished for a better start as they thrashed Gravesend 7–0 in their first fixture in 1 September 1990.'

At the end of the 1901–02 season Payne, aware of his own workload and his responsibility to the club, appointed King as the club's first full-time manager and charged him with the task of taking the Hammers to the top tier of English professional football.

So in 1902, the new manager began a period of 31 years' distinguished service to the club, culminating in the Hammers' election to the Football League in 1919 and their first ever Wembley appearance in 1923. In time Francis Payne's faith in his protégé was abundantly rewarded.

The new manager quickly imposed his management style on the club. Conscious of the Hammers' precarious financial position, King introduced a 'revolving door' transfer policy which did not meet with the approval of the club's growing band of supporters. It is tempting to imagine Syd King in the tradition of wheeler-dealer managers like Harry Redknapp. In truth he was more in the tradition of intelligent cricketing administrators like Trevor Bailey and Doug Insole at nearby Essex who were highly educated players with a passion for their sport and a real sense of responsibility for their club. King's activity in the transfer market was motivated more by financial pressure than anything else. He was forced to sell fans' favourites Charlie Satterthwaite, Dick Pudan and Billy Barnes soon after being appointed. Later, the controversial sale of the legendary Syd Puddefoot enraged the fans. However, this has to be balanced against some shrewd purchases including Billy Grassam, Fred Blackburn, George Kay and the incomparable Vic Watson. Overall, King's transfer record was positive, although he would have regretted the need to sell so many of the club's promising young players.

Syd King was the right man in the right place at the right time and had gained Payne's trust, but his task was immense. They say if you want a job done well and quickly, give it to a busy man. In the busiest time of his career, King even found time to write a short history of the club which he published in 1906. Here was a very special character. Best described as 'dapper', King sported a splendid moustache and was often photographed wearing a homburg or a straw boater at a jaunty angle. His photographs bring to mind the late Malcolm Allison rather than the more soberly attired, Barking Road, car-dealer image of Redknapp.

King was aware that Hammers supporters had high expectations and wanted to see their beloved club in the top flight. His managerial method combined a pragmatic day-to-day approach, with a more strategic long-term view of running the club. He also had clear ideas on his favoured playing style, which he worked out with assistant Charlie Paynter and a few senior players. It is conventional wisdom at Upton Park that West Ham's reputation as the academy with a commitment to a purist, free-flowing style of football evolved in the late 1950s under Ted Fenton. This philosophy was later nurtured by Malcolm Allison and Noel Cantwell, before being applied to glorious effect by Ron Greenwood and John Lyall. But the Hammers' standing in English football as the architects of the modern game can be traced back to the days of Syd King and Charlie Paynter.

A clear example of this can be found in the newspaper reports of the 1923 FA Cup Final, which refer to West Ham's attacking, close passing game being negated by the ruined surface, and the pitch being narrowed by the thousands of fans packed close to the touchline. Danger men Ruffell and Richards, with their wonderful wing play, just were not able to get into the game. Conditions were more to the Hammers' liking in the semi-final at Stamford Bridge where the side played some of the best football as they thrashed Derby County 5–2. The following day the *Daily Mail* was unstinting in its praise of the East Enders: 'West Ham have never played finer football. They were quick, they dribbled and swerved, and passed and ran as if the ball was to them a thing of life and obedient to their wishes…the ball was flashed from player to player.'

Some of the credit for this admired football philosophy must go to Syd King as manager, although Charlie Paynter's influence should not be underestimated. When Brian Belton interviewed Jimmy Ruffell in 1973, Ruffell had this to say:

'Syd King was a good manager. But he left a lot of the day-to-day stuff to our trainee Charlie Paynter. Syd King was more about doing deals.' In an interesting insight into the way football clubs were run at the time, Ruffell continued, 'A lot of the time we, the players, would decide what we were going to do. George (Kay) and Jack (Tresadern)…came up with ways of playing. But anything anyone had to say Charlie Paynter chatted about.'

Despite Paynter's undoubted influence on the team, King was the unquestioned boss at the club. His long reign as manager at West Ham was distinguished by success on the field and a period of financial stability off it – today's Hammers supporters can only dream of having someone of King's calibre leading their club. Like Francis Payne before him, King proved an able administrator and clearly enjoyed the responsibility of the job. In their first season in the Southern League the new Hammers finished in sixth place, falling away after an encouraging start. In 1901–02 the new Irons won six out of their first seven games thanks to the goals of Billy Grassam, but again suffered a bleak mid-winter, before recovering in the spring to finish in fourth place behind Spurs, Southampton and champions Portsmouth.

Syd King, who was still playing at this time, would have been delighted to see 17,000 fans turn up at the Memorial in November 1901 to see the Hammers lose 0–1 to Tottenham. He would have been further encouraged when visitors Portsmouth attracted a staggering 18,000 paying customers to East London on Boxing Day 1902. The gate receipts would have thrilled King and his directors, although losing both games would have been a huge disappointment for the fans. The Hammers continued their mid-table form for the duration of their stay in the Southern League, although they did finish in third place in 1912–13.

In the early days King showed his talent for buying and selling, again drawing heavily on the Scottish market. Top goalscorer Billy Grassam was sold to Manchester United and King shrewdly replaced him with the equally prolific Charlie Satterthwaite. By this time Charlie Dove had been transferred to bitter rivals Millwall, Roddy MacEachrane had left for Woolwich Arsenal and Charlie Craig moved to Nottingham Forest the same year. All this coming and going had no effect on the team's performances as they continued to hover around the middle of the table. At the end of the 1902–03 season, Syd King retired from playing to concentrate fully on managing the club's financial affairs, which by this time had started to deteriorate. They had lost the support of Arnold Hills, while a combination of a mounting wage bill, disappointing home attendances and paying the rent on the Memorial Grounds put a strain on King's meagre resources. West Ham were in real trouble and faced the possibility of being wound up.

Something had to be done. Francis Payne had guided Thames from Hermit Road to the Memorial Grounds, transformed the parent club into West Ham United and orchestrated the promotion from the London League. King, as the Hammers' first manager, needed to do something pretty drastic if the new club were not to be thrown out of the Southern League and Payne's legacy wasted. The club directors were in no position to criticise Arnold Hills over tenure and rent of the Memorial Grounds. The old puritan industrialist, one of the architects of working life in East London, was standing his ground. He originally supported the change from Thames to West Ham, under one condition – all players should take the pledge and become teetotal. It was probably at this point that the great man began to lose touch with his men and the changing times. Just imagine!

The future was looking very bleak indeed for the Hammers when serendipity intervened. Desperate to find a new ground for 1904–05, club officials happened to be watching a school match at the Boleyn Castle RC Reformatory School just off Green Street and began chatting to some of the school brothers about their concerns for West Ham's future. The school invited Syd King and his team to look at the Boleyn Castle field, which was owned by the Catholic Church, as a possible solution to the Hammers' problems.

King went at the project like a dog with a bone. He agreed a rent with the Church authorities, only to have their planning application rejected by the Home Office. King refused to be beaten and, with the help of his local MP, secured possession of the Boleyn Castle. The events surrounding the acquisition of the new ground – and effectively the future of West Ham – were led by King with great energy and determination. It was to be his defining moment and from that point his leadership of the club could not be questioned – the Syd King era had begun and his place as one of the most important figures in the history of the club was assured.

The field the club secured from the Catholic Diocese of Westminster was the home of local club Boleyn Castle FC. It is said that Ann Boleyn stayed at the former castle overlooking the ground, hence the name of both the old club and the new ground, which often confuses visiting fans. The bizarre association of the area with Henry's feisty and ultra-glamorous wife resonates with the modern Essex girls of today and her unfortunate end chimes with the line from 'Bubbles', 'just like my dreams they fade and die'.

From 1904 to this day West Ham's home ground is officially the Boleyn Ground at Upton Park. Such niceties would not have detained the pragmatic manager who had the tough job of preparing the ground for the Southern League by the end of August. As Colm Kerrigan tells us in his biography, 'Hurried improvements were undertaken during the summer to have the ground ready for the new season. While they were not finished on time, the ground was able to accommodate the 12,000 who came to see West Ham beat Millwall 3–0 on the opening day of the new 1904–05 season.'

The club had found its home thanks to the tenacity of Syd King, who worked tirelessly to ensure the new ground would be ready in time. King also had to employ his lesser-known skills of diplomacy. One of the conditions of taking over the ground of Boleyn Castle FC was that the best Boleyn players should have the opportunity to play for West Ham. In reality none of them were good enough to play for the Hammers, although a few did appear for the reserve team.

With West Ham established at Upton Park, King could turn his attention to his team. New players were brought from professional clubs around the country, including the outstanding inside-forward 'Chippy' Simmons from West Bromwich Albion. King released a number of players and some of his training staff and brought back Tom Robinson as first-team trainer. In the next few seasons the Hammers enjoyed a period of consolidation as the club settled into their new ground and found their level. The manager was satisfied with an 11th place finish in their first season at the Boleyn and would have been overjoyed that the club made a profit for the first time in their history – happy days! The next decade was preparation for King's ultimate ambition of West Ham being accepted into the Football League. The luxury of long-term planning is denied to modern managers at all football clubs, but King was in an unassailable position at West Ham at this time.

The Hammers' colourful manager was beginning to gain some popular notoriety as his confidence grew. In an unfortunate irony given what happened at the end of his career, the following message from the manager appeared on the reverse of a team photograph sponsored by Oxo: 'When training, Oxo is the only beverage used by our team and all speak of the supreme strength and power of endurance which they have derived from its use.'

If the team did enjoy the odd Oxo or two it certainly helped in their epic victory over Millwall in their visit to the Boleyn. The loyal fans had to make do with scalding, watered-down Bovril to sustain them through the cold.

A period of stability up to World War One enabled the club to settle and to work out some sort of strategy for the future, including Syd King's ultimate goal. In 1914–15, the last season before war interrupted most professional football across the country, the Hammers finished in fourth place in the Southern League, seven points behind champions Watford. In the FA Cup, King's men drew 2–2 with Newcastle before losing the replay. The

Newcastle tie helped to boost the club's finances as a total of 43,000 watched the two games. Legendary goalscorer Syd Puddefoot failed to score against the Geordies, but finished the season with 18 goals just ahead of the prolific Alf Leafe, who scored three times in the Newcastle tie.

Professional football resumed immediately after the war and 1919–20 was an historic season for West Ham United – it was their first ever in the Football League. West Ham had been invited into the top flight of British football, largely thanks to the ambition and drive of manager Syd King and the goals of Syd Puddefoot, a genuine pioneer in his own right.

Of course, King had a very different set of players after the war to the side that finished fourth in the Southern League in 1915. West Ham, like most professional football clubs, lost players in the war. Arthur Stallard, Bill Kennedy, Frank Costello and Frank Cannon were all killed in action in France, while George Hilsdon suffered the effects of mustard gas poisoning while serving for the East Surrey Regiment (Blows and Hogg, 2000).

Syd Puddefoot survived the war with no damage to his remarkable goalscoring abilities. The centre-forward's 26 goals in 43 League and Cup appearances helped the Hammers to seventh place in their first season in the Football League, 23 points behind champions Tottenham. King would have been happy with his team's performance in the higher League and thrilled with the receipts from the crowd of 47,646 who paid to see the Hammers lose 0–3 to Spurs in the third round of the FA Cup. The manager would have been less delighted with the result, but he knew he had a decent side with Bill Cope, another survivor from the Southern League, installed as captain and legendary 'keeper Ted Hufton in goal. With the remarkable feats of Puddefoot up front, the future looked promising. The Hammers struggled in mid-season but slowly improved and went on to win a total of 19 games that season.

The Hammers drew their first ever Football League match 1–1 with Lincoln City and the supporters paid one shilling to watch James Moyes score the Hammers' goal late in the game. Attendances at the Boleyn in the club's debut season in the Second Division averaged around 20,000, as the British people flocked to see professional football in the first year of peace. In the years up to 1922 King's careful stewardship saw the Hammers consolidate their status, finishing seventh, fifth and fourth in Division Two. Puddefoot's astonishing goalscoring, Hufton's exploits in goal and outstanding performances from Kay, Tresadern and Cope steered King's side to within reach of promotion to Division One. The club's dreams of promotion to the highest level of English football were realised in 1923, when King's side secured promotion by finishing second in Division Two behind Notts County. Not content with promotion in their fourth season in the Football League, the Hammers reached the FA Cup Final for the first time in their history.

The events of the White Horse Final of 1923 are well documented. Jimmy Ruffell pointed out how important reaching the Final was for the people of the area. 'It seemed like the most wonderful thing…as far…as West Ham were concerned. It was a hard time for most people around the East End. That was the best thing about it really: giving people, kids, something to smile about.'

Ruffell was right; in the 1920s an average of 150 British people died every year as a result of malnutrition. The Final was a welcome distraction from everyday life and Hammers fans began to dream of a glorious victory.

Despite being clear pre-match favourites, the Hammers were never allowed to play their fluent passing game in the atrocious conditions. In front of around 130,000 supporters, mostly Londoners, Bolton Wanderers won 2–0 and the Hammers returned to the East End with their tails firmly between their legs…'just like my dreams they fade and die'. But manager King and his directors knew the club was moving in the right direction – eight of the 1923 side went on to become internationals. His side scored a total of 63 goals in the League that year, conceded only 38, and enjoyed a period of 32 games with just one defeat, home to Manchester United, on their way to promotion and Wembley. Not bad for a former factory football team from the London docks. The team's progress was recognised by the board with an increase in the manager's salary to a princely £10 a week – a very decent sum in a time of economic depression, when most East End folk were fortunate to have a job of any sort.

West Ham being West Ham, a crisis was never far away. A huge shock to the Boleyn faithful came in 1922 when the great Syd Puddefoot was sold to Falkirk for a record £5,000, with King receiving a £300 bonus for this particular piece of business, presumably in a brown envelope. Around the same time the manager was awarded £1,500 in recognition of 20 years' loyal service to the club. The club's money was well spent. That the team survived the hammer blow of the loss of their principal goalscorer was due to a superb piece of management by King. He replaced Puddefoot with a player whose prodigious goalscoring feats eclipsed those of the wizard of Bow. Vic Watson was signed from Wellingborough in 1921 and played at inside-left alongside Puddy for a few games, but was bursting to take over the number-nine shirt. With the departure of Puddy, Watson had his wish and went on to break every goalscoring record in the club's history and in the process was selected to represent his country. Syd King had upset the fans with the sale of Puddefoot, but pulled of a masterstroke with his handling of Vic Watson.

Watson scored five goals in the 1922–23 FA Cup run, but failed to hit the net in the Final – the one blemish in his career. But he was the Hammers' top scorer in four out of five of their first seasons in Division One and his goals helped King's side to a creditable sixth place finish in 1926–27. The Hammers had gained the respect of the top teams in the country, not just for their results but for their attacking football. But King was a realist and knew that attractive football alone would not keep his team in Division One. Watson's goals were the missing ingredient which kept the Hammers in the top flight for eight splendid seasons, before they dropped, disappointingly, back to Division Two in 1932, when even the return of an ageing Puddy could not save them.

It is difficult to over emphasise the part Syd King played in turning West Ham from a local works side into a top professional club with a national reputation. In his time as manager King oversaw the move from the old Memorial Grounds to the Boleyn, now universally known as Upton Park, worked tirelessly to achieve election to the Football League and steered the club to Division One and the 1923 FA Cup Final. The club's first manager achieved all this through total dedication and commitment to his beloved West Ham as they went from strength to strength. In the 1926–27 season the Hammers finished in sixth place in Division One, a feat unequalled until 1958–59 under the great Ted Fenton. In Jimmy Ruffell, Ted Hufton and Vic Watson, King brought three outstanding players to the club. All three became West Ham legends as well as England internationals and formed the core of the team which graced Division One through the 1920s.

West Ham appointed King as a shareholder in 1931 in recognition of his outstanding contribution to the club's success, but when his team were relegated the following season, the inevitable happened. Boards of professional football clubs behaved no differently in the 1930s to how they do today. King was brutally sacked after the Hammers lost their ninth game of the season in the lower division – yet another poor defensive display, this time away to Bradford Park Avenue. The board acted with brutal decisiveness, but not only because the club had been relegated after years of stability in the top flight, or simply as a result of a run of bad results in Division Two. For some time King had struggled with what he had created at West Ham and strangely and inexplicably, his previously strong and determined personality had begun to unravel. He began drinking more than usual. Ted Fenton, who King signed as an apprentice in 1932, claimed that the manager used to send him out to buy cases of beer from the Boleyn pub next to the ground.

There were also rumours about financial impropriety in his dealings with the club funds. Concerned, the board appointed an official to take responsibility for all financial affairs, while King was gradually stripped of all of his responsibilities. On 7 November the board issued this curt statement: 'It was unanimously decided that until further notice C. Paynter be given sole control of players and that E.S. King be notified accordingly.'

At an extraordinary meeting the following evening Syd King was suspended for three months for insubordination and allegedly being drunk and disorderly at a board meeting. King was a Mason, as were many of the directors, but even this could not save him. The board decided unanimously to sever all links with their former manager and banned him from Upton Park, offering their former hero a miserly pension of £3 a week.

This exceptional character, the former Thames Ironworks full-back who led West Ham with such distinction for so long, left Upton Park in disgrace.

King was devastated. His world was shattered. He had lost his standing in the game, the adoration and respect he commanded in East London and the job he loved so much. Within a month he was dead. The disgrace was too much to bear and Syd King killed himself by drinking a deadly mixture of corrosive liquid and alcohol. The coroner said King committed suicide while of unsound mind. Tragically, there would have been little in the way of drugs, counselling or psychotherapy to help King with his depression in those days. King's death left a huge shadow over the club which took a long time to lift.

They say that the careers of all politicians end in failure. It is probably also true of managers of professional football clubs. Syd King was a complex character and probably difficult to work with, but he was hugely driven and successful. He loved nothing more than fielding a West Ham side which included eight or nine local lads. If he could achieve this he said he was in seventh heaven. It is unlikely that this will ever happen again, much to the detriment of this once highly esteemed club.

West Ham United owes Syd King an enormous debt and despite his tragic end, his place in the history of the club is assured. Many of the early pioneers owe their careers to the hard-working, if ultimately flawed, gaffer. It is not too dramatic to say that this greatest of the vintage Hammers gave his life to West Ham United.

George Webb: staunch Corinthian

One of the outstanding players of the King era was our next early pioneer, George Webb. A very interesting young character, Webb was born in Poplar in 1887, attended Shaftesbury Road School and played his first serious football for Ilford Alliance. He signed for the Hammers as an amateur in August 1905 and spent his first few seasons in the reserves. He made his senior debut against Leyton in April 1909 and played a total of four first-team games that season in which he scored two goals, including one on his debut. Webb was a genuine amateur and worked for the family's busy toy-making business. Work commitments meant he only played a handful of games in his debut season, but Syd King quickly recognised the potential of his young centre-forward and was keen to play him on a regular basis.

In the following season Webb found the time to commit himself fully to his football. He established a regular place in the first team and proved a key member of the side as the Hammers reached the third round of the FA Cup. They thrashed Carlisle United 5–0 in the first round before easily overcoming Wolves. With the Hammers forwards in dazzling form, the strong favourites were well beaten by a George Webb hat-trick and two Danny Shea goals in a 5–1 victory. West Ham were at their scintillating best. It was one of the best performances in their short history and the *Athletic News* reported, 'To say that West Ham sprung a surprise at Wolverhampton would put it mildly.'

George Webb's career was up and running. In the third round the Hammers were drawn against London rivals QPR and must have fancied their chances after their fine victory at Molineux. Webb got the away side off to a great start with an early goal, but Rangers scored a controversial equaliser, sending the tie into a replay. Around 18,000 people packed into Upton Park to witness a disappointing game which ended 0–0 after 90 minutes. Three minutes from the end of extra-time Steer scored for QPR and the Hammers' brave FA Cup run was over.

They were to do even better in the 1910–11 season. On a foggy day in East London, two goals from the prolific Shea gave the Hammers a 2–1 first-round win over Nottingham Forest. The second round brought celebrated Preston North End to the Boleyn. The Lancastrians had won the League and Cup double in 1888–89, but the Irons have never cared about reputations and ran out easy 3–0 winners, with all three goals scored by their sensational centre-forward, George Webb. With two great Cup victories secured, the

Hammers drew champions-elect Manchester United at home in the third round. Despite the club cynically doubling the admission price, over 27,000 squeezed into the Boleyn – at least they kept the programme price down to the usual 1d. The record crowd were privileged to witness one of the biggest shocks in English football as Caldwell's goal late in the game gave the Hammers a 2–1 victory. As you can imagine, celebrations went on long into the night in the Boleyn Castle pub and the streets around the ground.

The quarter-final draw brought Blackburn Rovers to Upton Park, in what was an anticlimax for the East Enders. Rovers were ahead twice in the game before the Irons, roared on by 20,000 fans, fought back to equalise. Cruelly for the home crowd, Welsh international Davies scored a late winner and West Ham's FA Cup dream was over for another year. Good Cup runs have been a feature of West Ham's success over the years, and the goalscoring partnership of George Webb and Danny Shea was crucial to their fine Cup campaigns during the early years of the 20th century.

Webb's great assets were his speed, hefty physique and thunderous shooting – a Geoff Hurst of the early 20th century. His goal-a-game record for the Hammers earned the centre-forward seven England amateur caps and representative honours with the Southern League. Webb is famously known as the first West Ham player ever to represent his country – the first in a very long line. In 1910 he was selected for England amateurs against Switzerland and the following year he was a key member of the side in the matches against Wales, Belgium, Germany and Holland. The selectors were so impressed with the goalscoring ability of the Hammers' number-nine that he was chosen for the full England side against Wales in March 1911. Webb scored in the 3–0 victory over the Principality and the following month was included in the side to play Scotland. Despite his international reputation as an outstanding centre-forward, Webb steadfastly refused to turn professional. In his attitude to the game he showed the same Corinthian spirit as old Arnold Hills and was proud to be part of an honourable tradition.

In his three years at West Ham George Webb scored 32 League and Cup goals in 62 appearances and topped the Southern League goalscoring list in 1909–10. But these bare facts tell us little about the man, so we are indebted to Steve Marsh's wonderful archive on his website *theyflysohigh*. Steve has collected over 8,000 images of Hammers players past and present. As a result of careful research undertaken by Pam Bloomfield, granddaughter of West Ham director George Hone, we are able to gain an insight into the character of the great West Ham centre-forward.

We learn that Pam's grandfather was an inventor in the manner of many late Victorians and had taken out two patents with Thames Ironworks' boss Arnold Hills. 'They must have been good friends', writes Pam, as she unearths more and more West Ham connections in her family. Pam discovers that George Webb was Hone's stepson and was brought up at Margery Hall, the family home in Forest Gate – in those days a relatively affluent part of East London. It transpires that George Hone invested heavily in the club in the 1900s and was rewarded with a seat on the board, just at the time when young George was performing his FA Cup heroics. His stepfather's business acumen must have rubbed off on George and his brother Jack. The two brothers opened a toy factory and shop in East London which became highly successful and was one of the reasons why George refused to turn professional – the toy business took up so much of his time. His goalscoring partner at West Ham, Danny Shea, once said that Webb led a too-crowded life for a top footballer and it is true that young George never played more than six games in succession, such were his business commitments.

Webb led a busy life. He had a young wife, his business, football, Masonic duties and a wealthy stepfather. This crowded life set him apart from the regular professional footballer of his day. In 1911 he left his home-town club for a short spell with Football League club Manchester City. The principled goalscorer left City when he discovered they had paid West Ham a transfer fee for his services. Disillusioned, he abandoned his football career and returned to his toy factory.

In 1915 George Webb died tragically of consumption at the age of just 28. We know little of the circumstances of his death, although at the time consumption was often a catch-all diagnosis for a whole possible range of diseases. What we do know is that Webb was an exceptional footballer and an extraordinary character. He made an immense contribution to the success of the Hammers in the club's early years and his story provides us with a real insight into life in East London at the turn of the 19th century. Webb packed a tremendous amount into his short life. There is no more interesting vintage Hammer than George Webb.

Danny Shea: the 'Artful Dodger'

One player who benefitted from King's enlightened approach was our next pioneer, Danny Shea, one of the most gifted players to play for the club in the early 20th century. Shea was born in Wapping in November 1887 to a poor family. His parents, Daniel and Julie, had nine children, of whom only six survived. Danny's father was a commercial clerk and his older sister Minnie was employed as a vegetable cook in a local restaurant, while young Emma worked in a local cigarette factory. We know from the 1911 UK census that his dad's widowed mother also lived in the family home. We also know that Danny did his bit for the war effort by working in munitions during the conflict.

Legend has it that Shea was spotted by Charlie Paynter playing for the Builders' Arms in Stratford, just a few miles from Upton Park. This was no ordinary pub team. Between 1909 and 1917 the Builders' went 119 games undefeated. The 'Artful Dodger', as Danny became known, was a handsome boy. Clean shaven, the youngster was a dead ringer for a young version of the famous actor and West Ham supporter Ray Winstone. The Hammers moved quickly to sign the youngster who impressed as a skilful inside-forward with an eye for goal. In his first season for the Hammers, Shea top-scored with an impressive 20 goals and soon established himself as a regular in the side. The Southern League was a big step up in quality for the former pub team player and replacing the legendary Billy Grassam did not make it any easier for the Wapping lad. Paynter need not have worried as Shea topped the club's goalscoring list for consecutive seasons between 1908 and 1912. Danny's exceptional goalscoring feats included four against Plymouth Argyle in 1908–09 and a hat-trick in the Hammers' 4–2 win over Swindon Town the same season. In 1910–11 he achieved the proud feat of being top scorer in the Southern League and was selected for the League representative side on a number of occasions. Charlie Paynter had clearly uncovered a gem of a player on the park pitches of Stratford.

Skipping over the difficult pitches, Shea's attacking play brought the East End boy rich rewards. His best season came in 1909–10 when he scored an exceptional 31 goals in 43 appearances. I like to think of Danny Shea as an early version of 'Budgie' Byrne, cheeky on the ball and able to open up opponents with a single defence-splitting pass. However, his goalscoring record was far superior to the Hammers' midfield wizard of the 1960s. If Byrne had Geoff Hurst to take the sting out of opposing defences, Shea had Freddy Harrison. Danny's partnership with Harrison reaped rich rewards as the pair scored 40 goals

between them in 1911–12, including two more Shea hat-tricks against Brentford and Norwich City. The young goal machine was described at the time as, 'An artful schemer and delicate dribbler who had the knack of wheeling suddenly when near goal and unleashing a thunderous shot.'

Quick, skilful players like Shea would have, of course, been hampered by the playing conditions of their time. In 1863 the FA introduced a rule which stated: 'No one wearing projecting nails, iron plates or gutta-percha on the soles of his boots is allowed to play.'

In 1886 Ellis Patent Boot advertised proper studs which they claimed were 'a wonderful improvement in making football boots suitable in any weather'. These studs were nailed on to boots of thick leather which stretched well above the ankle. The toe area was toughened to look and feel like modern working boots with shiny steel toecaps. Players would stand in a hot bath wearing their new boots to mould the boots to fit the size of their feet. In his book *Association Football*, F.N.S. Clark suggested that after buying a new pair of boots, the purchaser should 'sit on the edge of the bath with the boots soaking in tepid water for about half an hour'. It was vital to look after your clunky, thick leather footwear by daubing them with thick layers of dubbin after cleaning, before buffing them like mad to obtain a shiny finish. Dubbin would normally be applied with newspaper – in my case my dad's old *News Chronicle*. Better-off households would shine their boots with old shirts or other garments.

The great Geordie centre-forward Jackie Milburn used to wear his new boots down the pit to soften them up for matches and continued this somewhat extreme practice long after being selected for England. Lightweight boots with soft toecaps and screw-in or moulded studs were introduced in the mid-60s, but few park players could afford such luxury. Today's boots are like ballet shoes compared to the leather clodhoppers the old players were forced to wear.

The first professional footballers wore these clumsy and uncomfortable boots on bumpy, often heavy pitches. Crude shin pads were simply rolled-up copies of mum's old *Woman's Own*. If this was not difficult enough the old leather balls, with their porous cover and prominent leather lace, could look a couple of sizes larger when caked all round by an inch of thick mud. If we add cold water baths and washing your boots and face in the same grimy trough, you are about as far away as possible from the luxury enjoyed by today's Premier League stars.

Back in the 19th century more skilful, technical players would not only have been at the mercy of heavy pitches, uncomfortable boots and sodden balls, but also lenient referees who allowed aggressive defenders to thunder into opponents displaying the slightest hint of skill on the ball. West Ham has a tradition of playing technical football and developing skilful and creative players. This philosophy was severely tested in the early days, particularly when the appalling conditions of the 1923 White Horse Cup Final virtually handed the trophy to the more direct Bolton side. But Syd King stuck to his guns and continued to encourage skilful ball-players as he strove to establish the Hammers' reputation for free-flowing, attacking football.

The heavy boots and muddy ball failed to dampen the enthusiasm of the artful Danny Shea. During Shea's time at the Boleyn the club hovered around the middle of Division One of the Southern League, with a highest finish of third in 1912–13. But West Ham have always been a good Cup side, with their attacking style probably not suited to the weekly grind of League football. Shea's Hammers did enjoy several good Cup runs and reached the third round on several occasions. One particular Cup tie stands out.

On 14 January 1911 the Hammers were drawn at home against Nottingham Forest in the first round of the FA Cup. Forest were locked in a relegation battle and would not have fancied a trip to East London to face a ferociously passionate North Bank. Two goals from Shea saw the Hammers through to the next round in a 2–1 victory, their first against a top-flight club. The first half bordered on the farcical as both players and officials struggled to cope with a good old East London pea-souper. Fortunately, the fog partially lifted for the second half, but not before Shea scored twice, punching the ball into the net on both occasions. With the awful visibility, the Hammers' inside-forward got away with his two indiscretions in the mist. Years later Shea confessed that both goals should have been disallowed and Forest ought to have won the game. 'I punched both goals into the net in full view of several opponents,' he said.

But the mischievous handballs were rare slips in an otherwise unblemished career. It was inevitable that Shea's remarkable goalscoring record and great skill would attract the interest of Football League clubs. Sure enough, he was transferred to Blackburn Rovers in the middle of the 1912–13 season for a record fee of £2,000. He continued to score goals and helped Rovers to their second Division One Championship in three years, at which point war interrupted the League programme. Danny spent the war in East London where he worked in the munitions industry, playing 73 matches for the Hammers' London Combination wartime side, scoring 63 goals, including a run of 32 in 32 matches. Even in wartime his appetite for goals remained insatiable.

Shea returned to Blackburn after the war and stayed until 1920, making a total of 97 appearances and scoring 61 goals. In his time at Ewood Park, Shea gained two England caps and was selected to represent the Football League on a number of occasions – a relatively small return given his extraordinary statistics.

At the end of his career Shea returned briefly to Upton Park where he made just 16 appearances before moving west to Fulham. He continued his goalscoring exploits at Craven Cottage by netting 24 goals in 107 League and Cup games. His fellow players were quick to recognise Shea's qualities. Patsy Gallacher, the great Celtic player of the time, described him as 'One of the greatest ball artists who has ever played for England...Danny

Shea. His manipulation of the ball was bewildering. He was the Prince of Partners, the intellectual footballer.'

At the end of his playing career Shea took up coaching and had very definite ideas about working with professionals and how to get the best out of them. Shea came under the spell of the innovative Swiss coach Karl Rappan, famous for employing his bolt system with his successful national side. At the heart of Rappan's ideas about football was a focus on getting the players to pass and move at pace – this is what interested Danny. Rappan later said of Shea's work with footballers, '...he was ahead of his time...he began the "push and run"...that was to dominate soccer after World War Two'. (Belton, 2007). Shea explained his coaching ideas in the following way, '...it is better to build on what someone is doing more than get them to do what they're not doing'.

This simple but effective approach is reminiscent of the man-management skills of Brian Clough. Footballers did not easily take to over-complicating what is essentially a fairly straightforward game and intuitive coaches like Shea and Clough knew this.

Like Bobby Moore and Geoff Hurst after him, Danny Shea fulfilled every ounce of his undoubted potential and his prolific goalscoring earned him international recognition. He would have been delighted to have appeared in the same West Ham side as Puddy and Vic Watson – if only on one occasion. His rise from a promising pub footballer in Stratford to international honours was well deserved and a tribute to Charlie Paynter and West Ham United, who enabled the talented youngster's delicate skills to flourish in the era of leather boots, muddy balls and uncompromising defenders.

Brian Belton recognised Shea's contribution to West Ham United and football in general, '...his contribution to football was massive...the seeds of the modern game were sown by the likes of Paynter, Puddefoot, Kay, Tresadern and the sharp and lively mind of Danny Shea'. (Belton, 2007)

Daniel Harold Shea died in 1960 at the age of 73. He spent his retirement years coaching in Switzerland and Woking in England, before becoming a publican later in life. There is no question that Shea was one of the greatest players ever to have worn the claret and blue of West Ham and was, arguably, the greatest of the very early pioneers.

George 'Gatling Gun' Hilsdon

George Hilsdon was a true Cockney. He was born in Bromley-by-Bow, which remains to this day an area of extreme poverty, poor health and run-down housing. Set in the Lea Valley and surrounded by Stratford Marshes and Victoria Park, Bow is close enough to gritty Mile End and Limehouse to qualify as inner-city. The borough suffered extensive bomb damage in the last war and has been the subject of scandalous neglect ever since. Bromley-by-Bow is one of the East London boroughs from which West Ham draw their major support, and some of their best players. Players like George Hilsdon. The great centre-forward was born in 1885 in long-since demolished Donald Street. Of course, economic and social conditions in Hilsdon's time would have been markedly worse than they are today. For George, football provided the opportunity to improve his life and prospects and escape the hardship of living in the lower reaches of the Lea Valley. But for football George would have faced a precarious working life in the docks or one of the East End's numerous industrial death traps.

The Hilsdon's house had five rooms. George lived there with his parents, George and Katherine, sister Katherine and Betty Vance, a 62-year-old woman, who is described in the 1911 UK census return as a general servant, but was more likely to have been a widowed friend. Young George attended Marner Street School and later Plashet Lane when the family moved to East Ham. He was a talented footballer, captained his school team and played for East Ham Boys in the Corinthian Shield. A teammate, in what must have been a formidable school side, was the future Hammers player Billy Bridgeman. The young Hilsdon showed rare promise and even came to the attention of the local press: 'George Hilsdon, Plashet's crack centre-half, is one of the very best lads performing in the Corinthian Shield...he leads in a formidable manner...He tackles fearlessly...and has scored in every Corinthian match.' (*The South Essex Mail*)

Thanks to Colm Kerrigan's admirable short biography, *Gatling Gun George Hilsdon*, we are able to piece together a detailed and reliable account of his career, both at West Ham and later Chelsea. What is clear is that young George not only showed a real aptitude for the game but as a young man displayed natural leadership qualities. But as Kerrigan points out, we know little about Hilsdon as a teenager, except that he joined Boleyn Castle FC in 1904, the year West Ham moved to Upton Park. Syd King spotted the 19-year-old George playing in a local Sunday League match, much like Charlie Paynter had picked out Danny Shea. King signed the youngster for the Hammers in November 1904 and at Upton Park he joined up again with his old schoolmate Billy Bridgeman, along with an assortment of local lads and imported Scots. Today promising young footballers from the area struggle to compete with highly paid foreign players. For local lads like George Hilsdon it was imported Scots who provided the competition.

Hilsdon played his first game for the Hammers on 11 February 1905 against New Brompton. The youngster made a real impact with a goal on his debut and proved to his manager that he was well worth a place in the first team. His promise was confirmed when he scored a brilliant hat-trick that season in the 6–0 thrashing of Bristol Rovers. His performance moved the *East End News* football reporter to report with rare insight, 'The match was quite a triumph for the new West Ham centre-forward, who was responsible for three of the half a dozen…With a little more experience he will doubtless develop into a real first class player.'

Hilsdon had made a terrific start to his career and his future at West Ham looked assured. While his Bow schoolmates began their working lives humping sacks of sugar at Tate & Lyle, labouring in the sulphuric fog at Bryant & May, or taking their chances in the docks, young George was destined to be a famous professional footballer. However, life in East London in the early 20th century rarely ran smoothly and George picked up a number of injuries towards the end of his first season and lost his place at the start of the campaign. Billy Grassam and Harry Stapley provided stiff competition for places in the forward line at the Boleyn and young George's appearances in the 1905–06 season were restricted to nine games in which he scored just three goals. A combination of this competition and injuries led Syd King to consider the future of the promising boy from Bow.

It may seem odd to claim vintage status for a player who enjoyed the best years of his career at London rivals Chelsea. But this has been a regular phenomenon at Upton Park. For example, in recent times Hammers' youngsters like Joe Cole, Rio Ferdinand, Frank Lampard, Glen Johnson, Jermain Defoe, Michael Carrick and others have been sold to rival clubs just at the moment when their immense promise was about to be realised. Every one of these young players was sold to reduce the club's crippling debts. But Hilsdon was different. He was a home boy and only injuries prevented him from realising his potential at his home club.

Much to the bewilderment of Hammers supporters, the young Hilsdon left the club to join their West London rivals on a free transfer. Colm Kerrigan attempted an explanation for Hilsdon's departure.

> *It is difficult to understand why the shrewd Syd King was willing to let him go on a free transfer. Perhaps he had despaired of George ever getting over his injuries. Or perhaps, with Stapley doing so well as centre-forward with competent cover available in the form of Bridgeman and…Billy Grassam, he may have seen no place for him in his future team plans.*

This seems a plausible explanation for his leaving, but still does not fully explain why one of the best talents to emerge from the club in years was handed on a plate to a Football League rival – *plus ça change…*

Of course, Chelsea was a much bigger club than West Ham in the early part of the 20th century. In the 1904–05 season the West Londoners attracted a crowd of 60,000 fans into Stamford Bridge for a match against Manchester United. Hilsdon had joined a very serious professional outfit and he made a sensational debut. On 1 September 1906, he scored a remarkable five times in Chelsea's 9–2 victory over a shell-shocked Glossop. It was 50 years before the great Jimmy Greaves equalled this astonishing debut performance. Hilsdon's nickname, 'Gatling Gun', was well deserved as the centre-forward began rattling in the goals for his new club. The news of George's new-found success in West London must have been received on the North Bank with a heavy sense of irony.

But the youngster's spectacular debut gave him a lot to live up to and the Football League was a tough environment in which to learn the game. George soon became a marked man as his reputation quickly spread among the tough League defenders. A local West London newspaper reported on its sports pages that in a match against Fulham George received, 'A terrific charge after about 10 minutes and for the rest of the game he wandered about, a shade of his former self. In the dressing room at half-time he was writhing and twisting in pain.'

Welcome to the Football League, George. The *Fulham Observer* also reported that he 'found it difficult to do anything, as directly the ball came in his direction three opponents were on his track.'

But despite the close marking and robust physical attention, a determined George continued to score goals and demonstrate his class at this level. In a match against Worksop a few weeks later he scored an astonishing six times and notched an impressive 27 goals in his debut season for his new club. Hilsdon's impressive goalscoring was largely responsible for Chelsea gaining promotion to the top flight of English football in their first year as a professional outfit.

His prolific scoring rate and deadly shot soon attracted the attention of the England selectors. The *West London Press* described a typical Hilsdon goal, with Leicester City as the victims on this occasion: 'Hilsdon made a bewildering side movement which just for a second…nonplussed two Leicester players around him…in that brief space Hilsdon had flashed the ball past the astounded Lewis. It was a shot without the slightest element of speculation. It was a Hilsdon goal.'

Notes in the Chelsea match programme later described George's ferocious shots as 'unstoppable, and which travel like shots from a gun.'

The national press alerted the England selectors to George's prodigious talents: 'He commands the ball wonderfully, has a fine conception of a centre's duties, and above all, is a deadly shot.'

This early version of Geoff Hurst had taken the highest level of English football by storm and his achievements were finally recognised by the England selectors. Hilsdon was chosen for the match against Ireland on 15 February 1907. However, things did not quite go as well as he would have liked and by his own admission George had a poor match. Much to his disappointment he was promptly dropped for the next England game. But his goalscoring exploits for Chelsea meant that he could not be ignored for long and was recalled for the South v North England trial match in March 1908. This time George did grasp his opportunity, scoring all four goals in a match which ended in a 4–4 draw. His striking partnership with Tottenham's Vivian Woodward was a great success and the East Ender's career was back on track.

In Hilsdon's relatively brief international career he scored 14 goals in eight appearances, including four in England's 7–0 victory over Hungary and twice in games against Ireland, Austria, Wales and Bohemia. The *Fulham Observer* was unstinting in its praise for the Chelsea star, claiming that 'Hilsdon was now England's acknowledged greatest centre-forward.'

George Hilsdon did not enjoy a career of untroubled upward trajectory. It was full of ups and downs, although his brilliance was never in doubt. His international star did burn brightly for a time before it fizzled out in spectacular fashion. He was dropped by the selectors after an indifferent game against a weak Ireland side, despite scoring his customary two goals. He never played for England again. This was not a good time for George, because at the same time his club career went into steep decline as the goals began to dry up. Chelsea were relegated in 1909 and, having signed Vivian Woodward from Spurs, decided to release Hilsdon from his contract. In June 1912, in what must have been a humiliating experience for England's great centre-forward, he returned to West Ham on a free transfer and with his tail firmly between his legs.

In his Chelsea career Hilsdon scored 107 goals in 164 matches, represented England eight times and won a reputation as the most dangerous centre-forward in the country. But we know there is no sentiment in professional football, so he returned to the Boleyn in 1912 to eat humble pie and determined to rescue his career.

Despite receiving some early and predictable stick from the North Bank, Hilsdon settled quickly into a Hammers forward line that included Danny Shea and Freddie Harrison. As the *East Ham Echo* reported, 'Good as Shea has always been, he is 20 per cent better since the introduction of Hilsdon.'

George was nothing if not a fighter and returned to something like his old form in his second spell with the Hammers. His strong showing helped the club finish in third place in the Southern League. After a strong display against Southampton the *Echo* confirmed George's return to form: 'Hilsdon was once more the master of the attack and it would be difficult to estimate his share in placing the Hammers in 5th place…as against 12th at the same period last season.'

Without partner Danny Shea for the latter part of the season, George finished the campaign as top scorer with 17 goals in 36 League and Cup games. The following year proved to be a defining season for West Ham – and for George Hilsdon. In November 1913 Syd King signed a 19-year-old from Gillingham by the name of Syd Puddefoot. The newcomer promptly scored 13 goals in his first 11 matches. If that was not enough of a threat to Hilsdon's place in the side, Dick Leafe top scored that season with an impressive

21 goals. Suddenly and for the second time in his career, the great man was dispensable to his West Ham manager. His modest season's total of six goals in 17 games did not help his cause. West Ham finished in sixth place in 1914 and with the highly regarded Puddefoot in the side the future looked bright at the Boleyn. Even the ultra-realist King must have believed that honours were now a real possibility, even if George Hilsdon was not expected to spearhead the assault on the Southern League Championship.

With war imminent the country expected professional football to be suspended for the duration of the hostilities. However, the Football League decided the 1914–15 season should go ahead as planned. This must have delighted King – his team won six out of their first 12 matches, with Puddefoot scoring nine goals and Leafe and Hilsdon contributing seven between them. King must also have been happy to see the nearly veteran George acting as mentor and inspiration to the new kid on the block from Gillingham. The Hammers' Championship challenge was very much on track.

In the end the Hammers could only finish fourth that season and in the following year football was relegated into insignificance by wider events in Europe. In late autumn of 1914, with the reality of war beginning to bite, Lord Kitchener made his famous 'your country needs you' appeal. The ever-patriotic Football League supported the official line by backing Kitchener's emotional rhetoric, calling for all single professional footballers to temporarily hang up their boots and join their fellow countrymen on the Western Front. In December 1914 the 17th Service (Football) Battalion of the Middlesex Regiment was established and quickly recruited many London-based footballers.

Kitchener's cynical appeal to the patriot nature of the British people was not without its critics. The *Athletic News* vigorously rejected his call in the strongest of terms, claiming that it was nothing less than 'an attempt by the ruling classes to stop the recreation on one day a week of the masses…What do they care about the poor man in sport? The poor are giving their lives for this country in their thousands…'

For the *News* Kitchener and his political friends were nothing more than a 'small clique of virulent snobs'. Ouch! How the truth hurts. However, over 2,000 of Britain's 5,000 professional footballers bowed to this emotional blackmail by agreeing to enlist, including several Upton Park favourites. Jack Tresadern joined the Royal Garrison Artillery, Joe Webster signed up for the Football Battalion, while George Hilsdon was eventually recruited by the East Surrey Regiment, but not before he played a further eight games in the 1914–15 season.

We know that West Ham supporters formed their own Pals' Battalion in World War One. The 13th (Service) were part of the Essex Regiment and Brian Belton (2007) believes that the battle cry of the West Ham Pals was, of course, 'Up the Irons'. The battles they fought at the Somme, Ypres, Vimy Ridge and Cambrai took a terrible toll on the battalion's young men with over 34,000 wounded, killed or missing. Among the casualties of the war were six former West Ham players. Fred Griffiths, Frank Costello, William Jones, Frank Cannon, Bill Kennedy and Arthur Stallard were all killed on the Western Front, while George Hilsdon's striking partner, Freddy Harrison, was badly gassed and never played football again.

Arthur Stallard joined the Hammers in 1913 as a replacement for Syd Puddefoot who was rumoured to be on his way out of the club. Puddefoot never did leave at this time and struck up an effective partnership with young Stallard. It appeared that the club had unearthed another goalscoring sensation to equal Puddefoot, Danny Shea and George Hilsdon and, like the others, he was expected to go on and play for England. Sadly, young Stallard made the ultimate sacrifice and was killed in France on 30 November 1917, a few months after lighting up the Boleyn with his exceptional talent.

Like many of his teammates and West Ham fans, George Hilsdon fought in the bloody battles on the Western Front, enduring an horrific mustard gas attack at Arras in 1917, which badly damaged his lungs. But the old centre-forward survived the war, returned to civilian life and in 1918 returned to pick up the pieces of his shattered football career. He joined Chatham Town and scored a few goals, but a combination of waning enthusiasm, wartime injuries and permanent loss of form forced Hilsdon to retire from the game in 1919.

Like all professional footballers of his day, George never retired from the game with vast riches, nor did he receive the honours handed out to modern players with a fraction of his great skill. In his time professional football was not a way out of poverty. It was an opportunity to enjoy a few years doing what you loved the most and avoid spending the best years of your life in some dreary dead-end factory job.

There are many rumours surrounding George's post-playing days, most of which should not be taken seriously. One rumour alleges that George attempted to avoid war service by continually hiding from the authorities, before he was eventually discovered by the police hiding in a chicken run. The football press turned on George when he lost form, which would not have helped his confidence. In a veiled reference to his alleged drink problem, the *Fulham Observer* reported after one game, 'Hilsdon did very little at centre-forward…perhaps he is unable to concentrate on his game.'

East London footballer Reg Grove, who might have showed more understanding, claimed: 'He had become too sociable, too careless with his strength and vitality.'

Some claim Hilsdon liked a drink a bit too much and slid into alcoholism. Professional football in the UK has always been blighted by a strong drinking culture and few clubs have suffered from this more than West Ham. His alleged drinking may explain in part the sharp ups and downs in his career. But some of us prefer to discard these malicious rumours and show a degree of sympathy to the West Ham and Chelsea legend. He was not frightened of work, although as an old East Ender much of it was old-fashioned ducking and diving. As Colm Kerrigan tells us, George eked out a living '…in various ways, all of them on the right side of the law…just…One of his escapades…was to go around several East End pubs, raffling boxes of chocolates, but arranging for the prize to be won by…his wife'.

Perhaps we should put this down to the old East End spirit of survival rather than any devious criminal intent. With nothing to fall back on George was willing to try everything. For a few months he ran a pub and even briefly joined Fred Karno's famous circus. But his wartime experience had left the former England centre-forward with badly damaged lungs – a disability which prevented him from earning a living by more legitimate means.

George 'Gatling Gun' Hilsdon died in Leicester in 1941. The funeral of this great England footballer was attended by just four people; his son, daughter, son-in-law and grandson. There is no stone to mark his grave, no memorial plaque anywhere to acknowledge his considerable achievements in football. The funeral was paid for by the Football Association, an indication that the great man died in poverty.

Hilsdon may have made his biggest impact on the English game at Chelsea, but he was West Ham through and through. His humble origins in Bromley-by-Bow and his two spells at the Boleyn qualify him as a genuine pioneer. George was a wonderful footballer and one of the best to come out of the East End. Hammers fans should not forget the important contribution he made to the club's early years.

Syd 'Puddy' Puddefoot

With George Hilsdon and Danny Shea spearheading the attack, Syd King and Charlie Paynter believed they had assembled a side good enough to mount a realistic challenge for the Southern League title. King's combination of young local talent and a few experienced Scots achieved a third place finish in 1912–13 and hopes were high for the new season, despite the transfer of Danny Shea to Blackburn Rovers. The principal reason for such optimism was the arrival at the Boleyn of a 19-year-old from Bow, the incomparable Syd Puddefoot, one the greatest players ever to wear the claret and blue of West Ham United.

The manager would have been disappointed to see his team finish back in sixth place in 1913–14, as the return of George Hilsdon from Chelsea and the arrival of the inexperienced Puddefoot failed to compensate for the loss of Danny Shea. Clearly the young pretender needed a little time to find his feet. There was never any doubt that Puddy would make his mark in the game. At 5ft 11in tall and weighing an impressive 12st, Puddefoot set the Boleyn alight! He scored 16 goals in 20 League and Cup games in his first full season and would have scored more but for a serious ankle injury that put him out of action for a few weeks. As Northcutt and Shoesmith (1994) tell us, 'The 19-year-old Syd Puddefoot arrived and found the net on 13 occasions in his first 11 games…He proved he could find the net when opposed by a quality defence, scoring in both games of a replayed FA Cup tie against Liverpool.'

The outbreak of war in the summer of 1914 cast a dark shadow over the country and professional football became an irrelevancy. But as we have seen, the 1914–15 season was allowed to go ahead, despite many dissenting voices. In that war-torn season the young Puddy found the net 18 times in 35 appearances and helped his side to fourth place in the Southern League Division One. The boy from Bow took the Southern League by storm and King could now begin to dream about promotion to the Football League.

Sydney Charles Puddefoot was born just up the road from George Hilsdon, on 17 October 1894. He attended nearby Park School and played his early football for Limehouse Town. Syd's parents, Harry and Sarah, had a total of 13 children of which only five, all boys, survived into adulthood. This was an exceptionally high rate of infant mortality even for Mile End Town, one of the poorest boroughs in the UK. Thousands of undernourished young children died of scarlet fever, whooping cough, TB and influenza in the days before advances in medical knowledge and mass vaccination brought these killer diseases under control.

This enormous family lived in a five-bedroom house with an outside toilet and no bathroom. Young Syd's father, Harry, was a foreman horse-keeper and his older brother, Alfred, worked in the counting house of a china manufacturer. With at least three wages coming into the household, the Puddefoots were not poverty-stricken and were relatively free from the shadow of the workhouse. Nonetheless, life would have been tough for this respectable working-class East End family.

To make something of your life in these social conditions the Puddefoot children needed a combination of hard work and generous helpings of luck. Syd Puddefoot's fortune was to be born to score goals. He showed outstanding promise as a schoolboy and soon came to the notice of the selectors of the London Junior side. By a stroke of luck the Hammers' manager Syd King, on one of his many scouting trips, spotted the teenager playing for London against Surrey Juniors and quickly recognised the boy's potential. King knew he had unearthed a real gem and wasted no time in signing the promising centre-forward. The youngster made his first-team debut against Norwich City on 1 March 1913 and just three weeks later Puddefoot scored his first goal for the Hammers against Brighton.

With Danny Shea out of the picture and Hilsdon struggling to find his form, Puddy seized his opportunity. In January 1913 'our Syd' scored five times, including a hat-trick in seven minutes, in a magnificent 8–1 win against Chesterfield in the FA Cup – no banana-skin Cup shock for this West Ham side on this occasion. Puddy's goalscoring feat against Chesterfield remains an FA Cup individual scoring record for a West Ham player and the Hammers' biggest ever win in the competition.

Puddefoot quickly struck up a partnership with Dickie Leafe, who Syd King had brought in from Sheffield United as a replacement for Danny Shea, but it was the youngster who stole the glory. He scored a wonderful hat-trick against Exeter City in January 1915 which led the local paper to report, 'Some 14 minutes elapsed before Puddefoot, who completely outshone every other forward on the field, opened the scoring for his side and 10 minutes later he was again successful in finding the net.'

Puddy's goalscoring feats were becoming the stuff of legend. A photograph of Syd scoring one of his five goals against Chesterfield is a graphic illustration of the qualities of the player. The Hammers centre-forward is pictured rising high above the Chesterfield centre-half and goalkeeper, who despite their best efforts to knock him off the ball, fail to prevent Puddy from crashing a bullet header high into the net, much to the delight of the fans on the North Bank.

Puddy had made his mark at West Ham and established a growing reputation in the Southern League. In just over two seasons his physical courage, skill and goalscoring feats endeared the local boy to all Hammers fans. Syd King saw his young local hero as the heart of a West Ham side capable of promotion to the Football League. But all of that would have to wait until the most horrific conflict in European history played itself out on the fields of Northern France.

One of the many consequences of the war, and it is a fairly trivial one, was that attendances at League games fell away in the second half of 1914–15. Clubs were losing money and when the Southern League decided to bow to pressure and disband the following season, most professional footballers were laid off, with many joining the services as we have seen. But football did continue to be played through the war, if in a drastically reduced form. The British public cherished their football and with stories of brutality, butchery and rage seeping out from France, the on-field heroics of players like Puddefoot at least provided some much-needed distraction.

The London Combination was formed in 1915 as a League competition for the capital's major clubs and lasted for the duration of the war. Taking full advantage of the liberal registration rules, the Hammers took to the Combination like a duck to water. Many Combination teams were made up of 'guests' or 'ringers' as they would be known today. Danny Shea and Ted Hufton returned from the north and several players were signed from clubs like Glasgow Rangers and Everton. This hybrid mix of locals, ex-players and ringers served the club well and in the four years of the Combination the Hammers finished second, first, second and third. This impressive wartime record convinced the Football League to accept West Ham into the new Division Two when the war ended in November 1918.

Unlike most West Ham professionals, Syd Puddefoot was not conscripted to fight until late in the war and was therefore free to play for the Hammers in the Combination. Puddy made 126 appearances in the wartime League, scoring close to 100 goals including an amazing seven goals in a match against Crystal Palace. But it would be wrong to think that Puddefoot had an undemanding war while his former teammates were risking their lives on the Somme. As Brian Belton (2007) points out, 'Syd Puddefoot worked long hours, exhausting and often dangerous shifts in munitions factories.' Syd was doing his own bit for the war effort before he was eventually called-up.

When World War One finally ended in 1918 professional football quickly regained its place in the popular imagination. For West Ham and Syd Puddefoot in particular, the post-war years proved to be the most exciting phase in the club's history. By the time professional football restarted after the war, Charlie Paynter and Syd King had assembled a wonderful West Ham team which not only included the prolific Puddefoot, but terrific footballers like Jimmy Ruffell, George Kay, Eddie Hufton, Jack Tresadern, Vic Watson, Sid Bishop, Dickie Leafe, Billy Brown and Jack Young.

Sir Alex Ferguson has described his job at Manchester United as building a club rather than a team. This is just the philosophy that King adopted back at the beginning of the 20th century. King was in it for the long term and his sole aim was to lead the Hammers into the Football League. The club's outstanding record in the wartime London Combination and their consistent performances in the Southern League meant that King's dream eventually became a reality. Amid long celebrations in East London, West Ham were accepted into the newly-enlarged Football League for 1919–20 and with Puddefoot at centre-forward the manager would have been confident about his side's prospects at this elevated level.

King's side did him proud that first season in Division Two, finishing in seventh place behind champions Tottenham Hotspur. The Hammers achieved 19 League wins, largely through the efforts of Puddy, their principal goalscorer. The boy from Bow scored 26 goals in 43 matches as he cashed in on the chances created by the team's quick-passing, attacking style. With four against Nottingham Forest and a hat-trick in the match with Port Vale, Puddy was beginning to develop a national reputation. West Ham were certainly enjoying a successful first season in the dizzy heights of Division Two, which was only slightly spoiled by losing 0–3 at home to Spurs in the third round of the FA Cup. King's post-match mood would have improved when he was told that 47,646 people had crammed into the Boleyn to witness the contest.

In the early 1920s Puddefoot continued his goalscoring form for the Hammers and was the club's top scorer in both 1920–21 and 1921–22. Syd King had plucked the youngster from the obscurity of junior football and taken him to the heights of the Football League. Here was West Ham's centre-forward for the next 10 years. But things never go that smoothly at the Boleyn and in mid-season King dropped a bombshell that shook the club to its foundations.

In February 1922 West Ham sold Syd Puddefoot, the greatest centre-forward in the club's history, to Falkirk – yes, Falkirk – for £5,000. The club attempted to explain the transfer in the next match programme. The manager blamed Puddy's departure on his ambition to develop a business life outside football. This did nothing to appease the fans who were incensed and nearly caused a riot when they learned that Puddefoot had no wish to leave his beloved Hammers. The club was richer by £5,000, but the team had lost their priceless centre-forward. Predictably, without their top scorer, the Hammers failed to win promotion to Division One that season and without Puddy's goals dropped back to a disappointing fourth place. You could not really make this up – only West Ham could sell their best player to a minor Scottish club when he was at the top of his game.

Fortunately for our hero he returned to English football in 1926 with Blackburn Rovers, who paid Falkirk £4,000 for the ex-Hammer. Now 30 years of age, Puddefoot was warmly welcomed at Ewood Park as Mike Jackman (2006) argues: 'Puddefoot…was the type of gifted playmaker that the club desperately needed, and following his arrival there was an immediate upturn in results…Puddefoot remained one of the most gifted footballers of his era.'

Rovers' money was well spent. Puddy's goals took the Lancashire side to Wembley for the 1928 FA Cup Final, where they beat Huddersfield 3–1, Puddy scoring the opening goal.

During his time at Blackburn he won the first of his four England caps when he was selected to play against Northern Ireland.

As he reached the veteran stage in his career, Puddefoot yearned to return to his roots. In 1932, at the age of 37, he returned to East London in what turned out to be a vain attempt to save the Hammers from relegation – it was one move too many for the great centre-forward. He retired in 1933 having scored an impressive 146 goals in 375 Football League matches. His love of the game inevitably led him into management, which began not in the familiar environment of London or Lancashire, but in the steamy cauldron of Turkish football where for a short time he led Fenerbahce, before picking up the reins of rivals Galatasaray. Tony Hogg (2004) points out that the adventure '…proved to be a bad move when he was badly manhandled while trying to calm down fighting players and spectators during a big game.'

Chastened by his Turkish experience, Puddefoot returned to England and in 1937 was appointed manager of Northampton Town, where he remained until the outbreak of World War Two.

Puddefoot finally retired from the game he loved in 1963 and moved down to south Essex, where he did a little gentle scouting for Southend United. Puddy had a glorious career in professional football. The young lad from the overcrowded family home in Bow had conquered the North Bank at the Boleyn, had become a favourite at Ewood Park – a place not noted for its love of Londoners – and gained four England caps. For the record the young Puddy, much like fellow Hammers Bobby Moore and Geoff Hurst, was a decent cricketer, having played eight matches as a professional for Essex in 1922 and 1923. A right-handed batsman and medium-paced bowler, on his debut he captured the prized wicket of the Derbyshire captain, G.R. Jackson. Unfortunately, the great footballer had little success in his other seven matches and was released by the county the following season. Sadly, we do not know how Puddefoot, as a boy from the back streets of East London, was introduced to cricket. Perhaps it was through his father or a dedicated teacher, as it was for Graham Gooch 50 years later. There were few opportunities for promising young cricketers in the East End and it is a great credit to the young sportsman that Essex wanted to sign him as a professional.

But it was football and in particular his first spell at West Ham, that earned Puddy, not just pioneer, but legendary status at Upton Park. Sydney Charles Puddefoot died from pneumonia in Rochford Hospital, Essex on 2 October 1972. He was one of the finest players ever to wear the claret and blue of West Ham United. Historian Brian Belton has described Puddy as 'an innovative adventurer and one of the greatest ever Hammers' – an appropriate epitaph for a true East Ender.

George Kay: captain courageous

Like many Football League clubs, the Hammers built their team on a combination of young local lads, a sprinkling of northerners and one or two Scots. The spiritual leader of the successful King side of the 1920s was their centre-half and captain and our next pioneer, George Kay. In many respects Kay was the Bobby Moore of his day, the beating heart of a club that was clearly on the up.

Born in Manchester in 1891, Kay joined the Hammers in 1919 after spells with Bolton Wanderers and the Belfast club Distillery. In the words of a teammate Kay was, '...strong as I've seen a lad of his years. Nothing passed him. He's a big chap, but fast and bright.'

A World War One veteran, Sgt Kay served on the Western Front with the Royal Garrison Artillery before being sent home suffering from shell shock and the effects of gas. He played a few games for the Hammers while on leave and at the end of the war joined the club for a fee of £100. He made his debut against Barnsley at the beginning of the 1919–20 season and succeeded in keeping his place in a very good West Ham side which included excellent players like Puddefoot, Jimmy Ruffell, Vic Watson and Jack Tresadern. The centre-half impressed Syd King with his committed displays and his natural leadership qualities. In 1922, the manager decided to appoint Kay as club captain, a position he held for the next six seasons in which the Hammers reached the FA Cup Final and won promotion to Division One. George Kay was captain of one of the best teams ever produced at Upton Park.

In the years immediately following World War One professional football got back to some sort of normality. West Ham achieved Syd King's ambition to secure promotion to the Football League and the fans began to dream about a place at the top table of English football. For once, the club was financially secure as gates improved though the roaring twenties. Under King and Charlie Paynter, the club developed from a small works team in the London League into an established member of the English football elite, with a Wembley FA Cup Final appearance waiting in 1923.

In the country at large people were emerging from the desperate hardships of the war into a decade of relative prosperity. Down in the East End of London the 1920s brought some short-term social stability, but little in the way of increased opportunities in jobs, housing, education or health. HMS *Thunderer*, the country's largest dreadnought, was launched from the Thames Ironworks in February 1911, but was the last major commission for Arnold Hills' company. Thames gradually went into decline as orders dried up and the firm finally folded in 1912.

Arnold Hills died peacefully at his home in 1927, in the house known locally as 'Hammerfield'. The founder's sad death from an awful wasting disease stood in ironic contrast to the great Victorian's deeply held belief in the life-enhancing importance of sport and athletic endeavour, particularly to the lives of the poor. It was these values that led Hills to form Thames Ironworks FC. The great Victorian industrialist Hills continued to support his local football after the collapse of his business and lived to see his beloved Hammers reach the FA Cup Final in 1923. Hills made a huge contribution to East End life around the turn of the century. He was a decent employer and would have been devastated to lose the firm and the consequent loss of livelihood for hundreds of East Enders. When Thames Ironworks ceased trading a notice appeared on the gates which read, 'Do not let such a notice spoil your Christmas. The fight is not finished and no battle is lost until it is won. I will not desert you in the darkest hour before dawn. I bid you be of good cheer.' (Powles, 2005)

In the 1920s there were plenty of amusements to distract East Enders from everyday hardship. At their local cinema they could escape to a world of Fred Astaire, James Cagney or Judy Garland and later, Walt Disney. The wonderful Hoxton-born heroine of the stage, Marie Lloyd, performed in music halls throughout East London, belting out songs like *The Costers' Wedding* with provocative lines like 'I sits among the cauliflowers and the peas'. Lloyd was one of nine children herself, performed on picket lines, expressed support for the poor and never forgot her roots. In addition to the music hall, live music could be heard across the area in pubs like the Boleyn, the Royal Eagle Tavern and the Prospect of Whitby as Britain entered the jazz age. Close to the Boleyn was the wonderfully-named Herbert School of Dancing which attracted hundreds of young men and women looking for romance and a way to enjoy their hard-earned leisure time. Of course, those of Arnold Hills' disposition could spend their Sunday mornings worshipping in the dozens of splendid Hawksmoor churches in the area.

The Hammers went from strength to strength during this period. Crowds of 40,000 regularly squeezed into Upton Park on Saturday afternoons. We will never really understand why people go to watch football matches in such numbers. It might be a sense of place, ferocious in the case of Hammers fans, or it could be the sense of aesthetic pleasure found in watching the beautiful game played at its best. In the 1920s Hammers fans had everything to cheer about. The indefatigable spirit which shone through in wartime echoed around Upton Park as Syd King's wonderful attacking football shone through the foggy winters around the Barking Road.

But as all good coaches understand, free-flowing football needs to be based on a sound defence. At the heart of the Hammers' defence was the skipper, George Kay. The

Mancunian made 237 appearances in his seven seasons with the club and was, including Billy Bonds, the best West Ham player never to play for England. As a northern lad Kay won the cockney hearts of the club's supporters. Brian Belton (2006) acknowledged Kay's value to the club when he wrote, 'he was recognised as a deep thoughtful man, very serious about his football...He ate, drank, slept and lived for football'.

His passionate attitude to football was echoed down the years at Upton Park with Malcolm Allison, Noel Cantwell, Ron Greenwood and John Lyall – all deep thinkers about the game.

What an experience it must have been for Kay to lead the Hammers out at Wembley in 1923 for the FA Cup Final in front of around 130,000 people (although it is suspected that a great number more than that were actually present, with some estimates approaching 300,000) – just four days after the new stadium was completed. The skipper had led the Hammers in a glorious Cup run, with wins over Brighton, Plymouth, Southampton and Derby County. But the Final was a disappointing anticlimax for Hammers fans. Their Division Two side lost the White Horse Final on a pitch churned up by the encroaching crowd and a battalion of police horses. On the ruined pitch the Londoners were unable to produce their famous close passing game, with the conditions more suited to Bolton's no-nonsense approach. But success did come later that season when Kay's side finally achieved promotion to Division One. Leading his defence with gritty determination, Kay played 40 out of 42 games in the club's first season in the top flight. During the 1924–25 season, Kay became the first West Ham player to reach 200 League and Cup games. Here was a very special Hammer indeed.

After leading West Ham for seven successful years, Kay returned to the Manchester area with Stockport County, before retiring in 1927 following a series of career-threatening injuries. As a player Kay possessed outstanding leadership qualities and a career in management beckoned. If anything his achievements as a manager surpassed his considerable success as a player. After spending a few years learning his trade at Luton and Southampton, in 1936 Kay joined Liverpool where stayed until 1951. As Syd King would have known, Kay was born for club management. He had considerable success at Anfield, winning the Championship in 1946–47 and laying the foundations for the great years to follow.

As Liverpool manager Kay signed Stan Cullis, the legendary Bill Shankly and his best ever signing, Billy Liddell. At Anfield Kay has been dubbed the 'Shankly of his day' and was later described by Bob Paisley as 'one of the all-time great managers'. Even Sir Matt Busby said that Kay was a huge influence on his management style. Praise does not come any higher. There is no question that Kay turned a struggling Liverpool into a Championship-winning team. He was an innovative manager and coach in the modern style – years ahead of his time. The former Hammers captain had only been at Liverpool a couple of years when he organised a pre-season tour to Canada. It was an inspired decision with Britain in the grip of post-war rationing and the Canadians enjoying a healthy diet and a beautiful summer climate. Kay had organised a punishing schedule with 10 matches at stadiums strung out across this vast country. The trip paid huge dividends as the Reds, buoyed by their Canadian experience, began the 1946–47 season strongly and went on to lift the Championship for the fifth time in their history.

With players like Alf Stubbins, Billy Liddell and Jack Balmer in his side, Kay was desperate for more success. In 1950 Liverpool reached the FA Cup Final for only the second time in their history and the first time for 36 years. The Reds were strong Wembley favourites, but FA Cup Finals rarely go to plan. The day ended in disappointment and defeat for the Merseysiders as opponents Arsenal ran out comfortable 2–0 winners. For Kay, the defeat must have brought back unwanted memories of the 1923 White Horse Final, when his stirring defensive play failed to save West Ham from defeat. Kay had been ill for some time prior to the Arsenal match and left his sick bed to lead his team out at Wembley in front of King George V. The Liverpool manager was extremely unwell and it was soon apparent he could no longer cope with the rigours of managing a top-class football club. He battled against his illness with great courage but died in Liverpool on 18 April 1954 at the age of 63.

As Brian Belton suggests, Kay was a 'deep and thoughtful man' with a tremendous eye for detail. Like Bobby Moore after him, he was always immaculately dressed and extremely proud of his achievements in football. Unlike Moore, Kay followed a distinguished playing career with a long and successful spell in management. A chain-smoker, he suffered from ill health in later life and clearly felt the pressures and stress of football management deeply, but this did not stop him from helping to create the football giant that is now Liverpool FC.

For West Ham fans of the 1920s George Kay was a wonderful centre-half and captain who led the Hammers in one of the most successful periods in the club's history. As is the current custom, Kay's 1923 FA Cup Final medal was sold at auction in 2005 for £4,560, a pitiful sum when we consider his immense contribution to the history of West Ham. His leadership of the club was inspirational and George Kay stands out as one of the very best vintage Hammers.

Jack Tresadern, Billy Moore and Ted Hufton

Jack, Billy and Ted were key members of the West Ham side George Kay led out at Wembley for the 1923 FA Cup Final. Without our three heroes it is unlikely the Hammers would have reached the Final, or achieved the long-awaited promotion to the top flight of English football plotted by Syd King and Charlie Paynter for 15 years. We only need look at the semi-final against Derby County to confirm the immense value of Jack, Billy and Ted to Kay's exciting and talented team.

Over 50,000 people turned up at Stamford Bridge for the match. Derby were firm favourites, largely because they had dumped a very good Tottenham side out of the Cup in the previous round. The East Midlanders dominated the early exchanges and the Hammers were pinned back in their own half for long periods. We can let supporter George Kerr describe what happened next: 'Then Hufton took a goal-kick straight down the middle. Watson trapped the ball then swung around, hitting it out to the left about 10 yards to Jimmy Ruffell who carried the ball 20 yards before he swung over a slightly lofted centre which Brown volleyed into the top left-hand corner.' (Blows and Hogg, 2000)

The Derby defensive dam was broken and the Hammers poured forward with Moore and Tresadern at the heart of most of the action. Moore quickly scored the second before Brown and Ruffell sealed victory and ensured that West Ham would be in the first ever Final to be played at the new Wembley Stadium.

As we have seen, the chaotic conditions in which the Final against Bolton was played inhibited the Hammers' game, while the more pragmatic football of the northerners was far more suited to the damaged Wembley pitch. Jack, Billy and Ted did everything they could that day to bring the FA Cup back to the East End, but sadly it was not to be and the normally rowdy atmosphere in the Boleyn pub that Saturday night was unusually subdued. But the Hammers quickly recovered from their chastened Wembley experience and Tresadern, Moore and Hufton figured strongly in the remainder of the season as the Hammers continued to strive for promotion.

John 'Jack' Tresadern was born in Leytonstone on 26 September 1893. Like Bobby Moore after him, young Jack was a bright lad and on leaving school worked for a time as a cashier down in the docks. He showed early promise as a wing-half and was snapped up by Fred Hasle, manager of local side Wanstead. With Jack proving too good for park football, he left Wanstead for Barking FC, helping the Essex club to win the coveted London Senior Cup. He soon came to the attention of Syd King, who persuaded the young player to sign professional forms for the Hammers. He made his first-team debut

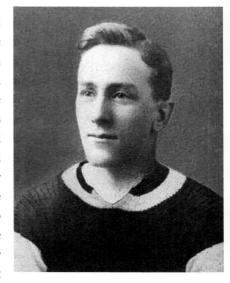

on April Fool's Day (no irony intended), 1914 in the 0–6 defeat at Watford, an inauspicious beginning to what was to be an illustrious career for the tough and tenacious left-half.

Like most professional footballers, war interrupted young Jack's career. He joined the Royal Garrison Artillery where his intelligence and leadership qualities impressed his superiors. Jack was quickly promoted to the rank of lieutenant, a notable achievement by the boy from the backstreets of Leytonstone.

Mercifully, Tresadern survived the war and returned to Upton Park where he re-established his place in the side and position in the club. 'Tres', as he became known, excelled for the Hammers in the years following World War One. The uncompromising half-back was adored by the Chicken Run regulars who appreciated his tenacious tackling and strong running. He was very much in the mould of Billy Bonds – a strong and committed character who could really play, a combination guaranteed to gain the approval of the passionate Boleyn crowd. Inevitably, his outstanding performances at the Boleyn began to attract the attention of the national press. For example, the *Daily Chronicle* described Jack as, 'An impertinent little fellow…he seems to steal the ball rather than win it in an honest, straightforward way.'

As we shall see, his playing style is one of the many similarities Tresadern shares with the most celebrated Hammer of them all, Bobby Moore.

Now playing in the top flight of English football and with West Ham impressing with their attacking approach to the game, Tres began to interest the England selectors. He was deservedly selected to represent his country for the match against Scotland on 14 April 1923. The match ended in a 2–2 draw and Tresadern's calm, if measured performance must have impressed the selectors. He was chosen for the friendly against Sweden a few weeks later, which England won convincingly 4–2. Young Jack did not quite repeat his West Ham form for England, but international debuts are difficult and the young half-back must have harboured thoughts of a long run in the England side.

Disappointingly, Tres' international career was restricted to these two matches and he was never selected to play for England again after the Sweden game. By his own admission he failed to produce his best form in either game. Following his international debut he later revealed, rather harshly, 'I was the best Scotland player on the park.' Tres returned to the Boleyn a little chastened by his England experience, but such was his character he continued to delight the West Ham fans with his wholehearted performances. At least, unlike Billy Bonds, he did get to play for his country.

Jack Tresadern was an intelligent footballer and a natural leader. He would surely have been the Hammers captain through their successful post-war period were it not for the presence in the side of the peerless George Kay. Teammate Jimmy Ruffell recognised the qualities of his teammate. 'Jack had a great football brain, we called him the little atom…He seemed to see the game a few passes ahead of us…He was undoubtedly one of the cleverest the West Ham club ever had.'

At the age of 31 Tresadern left his beloved West Ham to see out the last few years of his career at Burnley. He had played nearly 300 matches for the best Hammers team in the club's short history. His assured and confident performances in the West Ham midfield, together with his developed football intelligence, appeared to make Jack an ideal candidate for football management. However, again like Bobby Moore, his managerial career never quite reached the great heights of his playing days.

Following short spells in charge at Northampton Town, where he suffered the broken leg that ended his playing career, a spell at Crystal Palace and an undistinguished period at Tottenham, Jack moved to sunny Devon to take charge of Plymouth Argyle. He stayed at the south coast club for nine years before retiring from professional football in 1947. Like many ex-professional footballers he could not stay away long from the game he loved. Jack was happy to drop down to non-League football where he managed a succession of clubs, including Chelmsford City. In the words of Essex man Ian Dury, Jack's career in management had its ups and downs, but he was a full member of the West Ham academy of football management, following in the steps of Syd King and Charlie Paynter.

Jack Tresadern died in December 1959 at the age of 69. He was undoubtedly one of the finest and most popular West Ham players of his generation. His career spanned two world wars, reached its peak in the roaring twenties and ended in the years of the Great Depression. But Jack was more than a very good professional footballer. He was an extraordinary individual as Brian Belton confirms for us in his wonderful book, *War Hammers* (2007). Like many of his age, as a young man he fought courageously in World War One and lived through the Nazi bomb attacks on East London.

In Joan Littlewood's play of the 1960s, *Oh! What a Lovely War*, staged at the Stratford Theatre, one of the characters exclaims, '50,000 men left West Ham for the war without leaving a forwarding address'.

Jack Tresadern was one of Littlewood's men. His achievements included gaining promotion to officer rank in the Royal Garrison Artillery and a successful career in professional football, the highlight of which was helping West Ham to the FA Cup Final and promotion to Division One. Undoubtedly, the highlight of his playing career was being selected to play for England in 1923. Jack Tresadern was an outstanding early pioneer and fully deserves his status as a West Ham legend.

William 'Billy' Moore was born in Newcastle on 6 October 1894. Despite being a Geordie, Moore began his career at Sunderland following a stint at local club Seaton Delaval. Syd King brought Billy to West Ham in 1922 and the inside-left went straight into the side, making his debut against Bradford City. He joined Jack Tresadern in a strong midfield and provided King with the left-side balance the manager felt was lacking. Moore was extremely effective at Upton Park and was a constant provider of chances for Jimmy Ruffell and Vic Watson at the point of the West Ham attack.

Moore was a key member of the 1923 FA Cup Final side, although, like other creative Hammers players, his effectiveness was dulled by the churned-up pitch. He played brilliantly in the crucial 2–0 League win over Sheffield Wednesday just two days after the Wembley fiasco, a win which revived the Hammers' season and kept their First Division promotion bid alive. But perhaps his best game for his new club was against Leicester City back in February of that season. Moore scored a hat-trick as the Hammers trounced their promotion rivals 6–0. Little did the inside-left know that his goals would be worth their weight in gold in May, when his team secured promotion on goal average over none other than Leicester City.

As an inside-forward Billy Moore had many qualities, including the ability to score goals. He was a nimble, quick-witted player with a low centre of gravity who loved to drift into the opposition penalty area, much like a proto-Frank Lampard. In many ways he was more like an early Alan Devonshire, but a little tougher and stronger in the tackle. His teammate Jimmy Ruffell set out Billy's value to the West Ham side of the 1920s: 'You wouldn't wish for a better man alongside you than Billy Moore. He was nippy and clever and always surprising people. He didn't look tough, but he was wiry.'

Following the dramatic circumstances of their promotion to the top flight by the slenderest of margins in 1924, the Hammers struggled a little in Division One. But despite his team hovering around the bottom half of the table, Moore continued to score goals. This marked him out as a special player and his strong performances soon brought the England selectors to the Boleyn yet again. The boys in the blazers were

impressed by the Geordie lad and he was duly selected for the England team to play Sweden on 24 May 1923. Like Jack Tresadern, it had been a great year for Moore – FA Cup finalist, a member of the successful promotion-winning side and to cap it all, selection for the national team.

England won the Sweden game 3–1 and young Billy was outstanding in his favoured inside-left position, scoring twice and generally dominating the left side of the England attack. Back in Moore's day the England team was selected by a committee of long-serving FA officials. In fact, it was not until the appointment of Sir Alf Ramsey in the early 1960s that full responsibility for team selection was handed to the England coach. The national coach through the 1950s, Walter Winterbottom, in many respects a modern thinker on the game, had his team chosen by the suits of Lancaster Gate. So it will come as no surprise to students of the English game that, despite his two goals and eye-catching display, Moore was left out of the side for the next match and was never selected to play for his country again. The only crumb of comfort Billy might have found from such shoddy treatment was that he became, and remains, the England player with the best ever goals per game ratio. Not for the first time a West Ham player had been unfairly treated by the selectors, the price to pay for playing for an unfashionable club.

Being the kind of character he was, Moore wasted little time in worrying about the bizarre decisions of out-of-touch officials and returned to Upton Park to do what he did best – turn out consistently excellent performances on the left side of the Hammers' midfield. Eventually, the advancing years and the inevitable run of injuries led Billy to end his playing career at the close of the 1928–29 season. He was 35 years of age and now an honorary East Ender.

In his time at Upton Park, Moore had scored 48 goals in just over 200 appearances. He was a hugely popular player both with supporters and his teammates, as Jimmy Ruffell confirms. With his keen football intelligence he was, like many ex-West Ham players, another ideal candidate for coaching and eventually club management. The club recognised Moore's coaching potential and on his retirement immediately offered him the post of assistant trainer to Charlie Paynter, a position he held for three seasons. As many in the game predicted, Moore proved to be an inspirational coach and following his initial three years under Paynter, Billy was appointed head coach at the Boleyn, a post he held for 28 years until he eventually retired in 1960.

Billy Moore died in 1968 at the age of 73. Like his teammates he lived through two world wars and during his long years in football, saw the professional game change beyond recognition. He lived close to the Boleyn in Plashet Road and continued to visit the ground in his retirement. In his role as coach he guided the Hammers through difficult times and was a major influence on the club's celebrated philosophy of football. Along with King and Paynter, Moore was one of the founders of the club's famed coaching academy. There are few players and coaches in the history of the club who deserve pioneer status more than Billy Moore. He was much more than a terrific player and inspirational coach, but one of the most important figures in the history of West Ham United FC.

Arthur Edward 'Tiger' Hufton was born in Southwell, Nottingham on 25 November 1892. On leaving school Hufton joined a local works team before being snapped up by Sheffield United. He played just 15 games for the Yorkshire side before war intervened. The young goalkeeper enlisted with the Coldstream Guards and survived the war despite being wounded in action on the Western Front. While on leave recovering from shrapnel wounds, Hufton played 65 games for the Hammers during the war and clearly impressed Syd King. The manager promptly paid Sheffield United £350 to bring the promising young 'keeper to Upton Park at the end of the war.

It has often been said that you need to be a little mad to be a goalkeeper. Every Saturday and Sunday in parks across the country, thousands of young men and women volunteer to stand in goal for their team, dressed in an outfit designed more for Magaluf beach than for keeping goal on a freezing January afternoon on Hackney Marshes. Goalkeepers can win or lose matches; their errors are magnified and the subject of comic abuse by their own and the opponents' supporters. Robert Green's error against the USA in the 2010 World Cup defined England's abject tournament. It was as tragic as it was comical – it did not help that he played for West Ham.

When I was about 20 years old I had a close friend who was a promising professional 'keeper with a famous London club. One winter evening the two of us went to Wembley to watch an England international. It was a big match with over 80,000 in the old stadium. After the game my goalkeeping pal thought it would be a good idea to take a short cut to avoid the worst of the crush. This involved climbing a high chain-link fence – no problem to the intrepid young goalie who simply flew up the barrier, only to impale his right hand on some exposed barbed wire when he got to the top. I cannot remember how I got him down but I do remember the wound needing a handful of stitches. We made our way back to the stadium, jogged across the pitch and sought help deep in the bowels of Wembley. The medical men were brilliant and patched up the wounded custodian and we made our way back home to East London. The result of the ill-judged short cut was that my friend missed the rest of that season and his injury temporarily held up a highly promising career. His club never did find out about the real cause of his injury. Only a goalkeeper…

There have been some brilliant goalkeepers and one or two disastrous ones at Upton Park. The better ones included the great Ernie Gregory, Bobby Ferguson, young Mervyn Day (disappointingly sold to Leyton Orient at the top of his game), Phil Parkes and, arguably the greatest of them all, Ted Hufton.

King's faith in young 'Tiger' was handsomely repaid as his new 'keeper went on to play 456 matches during his seven years at the club – an achievement that places Hufton 12th in the all-time appearance list at West Ham. Tiger made his debut against Lincoln City on 30 August 1919 in the first Football League match ever played at Upton Park. Showing few nerves in front of over 20,000 excited fans, Hufton played solidly in a 1–1 draw, with the North Bank warming to his confident performance. He could not be faulted for the goal – an expertly-taken penalty by Lincoln's Chesser. The Hammers 'keeper continued to turn in consistent displays and was blameless in the 0–7 thumping at the hands of Barnsley in the second game of that historic season. West Ham settled for the rest of the campaign and conceded just 40 goals in 42 matches, a clear indication of the excellence of Ted Hufton in goal.

Of course, Hufton kept goal in the 1923 White Horse FA Cup Final. The Hammers' team photograph gives us a clue to the goalkeeper's personality. His thick, dark hair glistening in the rain, Hufton appears relaxed, assured and looking forward with confidence to the biggest match in the club's history. Despite the Wembley defeat, manager King knew this West Ham team was a very good one. The manager also knew he had a goalkeeper he could trust in his bid for promotion that same season.

The team's outstanding performances in 1922–23 led to England caps for Jack Tresadern and Billy Moore and it was not long before Tiger joined his teammates in catching the eye of the England selectors. Hufton made his England debut in the match against Belgium in 1924 and made a total of six appearances for his country. He was in and out of the England side, but like Tresadern and Moore, this was probably more to do with the vagaries of the selection process than any inconsistency on the part of the West Ham 'keeper. One of the reasons the selectors kept returning to Hufton may have been because of his reputation as a penalty specialist, saving 11 out of 18 spot-kicks in his first two seasons at Upton Park.

West Ham were relegated from Division One at the end of 1931–32, following a reasonably successful nine seasons in the top flight. The club's best ever generation of players were reaching retirement age, including Ted Hufton. As the great 'keeper's prodigious talent inevitably began to fade, he left West Ham for Watford. He played 401 League and Cup matches for the Hammers, but just two at Vicarage Road before he retired in 1932.

Supporter Jim O'Halloran recalls a story about Tiger Hufton which indicates how highly regarded he was at Upton Park. As a youngster O'Halloran spotted his hero Ernie Gregory leaving the ground one Saturday afternoon in the 1950s and approached the great goalkeeper for his autograph. The West Ham legend looked at the young O'Halloran for a moment, indicated his elderly companion and said to the boy, 'You don't want my autograph son, you want his. Ted Hufton was the greatest goalkeeper ever.'

The great Hammers manager Ted Fenton said about Tiger: 'Ted Hufton was another of my heroes, and he was always in the press room after a match at Upton Park, dispensing yarns and memories with the utmost amiability.'

The imposing Tiger was popular with fans and teammates as well as being one of the greatest goalkeepers ever to play for West Ham United. He was an influential member of the successful Hammers side in the inter-war years and his superb goalkeeping was one of the reasons the club remained in the top flight throughout the 1920s. Like others of his generation he fought bravely on the Western Front, but fortunately survived, despite suffering multiple injuries.

Ted Hufton died in Swansea on 2 February 1967 following a long period of ill health. Goalkeepers can make or break teams and in Hufton West Ham had one of the best of his generation. He fully deserves his place as a genuine pioneer and Upton Park goalkeeping legend.

Vic Watson: Cambridge goal machine

The player who had the greatest impact on the Hammers team of the 1920s and '30s was born in a small village in rural Cambridgshire, a long way from the grime and poverty of East London. At a difficult time, our next pioneer, Victor Martin Watson, raised the spirits of the East London club and gave the supporters many reasons to be cheerful. Vic Watson was born in Girton, Cambridgeshire on 10 November 1897 and despite being an outsider, Watson became as popular at Upton Park as any of the greatest legends in the history of the modern era.

West Ham were relegated to Division Two at the end of the 1930–31 season as Syd King's dream began to unravel. But such a sustained spell at the pinnacle of English football was a tribute to everyone at the club – the fans, the players and, of course, Syd King and Charlie Paynter. The dramatic departure of King in 1932 brought an end to an era of remarkable consistency, which included the 1923 FA Cup Final appearance. Following the drop in 1931, the Hammers were out of the top flight for 28 years. It took Ted Fenton's talented team of the late 1950s to restore the club back to its rightful position in English football. The achievements of Syd King and Charlie Paynter in the 1920s should not be underestimated and it remains one of the most successful periods in the club's history.

King's successor, the long-serving Paynter, took West Ham through the 1930s and the difficult years of World War Two. The 1930s were a particularly difficult time for the club and for the East End generally. The Wall Street crash in 1929 was the trigger for the Great Depression, the deepest and longest recession in history. Poverty, homelessness and 20 per cent unemployment returned to East London with a vengeance and Hammers supporters were forced to put their passion for the club to one side while they fought to feed their families in the most difficult of circumstances. The fascist elements of the British aristocracy attempted to recruit thousands of disillusioned working-class people to Hitler's cause. The East End was the site of one of the fiercest battles ever seen on the streets of London. The Battle of Cable Street on Sunday 4 October 1936 saw 300,000 people oppose a demonstration by the British Union of Fascists in a predominantly Jewish area of the East End, close to Shadwell underground station.

Soccer attendances declined in the 1930s, while people in the East End found other things to do in their well-earned leisure time. Ballroom dancing and the cinema grew in popularity and offered inexpensive nights out for local people. The Hammers provided little cheer as they bumped along in Division Two, with only the odd glimpse of promotion for frustrated fans in this most dismal decade. Spirits were low at Upton Park after the tragic suicide of Syd King, although Charlie Paynter, the last link with the club's dockland heritage, provided some welcome continuity. Throughout this period, Paynter was the club's centre of gravity and kept the Hammers on track during the turmoil surrounding King's last years. His inspirational style and innovative coaching methods made him a forerunner to the likes of Ted Fenton, Ron Greenwood and John Lyall.

Hammers fans were able to enjoy a couple of good FA Cup runs at the time, their side losing narrowly to Everton in a 1932 semi-final. But, in typical West Ham style, the Hammers spent the remainder of that season struggling against relegation. As the war clouds began to gather over a beleaguered country during the late '30s, the mood at football grounds across the country was unusually sombre and the Boleyn was no exception.

Despite the club's poor performances and a perceived lack of ambition in the 1930s, the fans had one consolation – the opportunity to enjoy the performances of one of West Ham's greatest ever players. He was not a local player born in the streets around the Boleyn or down by the docks in Canning Town, and he did not attend Park School in Plashet Road like Charlie Dove, Syd Puddefoot and Jim Barrett.

West Ham paid Wellingborough FC the princely sum of £50 for Vic Watson, initially as cover for fans' favourite Syd Puddefoot. But the bustling young centre-forward was to have an even greater impact on the team than the great Puddy himself. Between 1920 and 1936 Watson made 505 appearances for the Hammers and played a huge part in the club's progress in those years. But these bare facts scarcely do Watson justice – what a player he was.

Tony Hogg (2004) reminds us that, '…his goals were responsible for the Hammers' promotion to the First Division…and the club's appearance in the Cup Final'.

An old-fashioned, busy centre-forward, Watson scored an incredible 326 goals for the Hammers – 74 more than his nearest rival, the great Sir Geoff Hurst. The West Ham side of 1922–23, with players like Jimmy Ruffell, George Kay and Billy Moore supporting goalscorer-in-chief Watson, was one of the best ever seen at Upton Park. Ruffell stressed that, 'West Ham were a very good passing team. Most of the time you had an idea where the other players were – we were one of the few clubs to really practice that. Then with Watson…West Ham always had a chance at getting a goal.' Vic Watson's goalscoring feats for West Ham are the stuff of legend. However, as Hammers supporters know only too well, not everything always went to plan.

In their first ever season in Division One Watson broke a toe in the opening game against Sunderland, which kept him out of the side until the following April. But fortunately for the Hammers, the great man quickly recovered, regained his goalscoring

touch and continued to score a bucketful of goals throughout his career. In the 1926–27 season he finished top scorer with 34 goals and helped his club to a seventh place League finish. In 1928–29 he scored 29 goals in 34 games, including six in the 8–2 victory over Leeds United, a feat equalled many years later by his natural successor, Geoff Hurst.

Watson, however, reserved his best for the following campaign when he scored an incredible 50 League and Cup goals in only 44 games. In that year he achieved one of his career ambitions of being the leading scorer in Division One. His goals that season also helped his club to reach the quarter-finals of the FA Cup. Watson, with hat-tricks against Aston Villa and Leeds that season, was becoming the most feared forward in the top flight of English football. Leeds must have been sick of the sight of the marauding Hammer. In addition to his six against them in 1929, he scored a hat-trick the following season and another four in the 4–1 FA Cup victory over the Yorkshire side. Happy days for the Hammers striker and his adoring fans.

West Ham have won nothing since their FA Cup triumph against Arsenal in 1980 and the past 30 years has seen troubled times at the Boleyn. It is almost impossible to believe that in 1931 the Hammers trounced Liverpool 7–0 in front of just 14,000 at Upton Park. In the team that day were Ruffell, Barrett, James, skipper Stan Earle and of course, Vic Watson.

The Hammers won their opening game of the season against Huddersfield 2–1 and faced Liverpool on the following Monday night. The East End side began strongly with the midfield snapping into tackles and providing a string of defence-splitting passes to Ruffell and Watson. The home side were 2–0 up by half-time and in the second half produced some of the best football ever seen at Upton Park. With Man of the Match Jimmy Ruffell terrorising the Reds defence, the Hammers ran through Liverpool at will. Vic Watson was at the very top of his form and scored four goals that evening, including one of the best ever seen at Upton Park. Showing great strength and considerable skill, the centre-forward thrilled the supporters when he powered past five hapless Liverpool defenders, before slotting the ball calmly into the empty net, as though he was playing in a Sunday morning match at Hackney Marshes. The crowd rose to the great number-nine in joyful appreciation of his wonderful goal.

Following the Liverpool victory the Hammers sat proudly on top of Division One, but their outstanding form was not to last. In typical West Ham style they were thrashed 6–1 by Aston Villa in the next game and finished the season in 18th place, scoring 79 goals but conceding a shocking 94. The 1930–31 season was a microcosm of the fortunes of the club throughout its history – at times playing sublime football few teams can match, combined with atrocious, often comical defending.

Watson's record is incomparable and the Liverpool game in 1931 was a highlight in a dazzling career. It is no surprise that Blows and Hogg place him fifth in their list of West Ham all-time greats with only Moore, Hurst, Brooking and Peters ahead of him. His goals that year helped the Hammers to finish seventh in the top flight and reach the quarter-finals of the FA Cup. The one downside of an extraordinary career was in 1931–32. At the end of that season the Hammers finished 22nd in Division One and were relegated, despite Watson helping himself to a creditable 23 goals. But in the late 1920s it seemed there was nothing this goalscoring phenomenon could not achieve. A long England career seemed a certainty. We know that, just after the war, some of his teammates had won international honours on the back of the Hammers' promotion to Division One and selectors could not fail to recognise the claims of Vic Watson.

Watson won his first England cap on 5 March 1923 in the match against Wales. Inevitably, he scored one of the goals in the 2–2 draw. He was awarded his second cap later that season, this time against Scotland, and again was among the scorers. The Hammers' centre-forward had begun his international career promisingly and could look forward to many more caps. The *Stratford Express* echoed the thoughts and feelings of all Hammers supporters when their football reporter wrote on 3 March 1923: 'The choice of Vic Watson…to lead England's attack…in the match against Wales…has naturally given a good deal of pleasure and satisfaction to supporters of the club. A speedy and intelligent player, he is quick to sense an opening, and is a dangerous "raider". All "Hammers" will wish him success in his first international.'

Despite the confident start Watson made to his England career he was dropped after his two games and was out of the England side for seven years. He was recalled in 1930 when an avalanche of goals for his club could no longer be ignored by the selectors. He made a further three international appearances that season, scoring two goals against Scotland in the old Home Championship. Watson scored four times in his five appearances for England. It is hard to believe, given his record, that he was only selected to play for his country on five occasions. In Dixie Dean and Ted Drake he was up against strong competition for the England number-nine shirt, but Watson had excelled in his handful of international matches and was desperately unlucky not to have won at least 20 caps. It is a source of regret that Watson never had the impact on international football enjoyed by his natural successor at Upton Park, the illustrious Sir Geoff Hurst.

But Watson continued to score goals for his club following relegation. He scored 61 goals in three seasons in the lower division before he started to lose his greatest asset – his explosive speed. In 1935 he left West Ham to join his former teammate George Kay at Southampton, where he saw out the remainder of his playing career. The greatest goalscorer in West Ham's history, Watson reached double figures in 13 of his 15 seasons and on nine occasions scored more than 20 times. His 326 goals in 505 games says everything about our hero.

Like many players of his era Watson experienced life outside football. Like many of his fellow professionals, Sgt Watson was a veteran of World War One. We know that several East London professional footballers perished on the Somme, with the Hammers' neighbours Leyton Orient being particularly affected. Many more players returned with serious battlefield injuries. Most, like Vic Watson, returned from the war to pick up their careers where they had left them. He knew he was fortunate to be playing professional football after the war and made the most of his undoubted talent. As Hammers chronicler Brian Belton claims, Watson was 'perhaps the finest centre-forward in West Ham's history'. High praise indeed when you look at the impressive records of Geoff Hurst, Johnny Byrne and Johnny Dick.

West Ham fans accepted Vic Watson as one of their own, but he was more at home in the Cambridgeshire countryside than in the urban sprawl of East London. When he retired from playing, the great centre-forward returned to Girton and started a small, but successful, fruit and vegetable business. He also became active in the local community. Chris Horton, chairman of Girton Colts FC and a lifelong Hammers supporter, recently campaigned for a memorial to be erected in the Cambridgeshire village to commemorate their returning hero's remarkable record. Mr Horton makes a convincing case:

> *There does not appear to be a road named after him, such as 'Watson Way', and there is no plaque, statue or even a sign. This seems extremely unjust…how many other born and bred village people have played football for their country?*
>
> *Here we have had a very local sporting hero, someone that could inspire the kids and show them that anything is possible in sport. Vic's career shows it doesn't matter where you are from, you can still reach the top.*

Fortunately, Horton's campaign was successful and in June 2010 a plaque honouring the Hammers legend was unveiled in his home village. In 1988, deep into retirement, Watson reflected on his career:

> *I came home from the First World War and there wasn't any work about here, so I went to Peterborough. I lasted five weeks before I went to West Ham to play football – and they kept me. When I got into the game, I always felt I would like to get to top the Division One goalscorers. I managed with 42 goals. I scored six goals…for Cambridge City, Cambridge Town, West Ham Reserves, and then West Ham in Division One.*

Victor Martin Watson died in August 1988 at the age of 90. With an amazing 13 hat-tricks for West Ham, he had a wonderful career and was a proper pioneer and one of the very greatest players to grace Upton Park.

Jimmy Ruffell: West Ham's finest winger

If Vic Watson grabbed the headlines with four goals in the Hammers' 7–0 win over Liverpool in 1930, the Man of the Match was undoubtedly the mercurial winger, Jimmy Ruffell. Born in Doncaster on 8 August 1900, Ruffell's family moved to East London when he was a young boy. From then on we can safely and proudly refer to the Yorkshire lad as an East Ender. He played for Essex Road School, before turning out for a number of local clubs including Manor Park Albion and Chadwell Heath United. His eye-catching performances in local football meant that the young winger soon became hot property and the teenager was poached by West Ham from the intriguingly-named Ilford Electricity Board FC.

Football fans love to watch a dazzling winger who can ghost past full-backs at will and provide golden goalscoring opportunities for their teammates. Whether it is the direct running style of a Cliff Jones or Theo Walcott, or the dribbling skills of Stanley Matthews or Jimmy Johnstone, with one mazy run a winger can light up a dull game and get the crowd to its feet. A flying winger can raise our spirits and the hairs on the backs of our necks. Jimmy Ruffell brought that kind of excitement to the Boleyn. He was an outside-left of the old-fashioned kind. He was just 5ft 9in tall, with low-slung hips, a wonderful touch and blistering pace. With a drop of his shoulder he would repeatedly leave heavy-footed, bewildered full-backs stranded in the mud or flat on their backsides. His centre-forward, usually Vic Watson, waited hungrily for his deadly crosses. As we will see, the outside-left was no slouch himself when it came to goalscoring. He refused to let his strikers have all the fun.

Ruffell made his West Ham debut in September 1921 in the 3–0 home victory against Port Vale. He had a tremendous ability to hit pinpoint crosses to Watson and the pair formed a dangerous partnership. In many respects Jimmy epitomised the club's purist commitment. He had perfected the near-post cross – a West Ham speciality – and it is impossible to overstate the contribution Ruffell made to the team through the 1920s and '30s. Steve Marsh of the e-fanzine *theyflysohigh* once described Ruffell as 'immortal', an exaggeration perhaps, but an indication of the regard in which the winger is held at Upton Park.

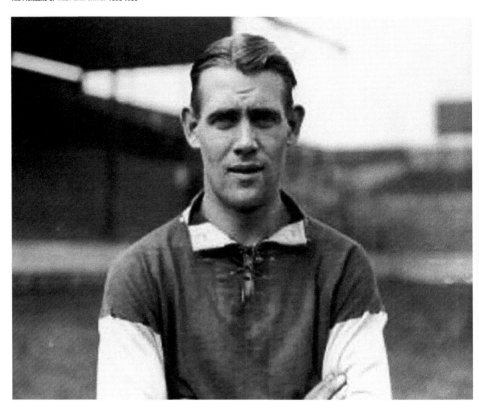

Ruffell blossomed under manager Syd King and the creative influence and encouragement of the man who laid the foundation stones for West Ham's philosophy of football, inspirational coach Charlie Paynter. The winger had pace, crossing ability and could score goals. He must have been a manager's dream and how the fans loved him. Club scribe Tony Hogg described little Jimmy thus: 'His record of appearances and goals bear no comparison.'

This is rare praise indeed as West Ham has had some wonderful wingers in recent times – Sissons, Redknapp, Stuart Slater and Johnny Ayres, but they all stand in the shadow of the great Jimmy Ruffell. Perhaps what marked Ruffell out from players of his type was that he played for the team. His contribution to the side was immense with his clever work in tight situations. His blistering pace and deadly finishing took his side on to another level. He made 548 appearances between 1921–37 with an impressive 166 League and Cup goals, often ending the season as the club's top scorer. His record of appearances lasted 36 years until it was surpassed in 1973 by the godlike figure of Bobby Moore. It is unlikely that Vic Watson would have been quite so effective without Ruffell's pinpoint crosses and penetrating through-balls.

Ruffell played in the White Horse Final when the appalling conditions reduced the impact of the most skilful player on either side. Jimmy was a first-team regular throughout the

1922–23 season when promotion to the top flight gave the club, players and fans a huge lift after the disappointment of Wembley. His match-winning performance in the 6–0 drubbing of Leicester City that year gave the Hammers the superior goal average that eventually secured promotion. Vic Watson would probably not have scored his three goals in the crucial matches against Leyton Orient had Ruffell not provided cross after telling cross in his usual manner.

Given his goalscoring exploits you would think Ruffell would have earned a hatful of England caps. In fact he played just six times for England, making his international debut against Scotland in 1926. He joined up with former West Ham star Syd Puddefoot, but unfortunately England lost the game 1–0. He retained his place for the 3–3 draw against Northern Ireland and played in four further Home Internationals before being discarded by the capricious England selectors. There is little doubt that international football is a step up in level and some players find the step a little too far. But Ruffell, Jack Tresadern, Vic Watson and Billy Moore were class players who all received shabby treatment from the England selectors. One can only assume the England hierarchy saw West Ham as a second-rate outfit, unable to develop players of genuine international class. How else do we explain that, between them, these great players gained just a handful of caps?

Although 128 West Ham players have won international honours since William Jones played for Wales against England back in 1902, the thought persists that it should have been many more – just ask Billy Bonds. Like Vic Watson, Ruffell faced competition for his England position with the likes of Cliff Bastin and Eric Houghton keeping him out of the side.

Jimmy Ruffell will be remembered at Upton Park as a pioneer of a particular style that has kept the Chicken Run enraptured for over 100 years. Sadly, Hammers fans have not seen his like in recent times, in these days of tracking back and tucking in when games become tight. We can only live in the hope that Ruffell's legacy has not been squandered and that we might again see the flying winger back at the Boleyn.

Tony Hogg captured both Ruffell's playing style and personality when he wrote: 'Portraying perfectly the cigarette-card image of the professional footballer, complete with centre-parting in his slicked-back hair, Jimmy set a dashing scene as he tormented his opposing full-backs, often leaving them with muddied backsides as he cut in to score yet another goal.'

Ruffell, who worked as a brewery representative after retiring from football, died on 6 September 1989. Jack Helliar, the West Ham historian who had watched him play during the 1920s and 1930s commented, 'I had the privilege of being a personal friend of Jimmy and his family…He will be sadly missed by all his friends and acquaintances throughout football, for as well as being one of the greats he was also one of the nicest people you could wish to meet.'

Jimmy Ruffell died on 6 September 1989 at the age of 89. He was one of the best of the vintage Hammers – the finest winger ever to play for West Ham United – a legend.

'Big' Jimmy Barrett

'Big' Jim Barrett was born in West Ham in 1907 and like some of his teammates, attended Park School. Jim's dad, Fred, was an iron founder in the docks, while his mum Flo looked after Jim and his brother and two sisters. He joined West Ham at the age of 15 from Fairbairn House Boys' Club. Like hundreds of East End youngsters, Jimmy and his family benefitted from the work of Fairbairn and other community-based initiatives. In the 19th century privileged old boys from Eton and Oxbridge became aware of the extent of poverty and destitution in the East End of London. They set up places like Eton Manor in Hackney, Durning Hall in Canning Town and Toynbee Hall in Shoreditch. The Dockland Settlements, as they were often known, provided a wealth of activities for young people and community services for the most disadvantaged in the area.

Fairbairn House was established in 1900 and completely renovated in the 1930s. Its elegant art deco facade and central staircase is a testament to the quality of the services that the donors were determined to provide. FH, as it became known locally, offered a whole range of sporting activities including boxing, football, cricket, cycling and swimming. Its superb facilities included a sports centre and playing fields at Burgess Road and a 60-acre campsite at Lambourne End out in Chigwell, complete with swimming pool, football pitches and an extensive and well-equipped campsite. The first principal of FH was Sir Ian Horobin MP, who many of the ex-members remember with a combination of fondness and fear. For local young people like Jimmy Barrett places at Fairbairn House were heaven-sent. Many of the boys went on to become professional footballers, while the Burgess Road centre produced a number of ABA boxing champions. These charitable institutions spurred local people to form their own clubs, the most noteworthy being the famous Repton Boxing Club.

Fairbairn House still exists today providing services for single parents and the homeless, and generally acting as a shelter for local people in difficulty. One former member looks back at his time as a member with affection:

> This was truly a great club and a great institution and together with my time at St Bonaventures school in Forest Gate they were, looking back, amazing life forming times and I'm glad and proud to have been involved in such a great institution. The Burgess Road ground was absolutely first class in every way and it's so sad to drive along the A406 these days to see it

derelict. My parents still live in Caulfield Road and although both were East Enders, Dad was a lighterman and therefore a rower belonging to Blackwall Rowing Club on the 'Island' and was never a Fairbairn boy. Great memories…

Jimmy Barrett was a perfect example of a Fairbairn boy and was a great credit to the institution. He had shown outstanding promise as a youngster and his play showed a presence and strength beyond his years. He played for West Ham Boys in the English Shield

Final against Liverpool in 1921 and in his first full season as a professional Barrett played 42 games, a real indication of his maturity and reliability as a defender.

Big Jim had to wait two years before making his first-team debut in the 1–1 draw against Tottenham on 28 March 1925. He went on to make 467 League and Cup appearances, scoring an impressive 53 goals over a West Ham career that lasted 13 years. In 1926 Barrett scored five goals in three games playing at centre-forward, an indication of his all-round ability which saw him play in every position for the club during his distinguished career. In a 5–1 victory over Bolton Wanderers at Upton Park in April 1930, there were goals for skipper Stan Earle, Watson and Jimmy Ruffell. But Man of the Match that day was the irrepressible Barrett who not only was the pick of the West Ham players, but managed to score two good goals himself.

Succeeding the great George Kay was a huge challenge for the young defender, but the barrel-chested Barrett had all the right physical attributes for a centre-half, including a heart like a lion. He was the bedrock of the West Ham defence in the 1920s and 1930s and played in every defensive position as Charlie Paynter tried to rebuild the great side of the '20s. Sadly, even Barrett's heroics and leadership skills could not prevent West Ham from a prolonged spell in the second tier.

Big Jim Barrett came along at just the right time. As we have seen the Hammers enjoyed great success in the 1920s. They had emerged from the Thames Ironworks to become fully paid up members of the highest echelon of English football. In Puddefoot and Watson they had two of the most prolific goalscorers in Division One and their goals ensured the Hammers remained at the top. In their different ways Syd King and Charlie Paynter achieved a small miracle in taking West Ham from a works side to a respected club boasting several internationals in their line up. Attendances were generally good and for a time the club returned a profit. The 1923 FA Cup Final helped the finances which were improved by attendances of 30,000–40,000 for most home games.

Hammers fans down the years have become hardened more than most to the realities of promotion and relegation. The drop back into Division Two in 1932, although a bitter disappointment to everyone at the club, was not completely unexpected. The Syd King era was coming to an end; perhaps the great man had been at the club too long and change was overdue, but no one could have predicted the tragic circumstances of his departure in 1933, with the club 20th in the Second Division. Under the guiding hand of Charlie Paynter fortunes improved slightly, with the Hammers narrowly missing promotion in 1935. But with Ruffell and Watson gone, the club remained mired in mid-table mediocrity. On a positive note Upton Park was a good stadium, the club had an excellent manager, ferociously loyal support and crucially they had, in Barrett, a rock of a centre-half at the heart of their defence.

As archivist Steve Marsh confirms, Barrett's name is 'inextricably entwined in Hammers' heritage'. A larger-than-life personality, Big Jim was one of the great characters of the inter-war period and anecdotes about his exploits are legion. It is alleged that during a Hammers tour of Holland, Barrett deliberately aimed a shot from outside the penalty area at a clock high in the stand behind the goal. Sure enough, Jim's pile-driver crashed into the clock sending one of the hands crashing to the ground.

There are many such stories about Jim of this kind, but it would be disrespectful to his memory to dwell too long on the light-hearted side of his character, which although often amusing, can disguise the sheer professionalism and dedication of one of the greatest defenders ever to appear for West Ham. This claret and blue legend became a household name in the East End, loved and admired by his own people.

Barrett retired in 1938, although he did play occasionally for the Hammers' various wartime sides, including keeping goal in one match. When the war ended in 1945 Jim's coaching potential was recognised by Charlie Paynter when he was appointed trainer to the club's A team. It would have given the old centre-half enormous satisfaction when, having come out of retirement briefly, he played in the same West Ham A side as his son Jim Jnr. It would have been a proud dad who watched his son's own successful career at West Ham and Nottingham Forest. The young Jim was born in November 1930 and signed for the Hammers in February 1949. He went on to make 85 League and two Cup appearances for the Hammers, scoring 25 goals. A decent enough career, but one firmly in the shadow of his famous father.

It is a familiar story that great West Ham players tend to be treated shabbily by international selectors, if we leave the World Cup-winning trio of 1966 and Trevor Brooking to one side. Barrett's one international appearance was for England against Ireland in 1928, a scandal for such a wonderful footballer. But at least Jim can claim his single appearance constitutes a record, if of somewhat dubious merit. His one game for the national side lasted precisely eight minutes before injury sadly ended his involvement in the match and with the England team. To this day Jimmy's international career remains the shortest on record.

Like Billy Bonds in the 1970s, Barrett was not going to let a temporary setback with the national side dampen his enthusiasm for football. He continued to be an invaluable asset to his club, not least because of his remarkable versatility which had seen him perform in every position for the first and second teams. His ability to switch from defence to attack is borne out by his tally of more than 50 League and Cup goals for West Ham. Perhaps the greatest compliment we can pay Jim Barrett is that he proved an even greater asset to the club than the man he replaced at centre-half, the great George Kay.

Big Jim Barrett died on 25 November 1970 at the age of 63, after suffering from ill health late in his life. He was a one-club man and claret and blue through and through. It is difficult to think of a more popular Hammer than Barrett. He was a local boy and a tremendous footballer who was one of the best Hammers defenders of all time.

Len Goulden: jewel in the crown

Players of Jim Barrett's time were the last of a line that began with Charlie Dove and ended with the beginning of World War Two. Syd King and Charlie Paynter had carried the Thames Ironworkers banner through the 1920s and '30s and created one of the greatest of all West Ham sides. Our final first-generation pioneer was at the centre of the success of the pre-war era and his career takes us to the end of the 1930s, before the second war in a generation engulfed the nation and the East End in particular. Leonard Goulden was born in Hackney on 16 July 1912, but his family moved across to Plaistow in 1915. The young Goulden was an outstanding footballer at school and one of the key players in the West Ham Boys team of the 1920s. Goulden's exceptional ability caught the eye of the England selectors and he was included in the England Schoolboys side to play Wales and Scotland in 1926. The young Hackney boy looked to have the world at his talented feet.

The Hammers were not going to miss a player of Goulden's ability and quickly signed the young inside-forward as an amateur – at 15 years of age he was too young to sign professional forms. Manager Paynter immediately sent young Len out on loan to Chelmsford City to toughen him up and expose him to the hard-nosed non-League defenders. After a successful spell with the Clarets, Goulden was brought back to West Ham where he made his first-team debut against Charlton Athletic on 8 April 1933. Two weeks later he announced his arrival in professional football by scoring his first goal for the club in the Hammers' 4–3 victory over Nottingham Forest. The youngster with the classical appearance of the 1930s professional footballer, centre-parting included, was on his way.

The following season he played in 40 of the 42 League games in a team that included Ruffell, Barrett and Watson. With his astute football brain, Goulden soon developed a lively understanding with his distinguished teammates, including a young Ted Fenton. Despite this group of talented players, West Ham could only finish in seventh place in Division Two in Goulden's first year as a professional, but he did manage to score seven goals, while the astonishing Watson ended the season as top scorer with 29 in 32 games.

Over the next few seasons the Goulden-inspired Hammers continued to do well without ever being able to clinch promotion back to Division One. They finished third in 1934–35, fourth in 1935–36 and sixth in 1936–37. Despite the club's failure to gain promotion Paynter knew he had unearthed a rare talent in the form of Len Goulden. Ernie

Gregory, a good judge of a young player, recognised young Len's exceptional ability: 'We've had some great forwards over the years at West Ham but Len was the greatest – the daddy of them all. He was the one I paid my money to see…I can still see Len now – controlling the ball, he killed it instantly…But don't just take my word for it, ask any of the old-timers – they'll tell you the same, Len was the tops.'

Given the quality of the players in the West Ham side at the time, this is rare praise indeed. With a growing reputation and continued good form, it was just a matter of time before he joined a few of his teammates in the England team. The selectors had watched Len's progress from schoolboy international with interest and despite the Hammers languishing in the lower division, the young inside-forward was selected for the game against Norway on 14 May 1937. This was quite an achievement for an inexperienced young player who faced competition from football legends such as Raich Carter and Cliff Bastin. Goulden repaid the selectors' faith by scoring in England's 6–0 victory. The young professional might have been forgiven for feeling a little nervous before the match as he changed alongside Bastin, Stanley Matthews and Stan Cullis. But the young forward played with great confidence and retained his place in the side for the matches that season against Sweden, Northern Ireland, Wales and Czechoslovakia.

Len Goulden had made a real impact on the international stage and had every right to look forward to a brilliant career in the game. But like many of the England players of his time Goulden was exposed to the harsh political realities of the late 1930s. In May 1938 England went on a European tour which included a match against Germany in Berlin. Chancellor Hitler was determined to use the match for propaganda purposes. Throughout the late 1930s Hitler's Nazi government had been threatening most of Europe in its attempt to spread its poisonous ideology. Hitler was not going to miss the opportunity to influence the England football team. In the final hour before kick-off, as Goulden and his teammates were getting changed, an FA official entered the dressing room. He told the players they had to give the raised-arm Nazi salute during the playing of the German national anthem. As Stanley Matthews later recalled:

> The dressing room erupted. There was bedlam. All the England players were livid and totally opposed to this, myself included. Everyone was shouting at once. Eddie Hapgood, normally a respectful and devoted captain, wagged his finger at the official and told him what he could do with the Nazi salute, which involved putting it where the sun doesn't shine.

The FA official informed the players he had a direct order from the British ambassador in Berlin. He explained to them that the political situation between Britain and Germany was now so sensitive that it needed 'only a spark to set Europe alight'. Placed in an impossible position by officials who should have known better, the England players reluctantly agreed to give the salute in front of 110,000 spectators, including senior British government figures and Nazi leaders. Despite their pre-match humiliation as a result of weak British politicians, the England team won the game 6–3. One of the goals was scored by Goulden and it was one of the best of his career.

The normally reserved Stanley Matthews described the goal as, '...the greatest goal I ever saw in football'.

According to Matthews,

> *Len met the ball on the run; without surrendering any pace, his left leg cocked back like the trigger of a gun, snapped forward and he met the ball full face on the volley. To use modern parlance, his shot was like an Exocet missile. The German goalkeeper may well have seen it coming, but he could do absolutely nothing about it. From 25 yards the ball screamed into the roof of the net with such power that the netting was ripped from two of the pegs by which it was tied to the crossbar.*

Both West Ham and England had found a wonderful player, a highly skilled inside-forward who could control the play and score breathtaking, opportunist goals. He played in the second match of the England tour, when Hapgood and Matthews both suffered serious injuries in the early part of the game. With no substitutes allowed England finished the match with nine fit men and lost the game 2–1. Goulden, now established in the side, also played in the final game which England won comfortably 4–2. The players had managed to put the anger and resentment surrounding the match against Germany solidly behind them.

It must have been a proud moment for Goulden when he later played alongside the young Tommy Lawton in a game against a FIFA XI, in which both players scored. In his mid-20s, Goulden was in the form of his life and the pick of a good England team. Lawton later argued that Goulden was so good that, 'he would have played for England in any era'.

We will never know what Len Goulden might have achieved had war not interrupted his career. He played in West Ham's first two matches in the 1939–40 season before Hitler ordered the invasion of Poland in September 1939. Two days later the prime minister of Britain, Neville Chamberlain, declared war on Germany. The government immediately imposed a ban on crowds assembling and for the second time in 20 years, the Football League competition was brought to an end.

On 14 September the government gave permission for football clubs to play a limited number of friendly matches with attendances limited to 8,000 for safety reasons. The rules were later relaxed and the crowd limit extended to 15,000. A 50-mile travel limit was imposed and the Football League, keen to keep their competition going through the war, divided the clubs into seven regional areas. As with county cricket, this allowed a limited range of competitive professional matches to continue, although not everyone agreed with professional sport being played in wartime.

Like most professional footballers Goulden committed himself to the war effort. He joined the police force in 1939 which enabled him to continue to play football. He played a total of 152 games for West Ham during the conflict, scoring 59 goals. He also played in six unofficial England international matches, in what should have been the best years of his career.

The FA Cup was cancelled for the duration of the conflict, just as it had been during World War One. The professional game had grown in popularity in the 1930s and many observers thought professional football would help with morale and every effort should be made to keep the game going. An East London police chief remarked at the time that local football should also be encouraged. After all, he continued, no one had suggested that people should stop going to church. He remarked rather persuasively, 'police cells would be full of young men with no outlet for their energies, if things like football were outlawed'.

The government accepted this argument and despite many of the grounds being taken over by the military, the Football League's proposals were accepted and allowed to go ahead. Upton Park, White Hart Lane and Highbury were all used for military purposes during the duration of the conflict, as was Wembley Stadium. Upton Park was under military occupation for most of the war and the old Boleyn Ground was hit during the Blitz, the offices in the West Stand suffering extensive damage. Temporary office accommodation was found at the Boleyn Castle pub just outside the ground which, for a time, was the home for the Football League administration staff and the official national football archive. The locals must have found somewhere more convivial to have a pint, perhaps the Black Lion at Plaistow.

But in 1939–40 the restrictions on professional football appeared a little heavy-handed as the country waited nervously for the war to begin in earnest. Taking advantage of the lull in hostilities, the Football League decided to introduce a Cup competition and in 1940 the grimly-named Football League War Cup was introduced to replace the FA Cup. The competition was a rare wartime opportunity for players like Len Goulden to display their talent on the national stage and a chance for the Hammers to challenge for some serious silverware.

West Ham managed to put out a decent side for most of the war and succeeded in reaching the first Final of the hastily-introduced competition. Their Wembley opponents were Blackburn Rovers and although crowds should have been limited to 15,000, over 43,000 fans turned up to see the big match. The vast majority of the crowd were Hammers followers anxious to see their team on one of their rare appearances in a Cup Final.

On their way to the twin towers the Hammers had good wins against Chelsea, Leicester City, Huddersfield Town, Birmingham City and Fulham. The club's fanatical fans, as always, travelled to Wembley expectantly, confident that skipper Charlie Bicknell would bring the trophy back to East London. Blackburn Rovers, an old and proud club, were bound to provide stiff resistance.

The stage was set as the two teams were presented to Mr Alexander, 1st Lord of the

Admiralty. The sides were evenly matched for most of the first half, then in the 34th minute the Hammers scored what turned out to be the decisive goal. Good link-up play between Len Goulden and Stan Foxall let in George Foreman for a shot on goal which the Rovers 'keeper failed to hold. Sam Small, an ambulance builder by trade, was the first to react, slipping the ball into the net beyond the helpless Barron in the Rovers goal.

The Londoners continued to dominate after the interval with future manager Ted Fenton prominent. But led stoutly by Bob Pryde, the Blackburn defence managed to withstand the constant threat of the Hammers forwards, above all tricky winger Archie Macaulay. The second half brought some encouragement to Rovers supporters, who had bravely made the hazardous trip to London, as a series of goalmouth scrambles threatened an equaliser. But the breakthrough never came.

As referee Dutton blew the final whistle West Ham became the first club to win the Football League War Cup and brought some much-needed cheer to the hearts of beleaguered Cockneys in the East End. The happy Hammers' supporters could not have imagined on that victorious day at Wembley the horrors that were to engulf them in the next 18 months. Len Goulden was outstanding in midfield on the heavy Wembley pitch and his confident performance did much to bring the trophy to East London. The medal Goulden took home that day was to be his only honour in what was an otherwise unblemished professional career. The match took place in the middle of the Dunkirk evacuation so held little interest for the country at large. Even the celebrations in the East End were subdued. As Dick Walker reflected in the *West Ham United Football Book* of 1968, 'Most of the lads had an informal Cup-winning reception in the Boleyn pub near the ground. We got back there in time to get in a few pints before closing time. I remember my medal going round and round the public bar.'

Ted Fenton gave us an insight to how the victory was received by the players who had been recruited by the army: 'Austerity was the watchword everywhere. The Wembley crowd was restricted in numbers by the police and after the game the players quietly split up and went straight back to our service units.'

Army duties prevented Ernie Gregory from attending the Final. 'We'd all joined the TA before the war,' he mused. 'So we were called-up straight away when it started. Archie Macaulay got away to play in the Final and the rest of us didn't even know what the score was until he got back to the unit.' (Blows and Hogg, 2000)

The cup remains in the club's Upton Park trophy room to this day.

Goulden was 34 years old by the time the Football League was reintroduced in the 1946–47 season. He was considered, rather harshly, too old to play for England and Charlie Paynter also had some concerns about Len's age and fitness. However, Chelsea were only too happy to sign the ex-England international and paid West Ham a handsome £5,000 to take the inside-forward to Stamford Bridge. During his time at West Ham Goulden scored

52 League goals in 239 appearances, figures which tell us little about the player who was one of the greatest ever to wear the claret and blue.

At Chelsea, Goulden had the opportunity to play First Division football for the first time in his career. Chelsea historian Tony Matthews described Goulden as, '...a brainy footballer, he could change the point of attack with one flash of brilliance, sweeping out a pass fully 40 yards'.

At Chelsea, Goulden teamed up with fellow new signing Tommy Lawton and the pair immediately struck up a useful partnership. Lawton later claimed that Goulden's passes were 'just the sort that centre-forwards pray for'. Despite the Lawton–Goulden partnership, Chelsea struggled in the League and over the next four seasons finished no higher than 13th in the top flight.

Goulden retired in May 1950. During his time at Chelsea he had scored 19 goals in 111 appearances. He tried coaching for a time, before being appointed manager of Watford in 1954. Following a short period in Libya, Goulden trained as a sub-postmaster and worked for a time at a US Air Force base in Northamptonshire. Like many of his contemporaries he found it difficult to adjust to the world outside professional football and in 1969 returned to the game for a short period as coach at Oxford United.

Len Arthur Goulden died in Cornwall on 14 February 1995. The great inside-forward rightly enjoys legendary status at Upton Park. He would have won far more than his 16 England caps if war had not disrupted his international football career and it was fitting that Bobby Moore became the first West Ham player to surpass Goulden's number of international appearances. As Blows and Hogg have written, he was the 'jewel in the crown' among the golden generation of the 1930s, one of the very best of the vintage Hammers. It was a real injustice that the only honour this great footballer won in club football was the medal from West Ham's victory in the Football League War Cup in 1940.

Dick Walker: natural born leader

If we look back into Hammers history we can identify several natural born leaders, great captains who stand out as inspirational characters. We think of Robert Stevenson, George Kay, Jim Barrett and in modern times, Billy Bonds. Bobby Moore is the classic example of a natural leader, while Billy Wright, Bryan Robson and Steven Gerrard possessed similar qualities. The best players do not always make great leaders on or off the field. In this unfortunate category we think of Ian Botham and Kevin Pietersen in cricket, while the captaincy of the England football team in the hands of John Terry and Rio Ferdinand has been less than inspiring. The ideal captain is the best player in the team and at the same time an inspirational leader. But the likes of Bobby Moore, as older West Ham fans will testify, come along once in a hundred years.

Our next pioneer, Walter Richard 'Dick' Walker, was such an inspirational figure, and takes our story of the Hammers' pioneers into the 1950s. Walker may not have been in the same class as the Hammers' revered number-six, but was a great West Ham captain. Dick Walker was born in Hackney on 22 July 1913, but brought up in Dagenham where the family moved when Dick was a young boy. The youngster was football mad and would have been thrilled, at the tender age of 13, to be selected to play for Dagenham Boys. Like many families in 1930s recession-hit Britain, the Walkers struggled financially, with young Dick's father out of work for long periods. Finding a few shillings for a pair of football boots would have been difficult for the Walker household. It is likely that the budding young centre-half played in second-hand boots and walked miles to away games when there was no money for bus fares.

Although he loved playing football young Dick Walker was no great fan of professional football and prior to joining West Ham had never been to a professional game. Being brought up in a council estate in Dagenham, Walker knew the value of money and it was this that attracted him most to playing football for a living. Although both his sisters had jobs, Dick was conscious that his father was on the dole and he needed to earn money to put food on the table and coal on the fire. As Charles Korr points out, 'Walker personified the East Londoner's need to work hard for anything he wanted.'

Dick found work hard to find when he left school and had no idea at this stage that he might have a future in the professional game. As a teenager he played football for Becontree Athletic where he was spotted by a West Ham scout, who was impressed by the teenager's ability and physical presence. In 1933, following an extended trial at Upton Park,

he signed professional forms and made his first-team debut against Burnley in August 1934. The staff at the Boleyn had recognised young Dick's qualities but also realised he was not ready to replace the great Jim Barrett, even though Big Jim was coming to the end of his wonderful career.

In the days before young players could be sent out on loan to learn their trade, professional clubs employed rather devious methods to keep their young stars happy. Dick was sent across to West London to play for Park Royal, a strong amateur club based in Shepherd's Bush. The club gave Dick a phantom job as an electrician, although he later admitted that he 'couldn't change a light bulb'. For his 'job' the youngster was paid £4 to £5 a week, which in 1933 was a small fortune for the boy from the backstreets of Dagenham. 'It made me the richest man in the world,' he said. Good amateur footballers received boot money from their clubs right up until contracts were introduced into the amateur game in the 1970s, when the distinction between professional and amateur became meaningless. Following the introduction of contracts, many gifted amateur players were provided with soft jobs as a way around paying boot money.

Walker excelled for Park Royal and impressed his new employers to such an extent that he was selected to play in a club match in Paris – a magical mystery tour for a boy from a poor family. West Ham watched his progress at Shepherd's Bush with interest and with Jim Barrett's immense powers on the wane Walker was brought back to Upton Park in 1934 to act as cover for the legendary defender. As a young professional Walker continued to live at home in Dagenham and helped his parents to pay the rent. He became a local hero, recognised in the streets and popular with the neighbours. Walker was an extremely friendly character and loved nothing more than to stop and chat with neighbours – here was a young man with his feet placed firmly on the ground.

The youngster must have felt all his boyhood dreams had come true when he sat down to change for his first-team debut alongside Hammers legends Barrett, Len Goulden, Jimmy Ruffell and Ted Fenton. He had a solid game at right-half in the early season match against Burnley, but was given only two more first-team games that season. The reason for his rare appearances can be explained in two words – Jimmy Barrett. Walker clearly had great potential but Barrett, despite his age, was proving himself irreplaceable in the Hammers' defence. The youngster had to wait until 1936–37 before he was assured of a regular place in the side. In their *Essential History of West Ham United*, Blows and Hogg summed up Walker's emergence at West Ham: 'Like his predecessor, Walker was a dominant figure at the heart of the Hammers' defence, but the similarities between the two legends didn't end there, for Walker too was a larger than life character who played his game with a swagger and played hard both on and off the field.'

Despite his bravado and swagger, Walker's estimation of his own ability was, to say the least, modest. He once said, 'I couldn't play but I could stop those who could.' In 1936–37, at last established as Barrett's successor, Dick Walker played 32 out of 42 League games. In the following campaign he made 43 League and Cup appearances and established himself as a fixture in the side, in a season in which West Ham finished an encouraging sixth place in Division Two. Charlie Paynter must have been delighted at having found such a reliable replacement for Barrett.

Stepping into the shoes of great players can be difficult and many have failed to live up to the challenge. How many times have we heard 'he is the new Bobby Moore or Geoff Hurst'? It has been the kiss of death to many promising careers. Walker showed he was more than up to the challenge. In his first two full seasons at the club he made a huge impression and his outstanding performances brought England selectors to Upton Park once again, despite the Hammers being out of the top flight of English football through the 1930s. A great future in the game seemed guaranteed for the young centre-half. But tragically, and it is a familiar story, war intervened to bring an end to any speculation at the Boleyn about the international prospects of their new centre-half.

In the late 1930s Walker produced some outstanding performances. In the season immediately before war brought an end to the League programme for six years, West Ham drew arch-rivals Spurs in the fourth round of the FA Cup. Both sides were challenging for promotion from Division Two and the tie promised to be one of the most keenly contested matches in the club's history. The fans must have licked their lips in anticipation of gaining revenge for the 2–1 League defeat by Tottenham earlier in the season – they were not disappointed. The match at Upton Park finished in a 3–3 draw as both sides threw themselves at each other in pursuit of victory. The replay at White Hart Lane also finished in a draw, this time a modest 1–1, but the real drama was still to come.

Over 50,000 spectators crammed into Highbury for the second replay. The two sets of opposing fans created a white-hot atmosphere in one of the most intensely passionate clashes in English football in the inter-war years. Spurs settled the quicker, scored an early goal and went in at the interval with their 1–0 lead intact. We will never know what Charlie Paynter or the senior players said at half-time down in the bowels of Highbury, but the Hammers came out for the second half like men possessed. But their total dominance and constant pressure failed to produce a goal. Finally, in the 60th minute their relentless assault on the Tottenham goal paid off. Foxall raced clear of the Spurs defence and fired his shot into the bottom corner of Hooper's goal, taking the match into extra-time.

West Ham dominated the extra period but the game remained deadlocked at 1–1 when Foxall produced another moment of magic. This time he provided Archie Macaulay with the simplest of chances which he took with relish, sending the claret and blue section of the crowd into dreamland. The irrepressible Foxall hit the post in the final minutes, but Macaulay's goal took the Hammers through to the fifth round. It was the sweetest victory for the Hammers and their delighted fans. One of the best players on both sides in all three games was Dick Walker, his superb defending keeping his side's hopes of FA Cup glory alive. How he must have loved the intensity of the Tottenham matches, which would have brought the best out of this tenacious and stubborn defender.

Walker continued to play for the Hammers during the war and was a prominent member of the side that beat Blackburn Rovers in the Football League War Cup Final, a game in which Walker defended with his usual passion and obstinacy. But, as Brian Belton reminds us, Walker played his part in the war effort and only appeared for the Hammers while on leave from the Parachute Regiment. Unusually, he volunteered for active service rather than take the easy option for professional sportsmen of joining the army as a physical training instructor. It would have been no surprise to his friends, or West Ham fans, that Walker served his country with distinction during World War Two. He fought in an infantry battalion in the allied campaign which stretched right from El Alamein to Italy in the east. Sergeant Walker was mentioned in dispatches on several occasions which must have made his anxious family very proud indeed.

Dick Walker's decision to apply for active service was an indication of the strength of his character and personality. He was a larger-than-life figure. As Belton recalls, in addition to his personal qualities of courage and bravery, Dick Walker was a real character known for his sense of humour and practical jokes. 'His leave from the Parachute Regiment during wartime to play for West Ham was premised by speculation about his current rank which seemed to be on a sliding scale between private and sergeant and back to private again.' (1999)

Charles Korr argues that Hammers supporters have a special affection for players who display a self-deprecating sense of humour – who can laugh at themselves. Korr tells us how Walker would exchange jokes with the fans standing close to the touchline in the old Chicken Run. But his jovial personality was combined with a commitment to the club he grew to love. Walker cared deeply about the game, always gave his best and knew how much West Ham meant to the fans in a time of poverty and hardship. Despite difficult times during the inter-war years, professional footballers in the East End were better off than most in the area. When Dick Walker married, he was able to upgrade to classier Chadwell Heath, close by the club's current training ground – a definite step up the social ladder from Dagenham to the Chigwell of its time.

After the war Charlie Paynter appointed Walker club captain in succession to Charlie Bicknell. He had distinguished himself in the war and played 24 times for the Hammers between 1939 and 1945, six years in which he would have been in his footballing prime. He may have been selected for his country if war had not intervened and would have almost certainly overtaken Jimmy Ruffell's record of appearances.

Dick Walker's record is impressive. He was born in Hackney and brought up in the tough, often mean streets of Dagenham, which came to be known as the Essex badlands before the Ford Motor Company brought relative prosperity to the area. He was raised in a poor family who must have been hugely proud when the youthful Dick signed professional forms for their local club. He was part of the Depression generation of the 1930s, fought in the war and achieved the rank of sergeant in his battalion. After the war he captained West Ham United and became one of the central figures at Upton Park as the Hammers sought to lay down a foundation for the future.

Dick Walker was a hugely popular figure at the Boleyn, despite having to follow in the footsteps of Jim Barrett. Ken Brown, a protégé of Walker and a loyal servant of the club, described Dick Walker as a 'wonderful man'. Brown continued, 'I lived in the same street as him…the kids would watch him walk the length of the road to where his mum lived and we would look out of the window and be amazed that this was Dick Walker.' (Belton, 1999)

The teenage Brown joined Walker and other senior players after training upstairs at Cassetari's café, just as Bobby Moore did in the early 1960s. Brown later bemoaned the fact that it was always the young players who paid for the teas, probably Walker's way of making sure the kids did not rise too far above their station.

In August 1950 Ted Fenton replaced Charlie Paynter as manager of West Ham United. Paynter had given Walker his chance and the centre-half never took to the new manager. 'I didn't like him and he didn't like me,' Walker said later. 'It was a matter of taking over from someone popular and wanting to show you're in charge.' Despite their differences Fenton kept Walker in the side and he continued to be the first-choice centre-half for the whole of 1951–52, although at this stage his future at the club was uncertain. The following season was Walker's last as a regular member of the senior side. He played his final game for the Hammers in the 0–1 home defeat by Plymouth Argyle on 18 February 1953, in front of just 8,000 fans, one of the lowest recorded attendances for a first-team match at Upton Park. Walker continued to turn out for the reserves and A team for the next few seasons, but his long playing career effectively ended in the match against Plymouth.

At the end of the 1956–57 season Walker's playing contract was not renewed by the club and instead he was offered a job as the club bootman on £4 a week. Walker interpreted this harsh treatment as a personal insult by Fenton, who may have been jealous of Walker's immense popularity at the club. In his last few seasons at the Boleyn Walker helped to coach the young players and generally took them under his wing, as Ken Brown remembers: 'I was a bit of a skinny lad and Dick Walker thought I should put on weight…Andy Malcolm had a car and Dick would take us up to Soho every Friday night for a glass of stout and a big steak and kidney pie, full of meat and gravy.' (Belton, 1999)

John Lyall, the club's most successful manager in the post-war period, praised Walker's attitude towards the young apprentices, who the upright Lyall described as 'Dagenham-type lads'. Of course, not so many years before Walker was one of those lads himself and he had not forgotten where he came from. In October 1957 Walker was awarded a deserved testimonial match against Sparta Rotterdam, before he left the club for a coaching spell at non-League Dagenham. He later accepted a job as a full-time talent scout for Tottenham, a role he thoroughly enjoyed as his son Mike tells us. 'He brought on many young talented players and did a great service to young players, finding accommodation for out-of-town lads and taking them back to his house where him and his wife, Tina, would feed them and make them feel special.'

Mike Walker's fond memories highlight the passion his father continued to have for the game which gave him so much. He stayed at Tottenham for an impressive 20 years, an indication of Walker's loyalty and commitment to encouraging and supporting young players.

In retirement Walker became ill and endured several spells in hospital. In the last couple of years of his life he developed Alzheimer's disease and became a virtual recluse. His old teammate, Ken Tucker, claimed that Walker became a tramp when he was reduced to sleeping rough. What we do know is that Walker was admitted to hospital in 1985 where he remained until his death in January 1988. It was a very sad end to a great life. Dick Walker had a happy but deprived childhood, saw active service in World War Two and enjoyed a long and successful career in professional football. He was an extremely popular figure with both players and fans and became a folk hero in his part of East London. There are very few players who deserve the status of distinguished West Ham veteran more than Richard 'Dick' Walker.

Charlie Paynter: one of the big five

Up to the cruel dismissal of John Lyall in 1989, West Ham United had built an honourable reputation for staying loyal to their managers through good times and bad. This policy of remaining faithful to the manager was part of the Hammers' claim to be a family club rooted in its local community. In the 88 years between 1901 and Lyall's departure in 1989, West Ham had just five managers – Syd King, Charlie Paynter, Ted Fenton, Ron Greenwood and Lyall himself. In the few years between 1989 and 2011 the club has employed an astonishing eight managers, a sure indication that all is not well at Upton Park, with the club ditching many of the cherished values which made the Hammers a special club.

Throughout the 20th century the ownership of the club remained in the hands of people with a real understanding of what the club meant to the supporters – people with an interest in the area like the Cearns and Pratt families. Over the past few years this once proud club has been bought and sold by unscrupulous businessmen whose motives have been at the best questionable. To emphasise the point about continuity, J.W.Y. Cearns was a founding member of the club and served from 1900 until his death in 1934. W.J. Cearns was chairman from 1935 to 1950 and F.R. Pratt, who became a director in 1924, remained on the board until his death in 1941. He was succeeded on the board by his son Reg Pratt. For most of the 20th century there has been at least one member of the Cearns family on the board and since 1924, the board has always included someone from the Pratt family.

W.J. Cearns established the construction and engineering company which built the original stands at Upton Park. The Pratt family made their money from timber and Reg Pratt, who was a local JP, lived out in affluent Wanstead, across the flats from Upton Park. With consistency at both board and management level for the first hundred years of the club's existence, West Ham went from strength to strength. Throughout this period the club's board, staff and players jealously protected West Ham's proud traditions. As we shall see, the sacking of Lyall in the summer of 1989 signalled the end of the values everyone at the club, including the fans, deeply cherished. It was over and the club has never really recovered.

It is to be hoped that the current owners David Gold and David Sullivan, both East Enders and Hammers supporters, will attempt to restore some pride in West Ham United. Business acumen may be a necessary condition to be an owner of a successful football club,

but it is not a sufficient one. When Avram Grant was unveiled as the man to replace the popular Gianfranco Zola at the start of the 2010–11 season, David Sullivan told the supporters, '…we are certain we have got the right man – Avram's arrival is just the latest reason for real optimism at the club,' before adding, without a hint of irony: 'Avram is a perfect fit for the club.' The Hammers were relegated from the Premier League at the end of Grant's first season.

How the supporters would love to have a Charlie Paynter character back in charge of their beloved Hammers. With Syd King, Paynter took a bunch of keen amateurs from the East London docks and turned them into one of the top clubs in England in just 20 years. Paynter was born in Swindon in 1879, but his family moved to Plaistow, just down the road from the Boleyn, when Charlie was a young boy. He attended the local Grange School before starting work as an apprentice electrician for the City of London at the age of 14. As a youngster Paynter was obsessed with sport, a healthy enough obsession for a young boy in the late 19th century. He loved nothing more than to spend time with groups of athletes and cyclists and soon began to assist them with their fitness training and preparation for competitions.

Paynter was a decent footballer and played for a number of London amateur clubs, including Victoria Swifts and West Norwood. But he was realistic enough to know that he was not good enough for the professional game and began to think about ways he could be involved in professional sport. As Brian Belton tells us, he spent a great deal of time around the new Memorial Grounds, the new home of Thames Ironworks. 'From an early age Paynter was an all-round sportsman and when the home of Thames Ironworks FC…opened in 1897 he began to spend most of his free time there, competing in athletics and coaching.' (Belton, 2006)

Young Paynter was a deep thinker about sport and developed an early interest in physiotherapy and coaching methods. He watched and learned from the old Hammers coach Abe Morris and when a serious injury ended his brief playing career in 1900, Paynter was offered a coaching contract by West Ham. Still only 21 years of age, Paynter seized this opportunity and so impressed manager Syd King that he was offered the post as reserve-team trainer for the following season. Paynter did not hesitate. He took the unusual, some thought reckless, decision to cancel his apprenticeship and join the club full-time. His long and distinguished career with the Hammers had begun.

Paynter was a quick learner and benefitted from working under Morris, Jack Ratcliffe and Will Johnson – all inspirational coaches at the Memorial Grounds and in the early days at Upton Park. In the 1904–05 season, the first at Upton Park, Paynter began working closely with Tom Robinson. He had known Robinson for several years, and described him as the 'dearest and kindliest soul in sport'. This is rare praise in a sport not known for kindly behaviour of any type. They worked together for eight years in which Paynter found his coaching feet and developed his ideas about the game. His views were heavily influenced by the first-team trainer and he 'learned to love the old chap as much as he loved his cigars'. When Robinson retired in 1912, Charlie was the obvious candidate and his commitment to the club was rewarded when he was handed his mentor's job as West Ham's first-team coach.

Charlie Paynter also learnt a great deal about coaching and man management from Syd King, to the extent that the older man was confident enough in his protégé to endorse Charlie's promotion. The new first-team coach's relationship with the Hammers' gaffer is one of the most intriguing in the history of the club. Jimmy Ruffell provided some insight into their relationship when he revealed that Paynter decided on team tactics and was closest to the players. King, as Ruffell admits, 'was a good manager' but preferred to concentrate on club strategy and buying and selling players than getting involved in everyday playing matters. It could be argued that it was Paynter, not King, who was largely responsible for developing the Hammers' famous free-flowing football style.

The relationship between King and Paynter was complex and not always harmonious, but there was always mutual respect between the pair. King was a mercurial character who nurtured a wheeler-dealer persona, perhaps more at home in one of the second-hand car dealerships that littered the length of the Barking Road. Paynter, on the other hand, loved nothing more than being with his players on the training ground, developing individuals and working through team tactics. King was a Mason, played golf and liked a drink, whereas Paynter, in the tradition of founder Arnold Hills, was teetotal. Different characters they might have been, but what is not in question is that in their 10-year working relationship, King and Paynter took the Hammers to their first FA Cup Final and into the top flight of English football – not bad for a bunch of dockers from Canning Town.

When King left the club in 1932, Paynter was appointed temporary manager. Given the turmoil and eventually tragic circumstances surrounding King's departure, it is not surprising that the Hammers narrowly avoided relegation to the Third Division at the end of that season. But as the new manager settled into his job the club's playing fortunes began to improve. Paynter bought shrewdly. The following season he acquired John Morton, Stan Foxall, Jim Marshall and crucially, Len Goulden and all four settled in quickly. The Hammers finished seventh in 1933–34 and third the following season, in which they were serious promotion contenders. The club reached the end of the 1930s in good spirits and well set for further promotion bids before war intervened.

In total Paynter spent 50 years with West Ham. As Jimmy Ruffell testifies, he was regarded as a father figure by the players and provided an ideal link between the team and the more distant Syd King. A clear indication of the respect in which Charlie was held in the English game was his appointment as trainer to the England team for the first international match to be played at Wembley in 1924.

As the *theyflysohigh* website editor Steve Marsh wrote, 'Paynter built a solid side that regularly occupied a top half position in Division Two before the Second World War shattered his ambitions and caused the inevitable break-up of the team.'

But even the horrors of the war failed to prevent Paynter from tasting Hammers glory in the 1940 Wembley Final against Blackburn Rovers. The directors showed their appreciation of Paynter's immense contribution to the story of the club when they awarded Charlie a testimonial match in 1950, 44 years after he was awarded a benefit following the injury that ended his playing career. Paynter led his team out against Arsenal at Upton Park in what has been described by Tony Hogg as a 'unique jubilee'. The match celebrated Charlie's 50 years at West Ham as player, trainer and, finally, only the second manager in the club's history. The match was attended by dozens of old Hammers players, many of them ex-internationals, who came to pay their respects to the great man. Among those paying tribute was the man who replaced him, Ted Fenton.

Charlie Paynter died on 1 December 1970 at the age of 91. He had the great satisfaction of seeing his successor, who he personally recommended, return his beloved West Ham back into the English Division One. Charlie's place at Upton Park is assured. He remains one of the three or four most important figures in the history of the club and how proud he would have been to see the Hammers conquer Europe in 1965 and win the FA Cup on three occasions between 1964 and 1980. Following the sacking of Avram Grant and relegation in 2011, caretaker manager Kevin Keen stressed the importance of West Ham getting back to their basic values, those that were established 80 years ago by the likes of Charlie Paynter – an authentic pioneer.

Ted Fenton: the great enigma

Charlie Paynter was always going to be a hard act to follow. His achievements included guiding West Ham into the Football League, promotion to the top flight and a Wembley Cup Final appearance. He led the Hammers through two world wars and was largely responsible for the club emerging from World War Two financially secure and with a decent group of players. But old Charlie knew that West Ham were ready for a younger manager with fresh ideas, someone who understood the capricious minds of modern professional footballers.

If he understood the need for change, Paynter was equally determined to maintain continuity between the Hammers' traditional values and the new post-war world of professional football. Most of all, he would have insisted that the new man had to have the Irons in his soul – he had to have claret and blue blood in his veins. Such a man was Ted Fenton. For Charlie Paynter, he was the only person who could take West Ham United from the austerity of the early 1950s to the comparative affluence of the swinging sixties. Paynter's judgement was spot on. The foundations laid by Fenton enabled Hammers supporters of the mid-1960s to witness the greatest days in the club's history.

When Fenton was appointed West Ham manager in August 1950 his starting salary was just £15, less than he had been receiving at his previous club, Colchester United. At the time West Ham were languishing in Division Two mid-table mediocrity. Fenton could have been forgiven for turning his back on his old club by staying at Layer Road, where he had enjoyed spectacular FA Cup success. But in the end he could not resist going back to his roots to take on the job he coveted – manager of West Ham United.

He left the comparatively affluent and breezy coastline of north Essex for a post-war East London damaged almost unrecognisably by war, with its people struggling to cope with poverty, unemployment and rationing. The fans looked to Fenton to produce a Hammers side true to its traditions, which would raise their spirits and provide a little distraction from everyday hardship. Fenton knew this and set about giving Hammers supporters just what they needed. Football journalist Bernard Joy hit the nail on the head when he wrote, 'West Ham's tradition of playing colourful football was a way of getting away from the drabness of life in the East End.'

Fenton had accepted a huge challenge and it would be some years before the fans saw any return on his £15 a week contract.

Bobby Moore was one of seven players in the 1964 Cup Final team signed by Fenton. Robert Frederick Chelsea Moore was a wartime baby, born in 1941 into an East End that had withstood the horrors of the Blitz with such stoic courage. After the war Moore's parents' generation set out to rebuild East London by restoring their neighbourhoods, renewing their community networks and resurrecting their sporting culture. Churches, allotment societies, Christmas clubs, sports clubs and adult education groups were all re-established as local people began to rebuild their social and cultural lives from the wreckage left by the Nazi bombers.

The job of rebuilding was formidable and took nearly 20 years, but by the early 1960s they had largely succeeded in their task. Within a few years local playing fields were back in full use, football and cricket leagues in East London and urban Essex came to life again, swimming clubs held their galas and boxing clubs reopened their gyms. By the end of the 1950s a rich amateur sporting culture had literally emerged from the ashes of war. This required a Herculean effort by local enthusiasts, as grounds had to be prepared, changing rooms renovated and equipment acquired. Many of the football pitches and golf courses had been dug up to prevent enemy planes from landing, or were used for growing vegetables as part of the war effort. Although still in the shadow of the war, East Enders had the will and tenacity to restore to their area the things they cherished most – and their local sporting facilities and institutions were very near the top of the list.

The generation of Moore's parents worked to build a new world on the graveyard of the old one. Rationing did not end until 1954 and local people had to cope with loss, hunger, unemployment, shortages and homelessness to a degree that we can barely imagine today, but they were determined to rebuild the sporting culture that had meant so much to the East End. C.L.R. James stresses the importance of sport to communities such as those in East London: 'A glance at the world shows that when common people were not at work, one thing they wanted was organised sport and games. They wanted them greedily and passionately.' (C.L.R. James, 1963)

London hosted the Festival of Britain in 1951 and the coronation of the young Queen Elizabeth II in 1953 captured the British post-war imagination. There was a sense in the country of a new world emerging from the old. By the end of the 1950s the stage was set for the emergence of an extraordinary local and national hero who was to conquer the world of sport and become a central figure in the social revolution of the 1960s. It is fitting that the nation's hero of 1966 came out of this forward-looking culture of renewal. If East London was a place of reconstruction in the 1950s, by the early 1960s local people began to enjoy the benefits of all their hard work and self-sacrifice. This was the positive environment that nourished one of the greatest careers in international sport. An environment partially created by Ted Fenton.

Bobby Moore grew up in this time of high activity, imagination, independence and cooperation. The community values that nurtured Moore and his generation meant that he was able to make the most of his talents. In West Ham he found a club that encouraged skill, creativity and forward thinking – it was not called the Academy for nothing. Ted Fenton played a huge part in creating the conditions for Bobby Moore and others to storm the football world.

Edward 'Ted' Fenton was born on 7 November 1914 in Forest Gate, close to the Hammers' new home at Stratford. He joined Colchester United on leaving school, but was tempted back home by Syd King and made his West Ham debut against Bradford City in 1932 at the age of 18. Young Ted quickly gained a reputation as a talented young player with an excellent goalscoring record, representing England Schoolboys against Scotland in 1932. The youngster had to compete for a place in the West Ham side with the likes of Len Goulden, Stan Foxall and Jimmy Ruffell and did not become a first-team regular until 1935–36. He played for the club up to the outbreak of war when he enlisted in the army, serving in both Burma and North Africa. When not on active service Fenton was employed as an army physical training instructor, a job which allowed him time to play for the Hammers during the war.

Ted Fenton was 31 when football resumed after the war and he made 37 appearances in 1945–46, but it was to be his last season for West Ham and he left to join Colchester in June 1946. In his final season at Upton Park he played four FA Cup matches, including the fourth-round defeat by Chelsea in front of 65,000 at Stamford Bridge. Fenton had been with the Hammers since 1932 and in his 14 years as a player at the Boleyn he made a total of 176 appearances and scored 18 goals. He also played 201 games during the war, scoring an impressive 44 goals. Nominally a half-back, Fenton was regarded as a utility player – in other words, a manager's dream.

Fenton joined Southern League Colchester United in 1946 as player-manager and made an immediate impression. He stayed at the Essex club for four seasons before being lured back to Upton Park following Charlie Paynter's retirement. The smooth-talking East Ender tempted some high quality players to Layer Road, including the old Essex cricketer Frank Rist and the legendary centre-forward Vic Keeble. In his first two seasons he put together a decent side, but even the ever-optimistic Ted could not have imagined that, under his guidance, his team would enjoy the greatest giant-killing FA Cup run in Colchester United's history.

After an early-round win against Wrexham, the U's drew Division One Huddersfield at home in the third round. Over 16,000 fans packed into the three-sided Layer Road ground to see the great Peter Doherty up against Fenton and his men. The player-manager superbly marshalled his defence, completely blotting out the Irish international. The veteran defender also showed his managerial promise in the Huddersfield match. He ordered the pitch to be narrowed before the game and with the crowd breathing down their necks and the Colchester players flying into their tackles, the Yorkshiremen succumbed to a 1–0 defeat. The *County Telegraph* reported that, 'Ted Fenton cannot visualise any opposition too strong for his team and manages to imbue the same spirit into the side which is making football history.'

It might have been the eccentric diet of oysters and the odd glass of champagne that lifted the players, but more likely it was the presence of Fenton, both on and off the pitch, that was responsible for Colchester's great giant-killing feat. After seeing off Bradford City in the next round the Essex side drew the Blackpool team of Mortensen, Matthews and Harry Johnston in the fifth round – away at Bloomfield Road. Fenton prepared his team meticulously, leaving nothing to chance. The players ran out in teeming rain in front of 30,000 excited fans with hundreds of Colchester supporters locked out of the ground. The scene was set for another act of giant-killing, but Stanley Matthews had other ideas. He produced a mesmerising display and ripped the U's defence to shreds in a convincing 5–0 victory for the Tangerines and Colchester's great Cup run was over, but Fenton's men returned to the Essex coast as heroes.

At Colchester Fenton ran the club single-handedly from a small shed in the corner of the ground. Club historian Bernard Webber wrote: 'The players called him the Governor and he was a born leader – tall, debonair, a snappy dresser, and always smoking a pipe. He had a sort of superior disdain to opponents.' (Webber, 2004)

When Fenton left Colchester for his beloved West Ham in the summer of 1948, the move came as no great surprise. He returned to West Ham as Charlie Paynter's assistant, before taking over as manager in 1950. In his first season at Upton Park the Hammers finished in 13th place in Division Two. Fenton had high ambitions and quickly realised he needed to recruit some quality players to have a realistic chance of challenging for promotion. He brought in Dave Sexton, Jimmy Andrews, Frank O'Farrell from Cork United and crucially Malcolm Allison from Charlton Athletic. They joined a side that included Dick Walker, Ken Tucker, Ernie Gregory, Derek Parker and Harry Hooper. Despite these exciting additions to the squad the Hammers continued to struggle, finishing no higher than 12th in the next few seasons.

In 1954–55 the fans began to see signs of improvement as Fenton's new men began to settle. The team was lifted by the famous signings, but the improvement was due mainly to the goals of the great Johnny Dick. Dick's 26 goals in 39 games that season helped lift the Hammers to eighth place in the League and rekindled some hope for the fans. Fenton welcomed his new players but was realistic enough to know that young players were the future of the club. He wrote in his autobiography, 'The only way to build the club was youth. There were lots of good players around, but I had no money to buy the key players we needed. There was always the problem of running a club on a shoe-string.' (Fenton, 1960)

Fenton introduced a youth policy which had spectacular results and was the envy of clubs across the country. The celebrated West Ham academy was to be the lynchpin of the club's success in the 1960s. Fenton's achievement in driving through his youth policy said a great deal about his determination to succeed in the job. Blows and Hogg (2000) tell an interesting story about the lengths to which Fenton went to secure the signature of John Dick. He had watched the Scottish international forward, who was billeted at Colchester while on national service, play for Eastern Counties works side Crittall Athletic. He knew he needed to convince Dick's parents that West Ham were the best club for the sought-after youngster, so he tramped the streets of Glasgow before eventually locating his target at Dick's parents' home in the Cardonald district of the city. Within an hour Fenton had persuaded Mr and Mrs Dick to sign, stealing the inside-forward from under the nose of Arthur Rowe of Tottenham. This kind of determination was almost bound to achieve results and he later showed the same single-mindedness when he signed Malcolm Musgrove from Lynemouth Colliery.

The classic West Ham combination of five or six locally produced young players combined with some experienced signings was something Fenton, and Greenwood and Lyall after him, saw as the future of the club. His side of the late '50s is a clear example of this policy. Fenton believed young players like Dick could achieve at the highest level and in the same spirit, he quickly promoted Malcolm Musgrove, John Bond, Ken Brown, Noel Cantwell and Andy Malcolm to the first-team squad. He sold Harry Hooper to Wolves for £25,000, transferred Dave Sexton to Orient and Frank O'Farrell to Preston. He brought in Mike Grice and Eddie Lewis and gave an opportunity to youngsters John Smith and Bill Lansdowne. As Fenton began to assemble a side he believed could win promotion, he knew there was still one piece of the jigsaw missing. The Hammers made a slow and disappointing start to the 1957–58 season and Fenton knew he had to act and act decisively. He had never forgotten his old centre-forward at Colchester, Vic Keeble, who was languishing at the time in Newcastle's reserves. Fenton telephoned his old teammate and said, 'I'm coming up Saturday. I fancy you Vic, I could put in a bid for you, I'll take a look at you, see how you do.'

Keeble scored two first-half goals in the match and the smooth-talking Fenton persuaded the centre-forward to leave Newcastle, who demanded a hefty £10,000 in return. The pairing of Keeble and Johnny Dick was made in Hammers heaven and their goals took the club into the promised land of Division One. Keeble was Fenton's most astute signing and his seemingly telepathic partnership with Dick brought back memories of Syd Puddefoot and Vic Watson at their very best.

The fans had waited a long time for it and their patience was finally rewarded when promotion was achieved in May 1958, when Keeble's 23 goals in 32 games clinched the Division Two Championship. Keeble and Dick have their own personal entries in this book and the pair certainly helped deliver their grateful manager's dream of getting the Hammers back to the pinnacle of English football for the first time since 1930. The 101 goals the team scored that season remains a club record to this day.

The great 2nd Division Championship winning side of 1957–58.

On their return to Division One the Hammers finished in a highly creditable sixth place behind champions Wolves, with the prolific pair of Dick and Keeble continuing to bang in the goals. But the Irons struggled for the next couple of years as the goals began to dry up and the pressures of the top flight began to take its toll on the club management. Promotion was a double-edged sword for Fenton. He was adored by the fans for winning the Second Division Championship, but the strain of managing at this level began to show on the normally confident and ebullient East Ender.

It probably did not help Fenton's confidence that his team was full of very strong characters, passionate about their football, ambitious and with strong ideas about the way the game should be played. Senior players started to ask questions of the gaffer who seemed to be, in the words of today's pundits, 'losing the dressing room'. At the heart of the struggle between players and staff was the outspoken Malcolm Allison.

Legend has it that Allison organised a players' revolt against his manager who had earned an alleged reputation for meanness and cheating players out of their bonuses. Allison claimed that 'Ted Fenton would cheat you out of anything'. Ken Tucker supported Allison's charge against his manager: 'The Arsenal players told me that they had got 10 guineas for a game with England Amateurs that was the FA's rate for such matches. When West Ham played against them Ted only gave us £5. Apparently the cheque had gone to Ted and he paid us in cash.'

Nothing is more likely to divide a manager from his players in the professional game than arguments about money. Aside from allegations of profiting from players' bonuses, it appears Fenton had other charges to face. The great Hammers' servant Dick Walker clashed with his manager on several occasions. Walker's damning accusations of Fenton's behaviour is a clear indication that the players badly missed Charlie Paynter. What we know is that Fenton refused to renew Walker's contract at the end of the 1956–57 season. Instead he offered the veteran defender a menial job at £4 a week. The former club captain had to accept a job he had done 25 years previously when he was a ground-staff boy. Whatever his motives it was a body blow to the great centre-half, who left the club shortly after falling out with his manager. Walker's accusations against his manager resulted in further rumours and allegations by players who probably should have known better.

Tucker poured further scorn on Fenton's man-management skills, claiming that, 'He [Fenton] was never straightforward. He was against the players…The players used to say he just pulled the names out of the hat.'

After one particularly nasty training ground spat, Tucker claims he threw his boots at his manager. The players were also incensed at Fenton's treatment of the popular Billy Dare. Mike Newman claimed that, 'Fenton once told Billy Dare, when the player asked him why he had been dropped, that he wasn't tall enough. Bill had done well for the club for years at that time and responded by asking Ted if it had taken him six years to work out that he was too small to play for the team.'

It is unusual for professional footballers to talk so critically about their manager in public. That they did is an indication of the level of unrest at Upton Park at this time and, perhaps, an explanation as to why they continued to languish in the lower reaches of Division Two in the mid-1950s. As we shall see in more detail in the following chapter, Malcolm Allison rose above this toxic training ground atmosphere to impose some sort of order. Ted Fenton eventually agreed that Allison should take over training and team tactics. From that moment Fenton's days at the club were numbered, despite the triumph of 1958.

The mood on the training ground was not helped by the players' criticism of club coach Billy Moore. Full-back John 'Muffin the Mule' Bond (he had acquired the nickname because his running style resembled that of the favourite 1950s children's puppet), was appalled by Moore's training methods. 'There was only two or three footballs in the entire club,' he claimed. 'You got out to training about quarter past 10 and ran around the pitch, ran a lap and walked a lap. You'd be doing this for about three-quarters-of-an-hour and you'd shout to Billy Moore to get the balls out. Billy would be standing at the entrance to the ground watching, with a fag in his mouth, that he never took out.'

Despite this torrent of abuse and criticism and accusations of losing the dressing room, Fenton had his supporters. Ernie Gregory disagreed with Allison's jibe that Fenton was a useless manager and argued that he was responsible for several interesting innovations: 'We were the first team to eat steak before meals.'

Not a startling innovation, but this was the 1950s. Gregory continued, 'We were told to put a ball between two players and you take two players out. John Bond and Noel Cantwell were the first of the overlapping full-backs…We used to train at Forest Gate ice-skating rink – it was narrow, so you could practice working in tight situations.'

Jimmy Andrews, a shrewd and perceptive coach himself, believed that, 'Fenton was on to one-touch football, and that was unusual at the time.'

Older supporters will remember the Hammers' close, intricate passing game of the late 1950s and early '60s. Bobby Moore used to say that the players trained on their toes to encourage them to go forward, always looking for attacking options. It was Fenton, on a foggy winter's day in 1956, who sent the club's property manager, Jack Turner, down to Flanders Fields in East Ham to 'go and watch a kiddy called Moore who's been recommended'.

If Fenton did have his strengths as a manager and thinker about the game, the evidence that he was not quite up to the job of running a modern football club is persuasive. Club scribe Brian Belton puts the situation in this way:

> As such, what happened at the Boleyn Ground in the Fifties can be understood as a kind of revolution, a series of culture changing events, that included worker (player) control…There was, as John Cartwright described it, a form of communism at the club. The players really ruled it. In short the dictatorship of the football proletariat.
> (Belton, 1999)

This seems to be an overblown way to describe what, in effect, was a power struggle between Fenton and Malcolm Allison. Allison triumphed for a few seasons before Ron Greenwood restored the status quo and the authority of the manager was, again, largely unquestioned.

Ted Fenton served West Ham United as player and manager from 1932 until his departure from the club in 1961. In his time as manager he established the highly-regarded West Ham academy through which he introduced young players to the club's famous free-flowing football philosophy, so loved by the fans. The academy has produced an impressive number of outstanding footballers including Bobby Moore, Geoff Hurst, Martin Peters, Frank Lampard Jnr, Rio Ferdinand, Michael Carrick, Joe Cole, Glen Johnson – the list goes on. Notwithstanding Allison's criticisms, it is difficult to imagine the success of the academy without Ted Fenton's guiding hand.

Fenton would have looked on with pride as the Hammers' youth team reached the FA Youth Cup Final twice in three years between 1956 and 1959. With the support of chairman Reg Pratt, Fenton encouraged his players to take their FA coaching badges, to develop their ideas on the game and to prepare for their futures. His greatest achievement as West Ham manager was, of course, winning the Second Division Championship in the 1957–58 season, taking the Hammers back to the top after so many years out of the limelight. At the time Hammers fans had certainly never had it so good.

It is possible to argue that Fenton never really received the credit his achievements warranted and that his players were ungrateful, disrespectful and downright bolshie. It is easy to forget that seven members of the FA Cup-winning team of 1964 had either been signed by Fenton or came through the academy. Fenton was a Cockney operator who brought his street skills to professional football – he was the Harry Redknapp of his day. His shrewd signings of Allison, Musgrove, Dick, Cantwell, O'Farrell and particularly Vic Keeble, paid off handsomely, even if the Allison signing did prove to be his ultimate undoing.

Most managerial careers end in failure and Fenton's was no exception. He left West Ham in March 1961 in mysterious circumstances which have never been properly explained to this day. There is little doubt that the players' revolt against his authority led to a deterioration in Fenton's mental well-being – the turmoil simply overwhelmed him. The team's form in Division One had been poor and the manager's health had suffered and he was eventually replaced by Ron Greenwood. He left Upton Park for Southend United where he stayed for four undistinguished years before he was sacked in 1965. He opened a sports shop in Brentwood, which he passed on to his son Alan, who played for the Hammers' A team in the 1950s.

Ted Fenton died tragically in a car accident near Peterborough in 1992, on his way to a family reunion. Although his place in the history of the club is secure, it is time for a reassessment of Ted Fenton's career at West Ham. His contribution to the great triumphs of the 1960s and the emergence of the club as a modernising force in the English game should never be underestimated. It is time he was given the recognition he deserves for leading the Hammers back to Division One after so long out in the footballing wilderness. His faith in young players, which remained a club policy until very recent times, established the foundations for the success of the 1960s. Fenton's academy innovation has been copied by most professional clubs and remains the best possible route to success for clubs like West Ham. Ted Fenton was a colourful character and an influential coach and manager. The club should find a way to repay their debt to a great pioneer.

Malcolm 'Big Mal' Allison

Malcolm Alexander Allison was born in Dartford on 5 September 1927. The son of an electrical engineer, he played for Erith & Belvedere FC as a teenager before joining Charlton Athletic as a professional in 1945. Even though he made his name in football away from Upton Park, Allison deserves his status as a Hammers pioneer for his influence on the club's success in the 1960s and in particular in his role as mentor to the young Bobby Moore. These bare and austere facts disguise the reality behind one of the most gregarious and high profile managers the English game has ever seen and he played for West Ham – a fact not generally recognised in the game.

Allison's potential as a future coach and manager became apparent early in his days as a West Ham player, following his £7,000 transfer from Charlton in 1951. Allison was a reliable and resolute defender and made 238 appearances for the Hammers between 1951 and 1958. His playing career was dramatically cut short following an operation to remove one of his lungs. The future manager of Manchester City was diagnosed with tuberculosis in 1957. His last competitive game for the Hammers was against Sheffield United on 16 September 1957, after which he fell seriously ill and he never played for the first team again.

Looking back, the years of West Ham's greatest achievements appear to be a carefree time compared with the grey and austere 1950s. On a serious note the '60s brought Vietnam, the Cuban missile crisis and the assassination of President Kennedy. But despite these momentous events, the early '60s did feel like a transition period between two very different periods of history. The BBC's Home Service and Light Programme gave way gracefully to Radio One and not so gracefully to the hugely successful and hip pirate, Radio Caroline. The venerable Victor Sylvester and Alma Cogan stepped aside for the Beatles and the Beach Boys – no contest really. Suddenly, the world seemed more colourful.

The designers of the official programme of the 1964 European Cup-Winners' Cup Final between West Ham and TSV 1860 München at Wembley – price one shilling and printed in black and white – seem not have caught the swinging sixties' creative design bug. Bobby Moore is listed as a left-half and the centrefold sets out both teams in the ancient 2–3–5 formation. The programme itself is interesting as an historical document. It includes four full-page advertisements – the *Radio Times*, Double Diamond ('the beer men drink'), the Hot Bovril Supporters' Club ('drink your health in Bovril') and Yardley ('a man's talc'). The Yardley cosmetics factory was situated on Stratford High Road in East London and was responsible for the sickly smell of sweet perfume mixed with the pungent aroma of ground bones which hung over the streets of the area for many years.

If the FA programme design for the match belonged solidly in the 1950s, the notes do pay a generous tribute to the Hammers. Peter Lorenzo of the *Daily Mirror* wrote that 'West Ham had gained a reputation as one of the finest ambassadors British sport has ever sent abroad and they have been a credit to themselves, their sport and their country.' Those who are familiar with West Ham's purist playing style over the past 40 years, inspired by Allison among others, will appreciate Lorenzo's comments when he continued: 'From all aspects, talent, intelligence, tactical ability and overall approach there are few, if any, better-suited flag carriers than West Ham United.'

There were few English clubs who experienced these rebellious times more deeply than West Ham. The club transformed itself from being a lowly Second Division club to a major force in European football within a few years. The Hammers team of the early '60s bristled with new ideas on attacking football and at the heart of the side were England's World Cup-winning heroes, Geoff Hurst and Martin Peters and of course, their incomparable captain, Bobby Moore. The best West Ham team ever played breathtaking football, scored hatfuls of goals and richly entertained football lovers across the country. The Upton Park faithful had every right to be proud of their local heroes, who were every football lover's second-favourite team. Moore's team brought glamour to the East End.

West Ham's emergence as a force in European football began in the period between the last few years of Ted Fenton's era and the appointment of his successor, Ron Greenwood, in 1961. One of the most influential and intriguing characters during this period was the flamboyant extrovert, Malcolm Allison. It was Allison who helped shape the team of the '60s and his radicalism was largely responsible for the attacking football that so distinguished the club in that period. He was at the head of a group of football thinkers at the Boleyn which included Dave Sexton, Frank O'Farrell, Malcolm Musgrove, John Lyall, Jimmy Andrews and Noel Cantwell. This passionate group of young professionals met regularly at Cassetari's café in the Barking Road to discuss their exciting ideas over endless cups of tea. The upstairs room in the old café was the crucible of the new football thinking that was to transform the future of this proud club.

Allison was a dominant, often overpowering character at the Boleyn and at the training ground at Grange Farm. His increasing influence on the other players led to a growing rift with manager Ted Fenton. But Fenton was no fool and quickly recognised Allison's leadership abilities and gave his new centre-half the club captaincy in 1952, soon after his arrival from the Valley. He respected the way his new signing took over from the legendary Dick Walker in the heart of the West Ham defence – much in the way Walker

himself succeeded Jim Barrett. There is no question that Allison's reputation in the game was earned as a manager rather than a player, but he had his moments at centre-half.

Martin Godleman (2008) offers us two matches in which Allison's resolute defending earned Division Two's Hammers FA Cup glory. In March 1956 nearly 70,000 fans crammed into White Hart Lane to see the Hammers earn a Johnny Dick-inspired FA Cup replay against a very strong Tottenham side. Skipper Allison led by example in the Hammers defence, providing stiff resistance against that great centre-forward, Len Duquemin and the flying winger, George Robb. Unfortunately, the Hammers lost the replay 1–2 on a muddy pitch in front of a disappointed capacity crowd of 36,000 at the Boleyn. In the 1958 competition West Ham claimed a convincing 5–1 victory over a Blackpool side who finished the season in seventh place in Division One.

Cruelly, Godleman also exposes Allison's limitations as a defender when he experienced a personal nightmare in a rare Hammers away win at Fulham in 1954. Allison was led a complete dance by the Fulham forwards, Johnny Haynes and Jimmy Hill. Complete embarrassment for the skipper was spared by goals from Dave Sexton, Tommy Dixon and two more from Dick which gave the Irons a deserved 3–4 victory. It is interesting to note that in the West Ham team of that day Allison, Cantwell, Sexton, O'Farrell, John Bond and Ken Brown all became managers of Division One clubs as the Hammers' revolutionary ideas began to influence the highest level of English football.

Allison took his captaincy duties extremely seriously and showed a profound interest in the direction the club was heading. His passion and strong ideas inevitably led the skipper to question Fenton's training methods and the way he treated his players. Perhaps he thought Fenton did not care enough. The rift between these two strong men caused serious divisions in the club and eventually led to Fenton's sacking and the appointment of Ron Greenwood as manager. In Allison, Fenton had created a monster – a football visionary who, in the words of Blows and Hogg (2000), '...would revolutionise the club's archaic regime and transform training, coaching techniques and tactics to secure promotion to Division One in 1958'.

This may be a little harsh on Fenton, who must take a great deal of credit for achieving promotion, but their comment does indicate the regard in which Allison is held at West Ham. For many, Fenton was stuck in the time warp of the '50s, while the innovative ideas of Allison were fizzing with the confidence and creativity of swinging London.

Allison's ideas about football, like most thoughtful observers of the game, were heavily influenced by the Hungarian national side of the 1950s. Shortly after Hidegkuti, Puskas and company handed out a lesson in modern football to the England team at Wembley in 1954, West Ham played AC Milan in a floodlit friendly at Upton Park. The Hammers side received their own lesson that night as they were torn to shreds by a Milan side which included five internationals in its forward line, including the great Uruguayan, 'Pepe' Schiaffino. Allison, Ken Brown and the others could not forget their 6–0 humiliation and immediately organised an unofficial players' meeting at their Barking Road café the following day.

In a heated inquest over egg and chips the players pored over every tactical move the Italians inflicted on them. Allison, Cantwell, Sexton and the others understood that there was a huge chasm between Continental football and its crude English counterpart. The Hungarians' technique, strategy and individual brilliance were years ahead of anything seen in Britain. Allison saw that you could combine possession football with speed and skill and he was desperate to try the Continental approach with a team of his own. How he would have enjoyed the Barcelona of Messi, Iniesta and Xavi.

The meeting that day at Cassetari's defined the future of West Ham for the next 20 years – standing tall over the discussion was Big Mal, as he was soon to become known to the football world.

Arguably, Allison's greatest strengths were his sheer enthusiasm and his drive to play a leading role in the changes that were beginning to overwhelm the English game. His qualities came to the fore at West Ham where he gradually took charge of coaching sessions, ran the academy set-up and began to take a decisive role in first-team tactics and selection. He desperately wanted to be at the forefront of the new Hungarian-inspired ideas on football and was not prepared to let Ted Fenton stand in his way. Fenton continued to give his determined skipper his head and allowed Allison to take charge of training sessions, help with the youth team and transform the club's outdated fitness programme.

Despite his undoubted ducking and diving abilities, Fenton was out of his depth as a modern football thinker. Allison was part of the bright new world of the 1960s where creativity was encouraged in all areas of life, even in the ultra-conservative world of professional football. Fenton knew this and was happy to hand over power to the new men, before events overwhelmed him. A pre-war player, Fenton was from the generation that had its antecedents in Arnold Hills' iron makers and Syd King, while Malcolm Allison's life became totally removed from the lives of first-generation Hammers like factory footballer Charlie Dove.

When he arrived at Upton Park from Charlton, Allison was appalled by the lack of ball work in training, the endless jogging around the pitch and the lack of tactical awareness at the top of the club. Allison was clearly shocked by what he saw. He later wrote the following damning passage in his autobiography:

When I was transferred from Charlton to West Ham I led myself to believe that the futility...was over. For a while I was happier but it was merely a change of environment which broke the monotony. Within six months I was more disillusioned than ever. Not only did West Ham know less about training than Charlton...but they asked for less effort.

The only difference in training sessions was that West Ham's were shorter. The facilities were disgraceful. We used to train on a pock-marked, scruffy little track at the back of the ground. We used to have to run in and out of trees...If he was alert he [Billy Moore] might spot blue cigarette smoke filtering through the trees.

My relationship with [Ted] Fenton was much closer than the one I had with Jimmy Seed...I did give him some problems but they arose chiefly out of my frustration with the way the club was run...I began to run the team with his tacit agreement. I was getting results.

As Allison's influence at the club grew he was joined by Noel Cantwell, John Bond and Frank O'Farrell in the West Ham players' equivalent of the Anfield bootroom. The leading players' commitment to change the club for the better and their confidence in their own ability was impressive and prepared the club for another visionary thinker, Ron Greenwood. The truth about the alleged conflict between Ted Fenton and Malcolm Allison at Upton Park in the late 1950s was that the two men represented two very different generations. Fenton had cut his football teeth in the pre-war years under the guiding hand of Charlie Paynter. It was a time when little thought was given to fitness plans or sophisticated team formations and tactics.

If Ted Fenton initially established West Ham's successful youth policy, Allison took it further and became recognised as one of the leading coaches in the professional game. Both men knew that to catch up with European football it was necessary to expose young players to the new methods from an early age – it became the West Ham way. In 1957 the Hammers' youngsters appeared in the Final of the FA Youth Cup, losing 2–8 on aggregate to the Busby Babes of Manchester United. Two years later the claret and blue youngsters reached the Final for the second time in three years, on this occasion losing to Blackburn Rovers 2–1 on aggregate, and this after drawing 1–1 at Upton Park. Despite these two defeats, the club's youth policy was a great success and a genuine team effort, until it was squandered in the 1990s. Allison loved working in a team and enjoyed the close support of chief scout Wally St Pier, youth-team manager Billy Robinson and first-team players John Bond, Noel Cantwell and Malcolm Musgrove.

Joe Kirkup, Jack Burkett, Eddie Bovington, Bobby Moore, Johnnie Cartwright, John Lyall and Terry McDonald all featured in at least one of those two youth Finals. Moore was one of nine West Ham youngsters who went on to represent England at youth level in the late 1950s. This was an impressive record by the standards of any club in the top flight of English football and much of the success could be attributable to Malcolm Allison. It was only a matter of time before his drive, energy and growing influence at the club extended to the first team. Terry McDonald, who later featured in the Orient side which famously gained promotion to Division One in 1962, had no doubts about who was running things at the Boleyn. 'Allison ran the team, there is no doubt about it. But don't just take my word for it, ask any of the players who were there at the time. He made West Ham.'

Allison was undoubtedly popular with the players and his contribution to the success of the youth team cannot be questioned. One of the club's young professionals found Allison's presence at the club inspirational. Allison was instrumental in turning a rather awkward young defender from Barking into one of the greatest footballers the world has ever seen. Nobody was more appreciative of Allison's part in his football education than Bobby Moore himself. The great defender paid this tribute to his inspirational mentor: 'When Malcolm was coaching schoolboys he took a liking to me when I don't think anyone else at West Ham saw anything special in me. I would have done anything for him. He was the be-all and end-all for me. I looked up to the man. It's not too strong to say I loved him.'

This is rare praise indeed from the normally rather reserved future England captain. The two men shared a deep love, almost an obsession with the game. Moore recounts how his mentor got him to think about his own game. 'We sometimes used to get the same bus from the ground and were sitting upstairs one day when Malcolm said, very quietly, "Keep forever asking yourself: If I get the ball, who will I give it to?". He told me that was Di Stefano's secret at Real Madrid.' (Powell, 1993)

The teenage defender was deeply shocked to learn that Allison was seriously ill. He was at Upton Park the day his revered guide and teacher received the dreadful news of his illness: 'Malcolm had been battling for months to recover from tuberculosis. I'd even seen him the day he got the news of his illness. I was a ground-staff boy and had gone to Upton Park to collect my wages. I saw Malcolm standing on his own…at the back of the stand. Tears in his eyes.' (Powell, 1993)

Moore was to play his own part in the departure of Allison from Upton Park, something which must have deeply affected the youngster. On 8 September 1958 the Hammers played Manchester United at Upton Park in a match that has a deep resonance in Hammers folklore. In the hours before kick-off it dawned on Allison that his playing days were probably over. Since his illness he had bravely and stoically made a modest comeback in the reserves and felt he was ready to return to the side against the high flying Red Devils.

Moore explained the situation at that difficult time: 'By the start of the '58 season we were battling away in the reserves, Malcolm proving he could still play. Me proving that I might play one day. After three or four matches we were top of Division One, due to play Manchester on the Monday night, they had run out of left-halves…it's got to be me or Malcolm.' (Powell, 1993)

Ted Fenton had the unenviable choice of selecting the ailing Allison or the young pretender for the number-six shirt. Fenton sought the advice of the trusted Noel Cantwell, Allison's great friend, who without hesitation nominated the 17-year-old for his debut. Moore played and the number-six shirt became his in perpetuity and his assured performance helped the Hammers to an unexpected 3–2 victory. One can only imagine how the young man felt as he watched his friend walk out of the Upton Park dressing room, for once in his life a beaten man. That night Bobby Moore became a man. He showed he had the strength of personality to turn a difficult situation into a personal triumph.

Moore later recalled that emotional evening in his biography.

I'd been a professional for two and a half months and Malcolm had taught me everything. For all the money in the world I wanted to play. For all the money in the world I wanted Malcolm to play because he had worked like a bastard for this one game in the First Division. It would have meant the world to him. Just one more game...

In her engaging book, *Bobby Moore: By The Person Who Knew Him Best*, Tina Moore provides a number of poignant and revealing insights into the close friendship that developed between Moore and Allison during the 1960s. His mentor was 13 years older than the future England captain and Tina claims that Bobby 'followed Allison around like a puppy', lapping up every piece of football knowledge he could from the fast-talking extrovert. Moore was also influenced by Allison off the field, although the future manager of Manchester City had not yet acquired the fedora-wearing, cigar-smoking playboy persona he adopted in the 1970s. Tina provides a glimpse of her husband's newly-acquired, Allison-influenced lifestyle: 'Malcolm Allison lived a social whirl and during this time he was friendly with a fishmonger's daughter. Bobby and I were invited round to the fishmonger's house on New Year's Eve and sampling it for the first time in his life, Bobby devoured an entire side of smoked salmon on his own.'

Moore's taste for high living began in a fishmonger's house – you can't get more East End than that. Tina enjoyed her new lifestyle but she would probably have drawn a line at Bobby's mates turning up on her honeymoon. Unbelievably, that is just what happened. The Moores had booked a fortnight in the sunshine of Majorca and guess who showed up on their first weekend? None other than Malcolm Allison and Noel Cantwell – on the newly-weds' honeymoon! With a hint of anger, Tina reveals that her new husband was easily led astray and could not resist a night out with Allison and Cantwell. Tina tells the story.

'True to form they showed up within a week. The three of them got plastered. Bobby was violently sick and spent the night in Noel's room and I ended up sobbing with his wife, Maggie.'

This was not the last of Moore's indiscretions, as Tina reveals, and Allison's example would have heavily influenced the impressionable lad from Barking. But Moore had something that Allison lacked. Despite the deep respect and affection Bobby had for the older man, Moore knew when to stop, as Jeff Powell explains that, 'The vision, however, did not blind Moore to the imperfections in Allison's lifestyle.' (Powell, 1993)

Fortunately for Moore he lacked the element of self-destruction that seemed to inhabit the older man's character. Moore draws this revealing conclusion on his friend's personality and style: 'Malcolm had a great life but he left some question marks behind him en route. As a manager I would have wanted to be part of my players. But only up to a point...how else could you discipline people?' (Powell, 1993)

Moore understood the need to keep a certain distance, a quality which made him such a natural and outstanding captain.

Allison left Upton Park soon after that fateful night in 1958 and simply drifted for a few years. He sold a few second-hand cars and let himself get involved in some slightly dodgy activities. Given the decisive contribution he made to their successful promotion campaign, most Hammers supporters believed the former centre-half would be offered a coaching job at the club. Sadly, it was not to be and we can only imagine what the Hammers might have achieved had he stayed at the Boleyn. Another lost opportunity!

After his brief period away from the game, Allison accepted an offer of a coaching role at Cambridge University and later the manager's job at Bath City, where he enjoyed modest success. In 1964 he crossed the Atlantic, accepting a generous offer from Toronto City. But the restless soccer dreamer quickly returned to the UK and in May 1964 joined Plymouth Argyle on the modest salary of £3,000 per annum. Allison made one of his best signings at Plymouth when he returned to Bath for full-back Tony Book, who later followed his boss to Manchester City. It is rumoured that Allison persuaded Book to alter his birth certificate, as the Argyle board would never had paid good money for a 30-year-old full-back with no League experience.

Allison's reputation as a visionary and successful coach in the game grew quickly and when Joe Mercer accepted the manager's job at Manchester City, he knew exactly where to go for an assistant. Mercer made Allison an offer he could not refuse. Mercer/Allison was a powerful combination. In 1967–68, under their inspirational leadership, City won the Division One Championship. The following season the Citizens won the FA Cup and triumphed in the League Cup and European Cup-Winners' Cup with great style and panache in 1970. The West Ham fans could only look on with envy as the team of Lee, Bell and Summerbee, ably supported by the old warhorse Tony Book, covered themselves in light blue glory.

Joe Mercer knew how to get the best out of Allison, but their relationship began to deteriorate when Mercer refused to stand down and let the younger man take over. Allison won the inevitable power struggle over his ailing manager and Mercer eventually left to join Coventry City, while one of the most innovative coaches in English football was given the job he coveted – manager of all-conquering Manchester City. But Allison needed Mercer more than he would admit. In the absence of the venerable Joe, City began to struggle and their fickle fans became uneasy and eventually hostile. Allison left the club in 1973 to join Crystal Palace where he enjoyed some FA Cup success and considerable media coverage – with his cigars, fedora and TV appearances he became the game's first celebrity manager. Allison loved the fame and attention, even gloried in it. But he wanted it for the wrong reasons and his life began to unravel as he failed to cope with the pressure of his celebrity lifestyle.

But Allison was lucky for most of his career and in one of those unexpected, even bizarre moments in football, the new City chairman, Peter Swales, persuaded Allison to return to Manchester to take over from his old friend Tony Book. But his return to the scene of his greatest triumphs ended in ignominy and failure and he left Moss Side again, this time in anger and frustration. Leaving City for the second time he became involved in an unsavoury spat with his successor at Maine Road, none other than his old West Ham mate, John Bond. Allison said at the time with typical humour, 'John Bond has blackened my name with his insinuations about the private lives of football managers. Both my wives are upset.'

Allison once said, 'you're not a real manager unless you've been sacked' – tell that to Alex Ferguson. Bond and Allison might have made a good team, had they not both been such strong characters.

In between his spells with City, the itinerant Allison managed abroad with Istanbul-based Galatasaray. After failing to delight the Turks, and returning for his unsuccessful second spell in Manchester, Allison continued on his travels. This time he washed up on the delightful shores of Portugal and a dream job managing Sporting Lisbon. The old magic had not altogether deserted him. His new club won the Portuguese League and Cup double in 1999–2000 and the irrepressible Allison earned himself legendary status in the capital city of that wonderful country.

Following his Lisbon adventure Allison drifted through the next 10 years in the lower echelons of professional football, a pale shadow of his former powerful self. He is now remembered as one of the great characters in football. In the age of George Best, Rodney Marsh and Bobby Moore he still managed to grab the headlines on both the front and back pages. Like Martin Peters as a player, Allison was 10 years ahead of his time as a coach. The ideas on the game he worked out on the Hammers' training ground at Chadwell Heath came to fruition in the glory days at Manchester City. As a personality he was headstrong, unpredictable and possessed a mischievous, wilful streak that got him into hot water on numerous occasions – not least on Bobby Moore's honeymoon. He loved, even courted controversy, but he was adored by the fans at Maine Road, Selhurst Park and Sporting Lisbon.

Malcolm Allison was a modest player at Upton Park, but in the late 1950s his influence on the club is unquestioned. Allison's part in the Upton Park transformation should never be underestimated, nor should his influence on the career of England's only World Cup-winning captain, Bobby Moore. Yes, he was a playboy and yes, much of his fame was image over substance. Those who remember his time at Upton Park fondly would have been sad to see his career descend into decline following his remarkable success with Manchester City.

In 2001 Allison's son – one of his six children – revealed his father was suffering with alcoholism and later we learned that this legendary manager was very ill with dementia. He died at a nursing home on 14 October 2010 at the age of 83. His funeral took place a few days later in Manchester where the cortege passed by the Eastlands Stadium on its way to the service. A large crowd gathered to pay their respects, draping sky blue scarves over the coffin. An ice bucket containing a bottle of champagne stood close by.

Simon Kuper's obituary includes the following acute observation of the life of one of the most iconic football figures of the 1970s:

> …*mostly he floundered without adult supervision. Wives and girlfriends came and went. He ended up alone with Alzheimer's in a bedsit in Middlesbrough. The Allison of Cassetari's café and Soccer of Thinkers had disappeared long before – his loss, and football's.*
> (The *Financial Times*, 23 October 2010)

The distinguished sports writer Brian Glanville offered the following summary of the great football thinker's personal life:

> *In 1979 he married Sally-Ann Highley from the Playboy Club, later describing it as 'the mistake of my life'. He proposed immediately after they had been in a car crash. From this union was born a daughter, Alexis. They split up officially in 1983. Next, for 17 years, came his long-term partner Lynn Salton, with whom he had a daughter, Gina, but by 2000 that relationship too was on the rocks, with Allison trying to smash down the door of her house.*

If Malcolm Allison lived a turbulent private life, he became a hugely significant figure in world football. West Ham United owe a huge debt to their former centre-half and captain for his drive and enthusiasm which helped to transform the club's fortunes in the 1960s. Malcolm Allison was a man of his time, a determined moderniser and a visionary claret and blue pioneer.

Noel Cantwell: elegant Irish full-back

At least two of the West Ham players featured in this book had the most successful periods of their careers at other clubs. George Hilsdon was one and the other is our next pioneer, the exotically named, Noel Eucharia Cornelius Cantwell. Irishman Cantwell, a defensive stalwart at the Boleyn in the 1950s, is generally accepted as one of the best full-backs of his generation, but his contribution to the advance of the club as a major force in English football goes far deeper than his elegant displays on the left-side of the Hammers' defence. He was the epitome of the modern footballer.

Noel Cantwell was born in Cork in 1932 and educated at the Roman Catholic Presentation Brothers College. As a youngster he was an outstanding all-round athlete, excelling at cricket, athletics, rugby and his first love, football. He joined local Irish League side Cork Athletic and although he may have dreamt about being a goalscoring centre-forward, he quickly developed into an accomplished full-back, without ever losing his attacking natural instincts.

Cantwell's father had plans for his son to enter the insurance business and a desk job at the Norwich Union was waiting. Neither father nor son would have given a career in professional football a moment's thought, despite Noel's passion for sport of any kind. By the time he entered his teens he had become a passionate Manchester United follower and modelled his game on the Reds' inspirational skipper, Johnny Carey. The youngster could never have imagined that one day in the future he would lead his favourite team out at Wembley in an FA Cup Final.

A visit to Ireland by two West Ham players changed Noel Cantwell's life forever. Frank O'Farrell and Tommy Moroney were both from Cork and often used to turn out for their old club on their occasional visits to Ireland. On one particular visit they both played in a friendly against Birmingham City and playing alongside the Hammers pair that fateful day was the young Cantwell. The tall and gangly full-back impressed O'Farrell and Moroney and when they returned to Upton Park they urged Ted Fenton to take a look at this promising young Irishman.

At the time Cantwell had his mind set on an amateur rugby career, but neither Noel nor his father could resist the persuasive Fenton and the youngster duly signed for West Ham, despite a little reluctance on the part of Noel's father. West Ham paid Cork £750 for Cantwell's signature, with the teenager pocketing a very tidy £150 – a small fortune

for the promising, but untried full-back. It was a very nervous and fearful young Irishman that arrived at Upton Park in 1952. He need not have worried as he set out on one of the most distinguished football careers of the 1950s and '60s.

Cantwell went straight into digs with Tommy Moroney who became his mentor and guardian. Having his fellow countryman as a guide and older brother was a great help to Cantwell and allowed him to settle quickly into his new life in East London. He was happy at the Boleyn and learned quickly from the likes of Sexton, Musgrove, Bond and O'Farrell, all deep thinkers about the game and passionate about their philosophy of attacking football. The young Irishman made good progress in his first season. He trained hard and grew in confidence as he settled into his new life – he loved the West Ham passing game and the way they encouraged their full-backs to go forward at every opportunity. He loved to attack down the left-hand side and the tall, handsome Irish boy with a twinkle in his eye quickly endeared himself to the Chicken Run.

Cantwell made just three League appearances in his first season, but in the following campaign became a regular in the side. He defended with rare maturity for a novice professional and his performances soon earned him the first of his 36 international caps for the Republic of Ireland. His exceptional maturity both as a player and an individual impressed Ted Fenton. The manager looked no further than Cantwell to replace Malcolm Allison as club captain. Fenton made the right decision. You could sense his enthusiasm and anticipation as Cantwell led his team out on to the Upton Park pitch as the new captain. In those days the teams ran out one at a time, not together as they do in the Premier League. Heaven help the away team who turned left out of the players' tunnel to warm up in front of the North Bank.

Cantwell's partnership with opposite full-back John Bond was one of the most successful pairings in the club's history, rivalled only by the later duo of Frank Lampard Snr and Billy Bonds. Cantwell and Bond were similar characters, both laid back and relaxed and natural full-backs, although both players did make a nuisance of themselves at centre-forward on a number of occasions in their long careers. Both were strong in the air and had excellent positional sense and although they were a natural combination, Cantwell was the better footballer. More relaxed on the ball, his surges down the left side of the defence were extremely effective. Much to his manager's dismay, he would often appear on the edge of the opponents' penalty area, looking for a crack at goal.

Cantwell took over the captaincy in the 1957–58 season when it became clear Allison was simply too ill to carry on. Cantwell was an intelligent skipper and in many respects West Ham was the ideal club for a progressive thinker about the game. He loved to bounce ideas off teammates like Malcolm Musgrove and Phil Woosnam. The Welsh international was educated to degree level and had a background in school teaching. Having players like

Woosnam in his team meant that Cantwell was more easily able to communicate his often complex ideas on the game to the players.

Woosnam, and later Bobby Moore, relished their new skipper's keen appetite for the modern game and blossomed in the exciting football environment he created. Cantwell's soon-to-be promoted side also included two forwards whose goals eventually secured the Hammers' promotion back to the top flight, John Dick and Vic Keeble. The partnership announced itself when the irrepressible Dick notched a hat-trick in Keeble's first game for the club – the 5–0 win over Sparta Rotterdam in front of nearly 20,000 fans at Upton Park. With Cantwell at the helm the Hammers were at last ready for promotion.

After an initial sticky patch when they lost three successive matches, under Cantwell's captaincy the Hammers went from strength to strength. They finally clinched the Second Division title in the away match against Middlesbrough at the end of April. Cantwell provided steady guidance to the side throughout and was a particular help to the young Ken Brown in the Middlesbrough game. That April afternoon, in front of a hostile crowd, the young Brown brilliantly snuffed out the danger of goal machine Brian Clough, who had already scored an incredible 40 goals that season. Cantwell encouraged the young defender through every tackle, while keeping an eye on Brown's positional play. Coolly led by their skipper, the Hammers' defence was unbeatable that day.

Ken Brown was not the only young player at Upton Park to benefit from their captain's guiding hand. Bobby Moore was not in the side on that historic occasion at Ayresome Park, but he later recalled Cantwell's influence on his fledgling career: 'When Malcolm was looking finished as a player I looked to Noel on the pitch. The first year West Ham were back in the First Division, before my debut against United, I went to Tottenham to watch them play. Noel Cantwell was left-back, Noel Dwyer in goal. It was the best display of defending and goalkeeping I'd ever seen.' (Powell, 1993)

After a promising start back in the top flight, the Hammers began to struggle and slipped down the League. They had acquired Phil Woosnam from Leyton Orient to provide some creativity in midfield and Dwyer to replace the ageing Ernie Gregory. The skilful John Smith was sold to Spurs in exchange for Dave Dunmore as Fenton tried to resuscitate his ailing team. Keeble and Dick managed just 26 goals between them in the second season after promotion, while the defence conceded a woeful 91 goals – the highest goals against tally of any team in the League. The problem was obvious to manager and captain.

The 1960–61 season was a defining one for the Hammers as they continued to struggle in Division One. Ted Fenton's long years of service to the club ended when he was replaced as manager by Ron Greenwood. There were some very good young players at the club, but some, like Harry Obeney, never quite fulfilled their early promise. In addition, some of the senior players were coming to the ends of their careers. Greenwood had inherited a team in transition.

At this time Matt Busby was attempting to reconstruct his Manchester United team following the tragic events of the 1958 Munich air disaster. Busby identified Cantwell as a key element in his planning for the future. Cantwell had been a Reds fans since he was a boy and with the Hammers struggling, he did not spend much time considering Busby's approach. He knew it was the opportunity of a lifetime – an offer he could not refuse. Cantwell duly signed for the Old Trafford club in November 1960 for a fee of £29,500 – a record for a full-back at the time.

Between 1953 and 1960, the Irishman spent eight distinguished years at Upton Park. The adventurous defender made 263 appearances for the Hammers and his attacking play was rewarded with a total of 11 goals. He featured in 33 Division One games in 1958–59, scoring an impressive six League and Cup goals. He was hugely popular with players and supporters alike and his influence on the development of the club was, like that of his great friend Malcolm Allison, undeniable.

Cantwell and Malcolm Allison made a great impression on the young fans at West Ham. As a boy I remember sitting in a darkened cinema at Forest Gate with some friends one evening when, to our utter amazement and shock, who should appear in the seats in front of us but the famous West Ham duo. We had never seen our heroes this close up and they looked huge in their expensive Crombie overcoats and sharp suits. We were too scared to ask for an autograph and just sat and stared in quiet devotion.

Cantwell left the comfort of East London for Manchester and a team that had been cruelly deprived of the talents of Duncan Edwards, David Pegg, Roger Byrne, Eddie Coleman and Tommy Taylor in Munich. Matt Busby made two other new signings at this time, the redoubtable Maurice Setters and centre-forward David Herd. Later Denis Law arrived from Torino and Pat Crerand from Celtic. Busby patiently rebuilt his team and by January all the pieces of the jigsaw were in place, including a place for the precocious teenager George Best. Busby's rebuilding quickly paid dividends when Manchester United won the FA Cup in 1963, their first trophy since Munich. The captain on that afternoon at Wembley was the ex-Hammers favourite, Noel Cantwell. The Irishman had come a long way since leaving Cork City as a raw young full-back.

When Cantwell arrived at Old Trafford he could not believe that such a great club employed such outdated training methods. It was no better than when he first arrived at Upton Park. Busby's training programme was dull and repetitive and according to Cantwell lacked tactical awareness, although he did respect the Scot's motivational powers. His West Ham days had left a deep impression on the Irishman and the last thing he wanted was to return to the old days of endless cross-country running and training sessions with a football nowhere to be seen. But Busby soon assembled a new team of coaches, including Jimmy Murphy. With new staff and the team he wanted, the rest, as they say, is history. Cantwell had six wonderful years at Old Trafford before he was replaced in the side by a fellow Irishman, Tony Dunne. Towards the end of his Manchester United career Cantwell was involved in an incident which affected him deeply and may have affected his future performances at the club.

In 1963 Manchester United drew Tottenham in the second round of the European Cup-Winners' Cup, with the London side winning the first leg 2–0 in front of a 57,000 crowd at White Hart Lane. After just eight minutes of the second match, Cantwell and the legendary Dave Mackay threw themselves into a 50/50 tackle which was to change the whole course of the tie. Cantwell picked himself up from the tackle, but was horrified to turn and see Mackay writhing in pain and clearly in great distress. The hard-tackling Scot had broken his left leg in two places in the most horrific of football injuries. It is difficult to tell to what extent Cantwell was affected by Mackay's injury, but he lost his form later in the season and as a result, his place in the side.

Cantwell was intelligent and forward-thinking and unlike many, was never going to be content with a place in Manchester United's reserve team. The former Hammer was so highly regarded in the game that in 1963 his fellow professionals elected Cantwell as chairman of the PFA. With his playing days behind him, a long and successful career in management appeared assured for the articulate and confident Irishman. There was talk about him staying at Old Trafford in a coaching capacity but nothing materialised, much to Cantwell's disappointment.

Then in 1967, a telephone call from the chairman of Coventry City fixed Cantwell's fate for the next few years. The extremely popular Jimmy Hill had taken the Sky Blues from the depths of the Third Division to the top flight of English football in a few short seasons. At the height of Hill's popularity nearly 60,000 people crammed into Highfield Road to see the Sky Blues play their deadly rivals, Wolves. Clearly, Hill would be a tough act to follow.

In the wake of Hill's departure, Cantwell did well to keep the Midlanders in the First Division, even if it was by the skin of their teeth. However, his young side improved sufficiently to achieve the club's highest ever top-flight finish of sixth place in 1969–70. The reward for this outstanding season was a place in the old Inter-Cities Fairs Cup. The Irishman had taken the Sky Blues back into the big time and had proved his credentials as a top manager. But following the legendary Jimmy Hill was probably beyond any manager and, despite Cantwell's relative success, a typical display of ego by the Coventry chairman led to him being controversially sacked in March 1972.

Cantwell had absorbed a great deal of football knowledge in his time at West Ham, Manchester United and Coventry City and needed a club with a sympathetic chairman where he could put all his experience to good effect. In 1972 he accepted an offer to manage lowly Peterborough United, who were about as far away from the glamour of George Best and Old Trafford as it was possible to get.

Peterborough won only one of their first 13 League matches in the 1972–73 season. Manager Jim Iley resigned and long-serving Jim Walker was appointed as his successor, but the results failed to improve and on 11 October 1972, Cantwell was announced as the new Posh boss. The ebullient Irishman immediately lifted the spirits of players and supporters. In his first game in charge, Cantwell's new club beat Doncaster Rovers 3–1 at home to record only their second win of the season. Cantwell recruited respected coach Dave Barnwell to assist him at London Road and the results continued to improve. Posh won 13 of their remaining League games, enabling them to escape relegation with ease.

In the following season Peterborough won the Fourth Division Championship and Cantwell was christened 'the Messiah' by the long-suffering Posh faithful. His revitalised team also enjoyed success in the FA Cup. The highlight of Cantwell's time at Peterborough was a fourth-round FA Cup tie against Tommy Docherty's Manchester United. The Stretford End had not forgotten their former defender and gave Cantwell a wonderful reception on his return to Old Trafford. He later reflected,

> ...they shut up Peterborough that day because it seemed everyone travelled up to Manchester and we received fantastic support. We didn't even mind when we went two down in the first 10 minutes. John Cousins did pull a goal back and we looked like getting an equaliser until Gordon Hill scored with a fantastic volley to clinch the game.

Despite his success with Posh, Cantwell could not resist the challenge of the emerging North American Soccer League. He stayed in the States for a few years, before returning to Peterborough for a second spell as manager and later general manager. At the end of his second period at London Road Cantwell was ready to retire from the professional game. In 1989 he left Posh to become licensee at the New Inn in Peterborough where his cheerful personality ensured a crowded bar. It seemed wherever he went people loved the extrovert Irishman.

Busy pulling pints one evening Cantwell was pleasantly surprised to receive a call from the England manager, Sven-Göran Eriksson. The Swede was keen to use some of Cantwell's great experience and wanted the Irishman to do some scouting for the national side. Cantwell was understandably flattered by the offer which he found impossible to resist. But shortly after receiving Eriksson's invitation his health began to deteriorate.

Noel Cantwell died on 8 September 2005, aged 73, following a courageous battle against cancer. One of the largest crowds ever assembled at Peterborough Cathedral came to pay their respects to the popular full-back and support his wife Maggie and their two daughters. Cantwell's popularity at Peterborough was confirmed in 2005 when he was inducted into the Posh Hall of Fame in recognition of his achievements at London Road. One Peterborough supporter remembered Cantwell's time at the club thus:

> *I had the pleasure of his company on several occasions and you always sensed when Noel came into a room as he had a certain aura about him. Suddenly, it would go quiet and the crowd would welcome him to spontaneous applause. I shall always remember his beaming smile with that Irish glint in his eye, in this truly remarkable man.*

His daughter Kate attended the Hall of Fame ceremony and talked about her father in an interview with Peter Lane of the Posh on-line fanzine. 'He liked his golf and horse racing, he would take me to the races. He loved having days out with his mates, he was a man's man and enjoyed their company. He loved also being with his family.'

Cantwell adored his grandchildren, Sam and Joe, and loved nothing more than kicking a ball around with them in the local park. Unlike his restless friend Malcolm Allison, Cantwell was happy in the relative backwater of rural England in the midst of his family. But football brought him fame and public affection. Reflecting on his brilliant career Cantwell revealed:

> *I don't think looking back upon my career I could have achieved much more than captaining West Ham, and being a friend of Bobby Moore who was a dear, dear friend of mine. Also at Old Trafford, captaining them, and then of course the great fun of playing for Ireland at that time. We could never ever win very much. It was so different than today.*
> *(www.bigsoccer.com)*

Under Johnny Carey, Cantwell was capped 36 times for the Republic of Ireland between 1953 and 1967, scoring 14 goals for his country. He achieved an enormous amount in the game both on and off the field. As chairman of the PFA he established the Provident Fund, the Benevolent Fund and PFA Education programme. While enjoying the respect of everyone in football, life for the Irishman was not without its tragic moments. His son Robert was killed in a road accident and his death had a profound effect on the rest of Cantwell's life.

An accomplished all-round sportsman, Cantwell played cricket five times for Ireland and in doing so became one of the very few Irish double sport internationals. A representative from Essex CCC, probably Doug Insole, watched the talented batsman make 47 runs against New Zealand and immediately invited Cantwell to join the county club. The left-hand batsman and right-arm medium pacer turned down the offer, saying that he did not want to spend his whole year in England. His great friend Bobby Moore was to receive a similar offer from Essex a few years later. Cantwell's last game of serious cricket was for Ireland against Lancashire CCC in July 1959.

Talented all-round sportsman, successful manager, accomplished administrator and convivial publican, Cantwell will be remembered by older West Ham supporters for leading their beloved Hammers back to the top flight of English football for the first time in over 30 years. They will remember an elegant, attacking full-back who gave hours of his time to developing the club's youngsters and for playing the game in the true spirit of West Ham United. Despite achieving wider fame at other clubs, few ex-players deserve the status of Hammers pioneer more than Noel Euchuria Cornelius Cantwell.

Ernie Gregory: loyal custodian

Most goalkeepers are like drummers in a rock band – part of the team, but not really proper footballers. Others like Gordon Banks and Peter Shilton are part of the team in every sense and played a crucial role in their team's success. There have been a few of the non-footballer type of 'keeper at Upton Park over the years, but Ernie Gregory was, like Banks and Shilton, a genuine footballer who was an essential part of the team. At West Ham Gregory ranks in the top three goalkeepers in the club's history alongside legendary stoppers, Ted Hufton and Phil Parkes.

It is difficult to get more claret and blue than Ernie Gregory. He was associated with the Hammers as a player, coach and administrator from 1938 until his eventual retirement in 1987. Gregory was born in Stratford, like many of the Hammers' pioneers, on 10 November 1921. As a youngster he represented West Ham Boys and was spotted by trainer Charlie Paynter playing at Upton Park in an English Schools Trophy Final against Preston North End. In 1936, at the age of 15, he joined the ground staff and began a long and magnificent career at the Boleyn.

In the pre-war years, ground-staff boys were encouraged to continue playing for their local amateur clubs for the experience. In the 1930s Gregory played for local club Leytonstone in the Isthmian League until the outbreak of war in 1939. The standard of London senior amateur football was extremely high at this time and some of Gregory's teammates at the 'Stones ground in Granville Road would have been good enough to play for most professional clubs. A young would-be professional could not have had a better grounding in his trade.

Leytonstone FC was a stalwart of the Isthmian League for nearly 100 years. Formed in 1886, the club's record is one of the most impressive in the long history of English amateur football. Always close rivals of their neighbours Walthamstow Avenue, Leytonstone won the prestigious FA Amateur Cup in 1947, 1948 and 1968. Between 1933 and 1952, in addition to winning the Amateur Cup twice, the club were Isthmian League champions a remarkable seven times. The club's ground on the high street was adjacent to the Midland railway station and on Saturday afternoons you could watch the match from the station for the price of a platform ticket. The ground had one covered, corrugated-iron stand and three terraces that were open to the elements. As schoolboys we paid the princely sum of 2d admission and a further 2d for a bag of Percy Dalton peanuts. The pre-match

entertainment for the 5,000 or so loyal supporters was provided by the Leyton Silver Band and at half-time you were encouraged to throw your loose change into a blanket carried round the pitch by willing club officials.

The Leytonstone pitch was always in excellent condition and lovingly cared for by groundsman Alf Walters, who owned the flower shop in the High Street next door to the police station. The club was a breeding ground for Leyton Orient and produced many of the O's local players, including Frank Neary and Bunny Groves of the footballing Groves family. One of the great characters in the history of the club was Leon Joseph who had a menswear shop under the arches near the railway station. With his good looks and fine singing voice, Joseph was a local heart-throb who regularly sang at the club's Saturday night socials. Much to the delight of the fans, the film star Jayne Mansfield made an appearance at the ground in 1962. It is said that she had an 'association' with one of the players and that player could only be Leon Joseph.

My cousin Kenny married into a Leytonstone FC family. His father-in-law was Ernest Morgan, club treasurer from the immediate post-war period up to the late 1950s. He was heavily involved in all the club's activities which included children's parties, beanos and holidays. The club organised regular Bank Holiday outings to Dimchurch, Bognor Regis and Walton-on-the-Naze and one Christmas put on a trip to Margate and an overnight stay at the delightfully-named Kittiwake Hotel.

One thing that older Leytonstone supporters will remember is that the club had a real live goat as their mascot. It lived in the back garden of the Morgans' house not far from the ground and before every home match the family would walk the proud quadruped along Leytonstone High Road to the ground, where it would be paraded on the pitch. The goat would be escorted back home after the game, much to the delight of local children out shopping with their parents. Later the Morgans moved a couple of miles up the road to Forest Gate, closer to the East End, but continued the Saturday match-day ritual with, perhaps, the most curious club mascot in senior amateur football. Sadly, Leytonstone FC closed their doors in 1979 and their ground, full of rich football memories, was sold off for development. Leytonstone collapsed because they could not cope with the financial demands imposed in the 1970s by the introduction of player contracts, which signalled the end of senior amateur football in London.

The three years Ernie Gregory spent at Leytonstone was an ideal preparation for a young goalkeeper. Winning the Isthmian League title in 1938 and 1939 gave the young Gregory the experience he needed in a tough competitive environment. His improvement in the hothouse of senior amateur football was noted by Charlie Paynter who, just before the war, gave his young 'keeper several games in the Hammers' midweek side.

During World War Two Gregory served with the Essex Regiment and the Royal Air Force. The Hammers 'keeper was a member of the Territorial Army and as a result was called-up immediately war was declared. Like some of his fellow West Ham players, army duty prevented Gregory from playing in the first wartime Cup Final in 1940. Only inside-forward Archie Macaulay of serving soldiers at the club made it to Wembley for the match against Blackburn. But Gregory continued to play for the Hammers when on leave, despite being on active service for long periods. He managed to find time to appear in over 60 games for the Hammers during the war.

Gregory eventually made his League debut in the match against Plymouth Argyle at Upton Park on 28 December 1946. The Hammers won 4–1 in front of a crowd of 17,000. He played a further eight games that season in a team which included Macaulay, Charlie Bicknell, Norman Corbett, Ted Fenton, Sam Small and Dick Walker. Gregory was a local boy and showed great patience with West Ham and considerable loyalty. He had joined the club as far back as 1936 and waited 10 years for his first-team debut. His patience finally paid off when, in the 1947–48 season, Gregory played in all 42 League games. He was also an ever present in 1948–49 and 1952–53 and in the promotion season of 1957–58. After a 10-year wait, Gregory's time in the West Ham goal had finally arrived.

Gregory was a solid and dependable 'keeper in the manner of Jim Standen, rather than spectacular like Phil Parkes or Mervyn Day. Charles Korr (1988) argued that, 'He gave the impression of solid imperturbability, although anyone standing close enough to the West Ham goal might have heard some rather colourful language.'

One of Gregory's greatest games for the Hammers was the FA Cup third-round tie against high flying Blackpool in January 1952. The game features high in the West Ham greatest games list and was one of the first in which new manager Ted Fenton showed his true worth to the club. The legendary Stanley Matthews ensured a good crowd and an impressive 38,500 – a new post-war record – crammed into the Boleyn to see the tie of the round. Fenton came up with his 'F-Plan', which involved winger Ken Tucker exploiting the Seasiders' ponderous but highly skilful midfield. Fenton's brainwave paid almost immediate dividends when, in the 12th minute, Tucker cut inside the Blackpool defence and his excellent cross fell to Jimmy Andrews whose volley flew into the net.

Roared on by the North Bank in the second half, the Irons scored a second when Frank O'Farrell drove a shot through a crowd of players and into the Blackpool net. The 1950–51 Footballer of the Year, Harry Johnston, pulled one back for the away side late in the game, but the Irons held on to secure a memorable victory. The hero of the evening was Ernie Gregory. The Hammers' 'keeper needed to be at the top of his game to hold back the famous Blackpool forward line. Andrews and O'Farrell were the goalscoring heroes that day, but as Martin Godleman (2008) explains, 'Another of their heroes was the man they called the best uncapped goalkeeper in the country, which he was. That description belonged to Ernie Gregory who…pulled save after save out of the bag to keep West Ham in the tie.'

Gregory performed Blackpool-type heroics season after season in his 14 years at the Boleyn. Unfortunately, his performances earned him just one international cap, when he was selected to play for England B against France in 1952. The opponents in the match were the France Espoirs, the French Under-23 side, who thumped England 7–1. At least Gregory would have had the honour of playing against the incomparable Raymond Kopa, arguably the greatest player ever to play for France. The young Frenchman was unstoppable and taught the England players a few lessons that day. Kopa later developed a devastating partnership with fellow forward Just Fontaine, as France emerged as the best team in Europe in the 1950s. If Gregory's single England appearance was undistinguished, he also had strong rivals for the England green jersey in Wolves' Bert Williams and Gil Merrick of Birmingham City.

Gregory made 406 appearances for the Hammers in his 24 playing years at the Boleyn. He was a committed and loyal Hammer who rejected a move to fashionable Arsenal – a move which would surely have enhanced his England international prospects. Gregory's last season for the Hammers was in 1959–60 when he played just one game, against Leeds United, his last for the club. The previous season he made 32 appearances in the Division One side, including a handful alongside a youthful Bobby Moore.

The club rewarded Gregory's loyalty with a testimonial against LD Alajuelense of Costa Rica. But the long-serving Gregory was not finished with West Ham just yet. He remained at the club in a coaching capacity until he finally retired from the game in 1987. The Football League also recognised Gregory's outstanding contribution to the game; the Hammers' distinguished 'keeper was one of eleven players to receive a special statuette for serving 20 years or more with one club. Among the eleven were such soccer notables as Tom Finney, Billy Wright, Jimmy Mullen, Nat Lofthouse and Billy Liddell. He was in very distinguished company indeed.

Following his official retirement, Gregory continued to attend first-team matches and helped out occasionally with a little coaching. But the club had moved on with a new manager and were about to enter the most successful period in their history. His long career in the game was now at an end, but he desperately wanted to continue to serve the club he loved so much.

After suffering a serious stroke at the end of 2011 Ernie Gregory died in hospital on 21 January 2012. He had previously been in a nursing home for a year or so.

Former colleagues of the 1960s, Billy Bonds, Ronnie Boyce, Geoff Pike and Brian Dear all visited Gregory in hospital in the last few weeks of his life, a clear indication of the affection in which he was held by the young players around him. The *Knees Up Mother Brown (KUMB)* website gave its readers an opportunity to pay their respects to the old West Ham 'keeper. Paul Walker spoke for most of the respondents.

Ernie, you are a true Hammers legend. My late dad, who sadly passed away in January, first took me to see you and the Irons in '59, soon after our promotion back to the top flight. We all owe you so much. You are a big part of our history and underline what is really great about our club. A loyal, one-club man who contributed so much on and off the field. Don't ever think you are not remembered.

Another tribute refers to a highly amusing story about an incident between Gregory and full-back John Bond. In a match against Leeds United at Upton Park, Gregory gathered a loose ball in front of the South Bank and threw a pass out to Bond in the right-back position. The 'keeper, with the ball out of harm's way, then turned and walked back to his goal. Everyone in the ground, Gregory included, expected Bond to knock the ball upfield, but instead he hit a perfect chip back over the oblivious Gregory, who watched helplessly as the ball dropped over him into the net – the perfect own-goal. Gregory and Noel Cantwell, standing close by, delivered some well chosen words in the direction of the hapless Bond, who must have wanted the Boleyn to swallow him up. The story had a happy ending because the Hammers won the match. But the incident was one of the most comical seen at Upton Park – which is really saying something.

Michael Morton, an ex-pupil at Plaistow Grammar School, remembers watching the Hammers in 1948–49 and offers an interesting insight into the lives of professional footballers in the period just after the war. One day in the summer school holidays he heard a group of men working in the garden of the house next door:

They were digging out a World War Two air raid shelter, dug deep below the surface. I suddenly began to recognise some of the men as regular first-team players from West Ham. The group included Dick Walker, Ernie Gregory…and Ernie Devlin…they were all very friendly and enjoyed chatting with this very young supporter.

This was an era when players' wages were very low and almost non-existent during the summer months so they had to take on labouring work to keep the wolf from the door. How times have changed!

Ernie Gregory was a loyal Hammers servant for over 50 years. The old 'keeper was loved by players and fans alike as goalkeeper, trainer and administrator. We tend to throw the word legend about these days, but Gregory, almost above all others, deserves the accolade. He would certainly be in goal for the best West Ham XI of all time and occupies the highest rung on the club's ladder of esteem.

John Dick: a proper forward

West Ham United manager Fenton discovered John 'Jack' Dick during their army years together. Dick was one of a long line of good Scottish players recruited by the club throughout its history. The tradition goes back to former skipper Robert Stevenson who made his debut for the Hammers in 1898. Scottish players were tough characters who could be picked up relatively cheaply and were good value for money for a club like West Ham.

John Dick was born on 19 March 1930 in Glasgow's tough Govan district, the same neighbourhood as Alex Ferguson and the loveable TV rogue, Rab C. Nesbit. Dick's character was forged in the combination of a tough childhood on a poverty-stricken Glasgow estate and two character-building years of national service. On leaving school he became an apprentice machine tool operator, but football was always his first love. He was spotted by a scout playing for his local side and was picked for the Scottish Junior team and his long career was on its way.

In 1950, Dick was enlisted into REME (the Royal Electrical and Mechanical Engineers) for his stint with the forces and was stationed in Colchester in Essex. He was soon playing football for the army representative side and his local club, Braintree FC. Dick was signed by West Ham in 1953 at the end of his national service after West Ham scouts had watched his impressive performances for the Essex works side, Crittall Athletic. His career crossed the generations at Upton Park and in his last season at the club he played with many of the next cohort of Hammers stars, including Bobby Moore, Martin Peters, Geoff Hurst, Johnny Byrne, John Bond and Kenny Brown. We should say at the beginning that John Dick is in the first rank of West Ham players of all

time. He is the joint-third leading goalscorer in the club's history, making 351 appearances in which he scored a remarkable 166 times.

The Scotsman was made club captain by Ted Fenton in 1960 and was runner-up to Bobby Moore for Hammer of the Year in 1961–62. Dick became the first West Ham player to be picked for Scotland when he played against England in April 1959, replacing the injured Denis Law. On that day, England captain Billy Wright gained his 100th cap in England's 1–0 victory. But as we shall see, it was not a particularly happy occasion for the West Ham number-10.

Always a popular local figure, Dick married his young wife Sue Culley in Barking Abbey Church in 1956 and they set up home in a club house out on the East London/Essex border at Hainault, close to the Hammers' training ground at Grange Farm. They later bought the neat semi-detached house under new right-to-buy legislation. Sue has lived in the quiet terrace for over 50 years and her pretty house is adorned with photographs of her late husband and their family. She tells an interesting story of a young and shy Bobby Moore spending his weekday afternoons at the Hainault house, enjoying a cup of tea and amusing the girls and their friends. She is clearly proud of her husband's career in professional football and has a wonderful collection of old contracts, letters and other documents relating to Dick's 50 years in football.

East Ham-born Sue, who grew up with five brothers and three sisters, met her future husband at the old Harmony Hall, Stratford, later revamped as the more fashionable Lacy's nightclub. The tall young Scot must have been an imposing figure, but his wife-to-be was more taken with John's sense of humour. Sue joked recently that she came fourth in John's life behind football, the children and grandchildren in the family pecking order. But as she said, 'we were always great friends'. Their marriage lasted 44 years until John's sudden death in 2000.

John went on some of West Ham's more ambitious tours to South Africa and Europe and brought back mementoes of his travels for his family. These tours were not always as glamorous as they sounded, with the team staying in the most basic accommodation. But, as Sue has said, it made for an interesting life for the couple who had a wide circle of friends in the game and a full social life. At the centre of their crowd were the Cantwells and Allisons – not for nothing were John, Noel and Malcolm referred to as the 'Three Musketeers'.

John adored his two daughters and was proud to see them establish their own careers. Jennifer became a secretary and lives close to her mother, while Gillian, who lives in Elstree, retrained as a primary school teacher after a spell as a shoe designer. The family are very aware of John's many achievements in football and I am sure Gillian would have been inspired to become a teacher by her dad's example. John doted on his two grandchildren and even forgave them for becoming Arsenal supporters.

Bobby Moore's first wife Tina remarked in her autobiography that football in the early 1960s 'was a much smaller game'. I think she meant there was a lot less media attention and players and their families were much closer to the fans than the celebrity footballers of today. Footballers' wives were certainly treated rather differently back in the day – more tea and cakes than chardonnay and prawn sandwiches. Sue Dick remembers the players' wives had a hospitality suite at Upton Park, which was no more than a wooden hut in the corner of the club car park. Tina recalls going down to the Black Lion in Plaistow on Saturday nights with Bobby, accompanied by the Lampards and Allisons, enjoying the company of the local supporters and free of media harassment. The close link between professional footballers and local people is why so many locals became West Ham fans – sadly, that local link disappeared with Moore's generation.

The West Ham side of the late 1950s was one of the best for many years. Alongside John Dick was the prolific centre-forward Vic Keeble, and what a goalscoring partnership they made. Their goals ensured Hammers' promotion in the historic season of 1957–58. With them in that side were Malcolm Allison, Noel Cantwell, John Bond, Malcolm Musgrove, Ken Brown and Bill Lansdowne. Dick usually wore the number-10 shirt, but was not a traditional inside-forward. He played as a striker in the manner of Geoff Hurst, his successor in the side in that position. Fenton's innovation of playing twin strikers in Dick and Keeble was ahead of its time and there is no question that Hurst in particular built his game around Dick's attacking style.

There were games in the late '50s when Dick was at his unplayable best. It is difficult to do full justice to his immense contribution to the Hammers' improvement in the mid-to-late '50s and their emergence as a real force in the early '60s. But several games, where his goals made the difference, stand out.

In January 1954, the Hammers made the short trip across London to Craven Cottage, their long-suffering fans expecting the usual away defeat. But on this occasion their loyalty was rewarded with a stunning victory against promotion-chasing Fulham. The game was a real roller-coaster with West Ham 3–0 down with just a few minutes to go to half-time. But somehow the Irons found some fighting spirit – not a quality usually evident in such circumstances. In the last five minutes of the first half the game was turned upside down as first Dave Sexton, then Tommy Dixon scored, reducing the arrears to a single goal.

The second half began in equally frantic fashion and within a minute West Ham were level as John Dick crashed home the equaliser. Ten minutes later a typical piece of Hooper magic set up Dick who, without breaking stride, thundered a drive past Black in the Fulham goal. The Hammers had turned a 3–0 deficit into a 4–3 lead and there was still half an hour to go. But for once the East Londoners held on, despite the best efforts of Johnny Haynes and Jimmy Hill to deny them victory. Martin Godleman (2008) describes West Ham's rare failure to roll over in an away match: 'Part of this failure could be put down to the arrival of John Dick for his first season at Upton Park. The free-scoring Scot had hit a hat-trick against Bury in November and four other goals going into January…'

Slowly, the fighting spirit of John Dick roused his teammates as the Hammers began to believe they were good enough to challenge for promotion. A couple of seasons after the surprise away win at Fulham, the side drew Division One Tottenham in the quarter-final of the FA Cup. The game is fixed in the collective memory of West Ham United as one of the greatest games in the club's long history. Billy Nicholson, the Tottenham manager, was beginning to assemble the best ever Spurs side and over 69,000 packed into White Hart Lane to witness the encounter. Drawing on their new-found confidence, the Hammers were in no mood to surrender to their illustrious opponents and attacked from the kick-off. Their positive play was quickly rewarded when Dick put his side ahead with a clinical finish from a perfect pass by Albert Foan. The away fans experienced a collective nosebleed when Dick scored a second, this time heading in Tucker's accurate left-wing cross.

Stunned by going 2–0 down at home to a Division Two side, Spurs began to fight back. As the tricky George Robb began to run at John Bond, Spurs started to dominate and reduced the deficit when Tommy Harmer converted a penalty. But the home supporters' euphoria was short-lived. They received a real hammer blow when Dick sped on to a superb through-ball from Hooper to slot in the Hammers' third. Tottenham were not out of the Cup yet and within minutes Robb headed in from a corner. The teams went in for the break with the Hammers leading 3–2 courtesy of a famous hat-trick from their outstanding number-10.

Dick completing yet another hat-trick v WBA, March 1959.

Dick scoring again. This time in front of the South Bank at Upton Park.

Five goals were scored in 15 first-half minutes, but the pace of the game settled after the break as West Ham sought to preserve their slender lead. But Spurs' pressure finally told on the tiring away side when Len Duquemin exposed a gap in the Hammers defence to head in yet another Robb cross. The game finished 3–3 and Spurs went on to win the replay 2–1 at Upton Park. But the Hammers had achieved a kind of victory in the first game at White Hart Lane. The first match was a real confidence-booster and a further step on the road back to the top flight of English football. The game was a personal triumph for the Hammers' free-scoring Dick and one of the most memorable in his distinguished career.

Another stand-out game for Johnny Dick was the Championship-clinching 3–1 victory at Middlesbrough at the end of 1957–58. The Dick/Keeble partnership was in full swing and inevitably, both forwards scored in the match, with a third added by Malcolm Musgrove. The Hammers won the Division Two title by a single point from Blackburn Rovers that day, largely thanks to the 46 goals Dick and Vic Keeble scored between them, finishing the season with 23 each. The club celebrated with a dinner and dance at the Café Royal with entertainment provided by the popular chanteuse of the day, Anna Neagle.

Of course, John Dick scored West Ham's first goal back in Division One and ended the 1958–59 season as top scorer. He led the side by example and adjusted to the new level without breaking stride. Two games from that first season back in the top flight are worth a mention and both were against Manchester United.

The first was the early season home match against the Reds which was notable for two things; the debut in defence of the 17-year-old Bobby Moore and a terrific 3–2 win against a strong Manchester side. Dick scored as early as the eighth minute and further goals by John Smith and Malcolm Musgrove secured the victory. Players and fans grew in confidence that day as they realised their team was good enough to win against the best teams in the country.

In December 1961, in a reversal of the normal order of things, the Hammers were fourth in the table, while Manchester United were down in 20th place. In two seasons, new manager Ron Greenwood's West Ham had proved they could compete with the very best teams. Dick, now reaching veteran status, continued to score goals, despite the absence of his former partner Vic Keeble. United came to Upton Park that December low in confidence following their poor start to the season. The club was still recovering from the effects of Munich as Matt Busby tried to rebuild his young team. But Manchester United should never be underestimated and they had match-winning players of the quality of David Herd and Bobby Charlton, who could and did win games with a single piece of individual brilliance.

On a gloomy and cold Saturday afternoon at Upton Park, the Reds took a surprise early lead when Herd took advantage of some sloppy defending to slide the ball past Lawrie Leslie. Slowly, Woosnam and Musgrove began to take control of midfield, but the Hammers failed to equalise and went in for the break a goal down. The second half brought a dramatic improvement as the Hammers poured forward in search of an equaliser, as Martin Godleman writes: 'The equaliser didn't come until a quarter of an hour from time, but it was from the trusty left foot of Scottish striker John Dick, hitting his 15th goal of the season.'

Man of the Match Dick scored a second in the 85th minute, ensuring his side took both points. His second was his 15th of the season and he finished the campaign with an impressive 23 goals, but it was to be his last full season at Upton Park as the new manager sought to impose his own ideas. The future for Greenwood lay in the hands of Bobby Moore, Johnny Byrne and his new number-10, Geoff Hurst. John Dick was unceremoniously sold to Brentford in September for a sizeable fee in those days of £17,500. He had scored 166 goals for West Ham in 351 League and Cup games, but his career was far from over as with typical enthusiasm, he threw himself into the challenge of playing in the lower divisions.

Back in the 1950s professional footballers were paid a regular wage supplemented by win and appearances bonuses. John Dick's contracts from his Division Two days at Upton Park show he was paid £15 a week in the season and £12 in the summer. Weekly wages would have been boosted in 1957–58 by bonuses of between £5 and £10 for every game the Hammers won. Dick's contract was improved in 1961–62 to £30 a week, with £5 for first-team appearances, plus win bonuses. Of course, there was no free car or house and no expensive hotels on away trips. But with their rented club house in Hainault and Sue working, the couple were comfortable in comparison with other local working-class families at that time, many of whom worked at Ford's Dagenham plant.

Surprisingly, things improved financially for John and Sue when Dick was transferred to Brentford. In 1964–65 his contract with the Bees shows he was paid £20 a week with £10 appearance money, £12 for appearances in the Football League, plus a car – a real indication of how his new employers looked after their players in comparison with West Ham. Dick proved to be an excellent signing for Brentford, making 72 appearances in which he scored a highly impressive 45 goals. He committed himself fully to the Bees when he might have chosen to ease himself into retirement at his new club. He loved and respected the game too much and never gave less than his very best, which was good enough to help Brentford gain promotion in 1963. The Griffin Park club certainly upstaged the Hammers with their celebrations, hiring the glamorous Sophie Tucker to get their promotion party started. John and Sue would have enjoyed themselves that evening – the irrepressible Scot had won League titles with both West Ham and Brentford in the space of a few years and no player deserved the rewards of promotion more than the great Govan goalscorer.

For such a prolific striker with a proven record in the top flight of English football, Dick, like many of the Hammers' early pioneers, seriously underachieved at international level. It remains a mystery why one of the most lethal finishers in football made just one appearance for his country. His only Scottish cap was awarded in the match against England at Wembley in April 1959. The match, part of the old Home Championship, was played in front of a huge crowd of 98,329. England won the game 1–0 courtesy of a Bobby Charlton goal late in the second half. Scotland manager Andy Beattie selected Dick after Denis Law pulled out of the match with a recurrence of an old knee injury. By his own admission, the Hammers striker failed to grab this rare opportunity to impress the Scottish selectors. He later recalled, 'The game at Wembley was my only appearance for Scotland and the way I played I didn't deserve another one. I was awful. I'd never been so nervous before a game and it was one of my worst performances of my career.' (The *Guardian*, 13 November 1999)

It is easy to see why a Second Division player, even one with Dick's record, would be intimidated by the occasion. A look at the Scotland line up that day helps to explains why he simply froze on the day.

Bill Brown, Duncan McKay, Eric Caldow, Tommy Docherty, Bobby Evans, Dave Mackay, Graham Leggat, Bobby Collins, David Herd and Willie Ormond is a team of Scottish legends, only weakened by the absence that day of the incomparable Denis Law. Dick admitted he was in awe of the likes of Dave Mackay and Tommy Docherty and later

The Hammers' great No.10 being introduced to Harold MacMillan with Tommy Docherty to his right.

revealed how he felt at the end of the match. 'I should have done better...and it hurt. It meant so much to me to play for Scotland. I've still got the cap somewhere but I've put the whole experience far behind me. It's not a good memory.'

John Dick may not have had the glorious international career his prodigious talent deserved, but he had every reason to look back on his playing days with real satisfaction. The single Scottish cap can be dismissed as a mere aberration and his lack of success at international level failed to dampen his enthusiasm for the game he loved. Dick had gained his FA coaching badges during his playing days and following his retirement from

John Dick on target for his country against England at Wembley. The match was a huge disappointment to the Upton Park favourite.

professional football at the end of the 1964–65 season, he embarked on a second career as a coach for Hackney Council and later the Inner London Education Authority (ILEA).

The East Marsh Centre was set up by Hackney Council in the 1960s to provide sporting opportunities for young people in the area. In addition to football, the team of coaches offered tennis, archery, rugby and other sports. When Hackney's education and leisure was absorbed into ILEA, East Marsh became even more popular, largely due to the appointment of a new head of PE, none other than the hugely popular John Dick. Along with a team of coaches that included his old teammate John Cartwright and Hackney teachers like Malcolm Williams, Dick developed East Marsh into one of the busiest and best sporting facilities for young people in London.

In addition to his considerable coaching duties in Hackney, Dick ran Santos FC, a Sunday youth team, whose ground was just a few minutes from his home in Hainault. When a neighbour asked John if he could spend an hour or two with a group of mustard-keen nine-year-olds, he simply could not refuse. He stayed with the same group of kids for 10 years and turned them into one of the best youth teams in Essex. In the early '70s Dick also spent a successful year coaching a West Ham youth team back at Upton Park, assisted by full-back Frank Lampard.

Following a distinguished playing career, Dick had 25 wonderful years coaching and organising sports programmes for young people. He became something of a legend to youngsters in Hackney and Hainault and enjoyed this part of his life just as much as he enjoyed playing. Dick retired from his coaching job in 1992 and few people in the game deserved their retirement more than the genial Scot.

Sue Dick recalls that her husband's weight remained the same throughout his working life, but when he retired he became dogged by ill health and much to his frustration, began to pile on the pounds. John, now nearing 70, had experienced some heart problems and in early 2000 doctors decided he needed a quadruple by-pass operation. He was never really the same again. John 'Jackie' Dick died suddenly later that year at the age of 70 following a massive stroke. The operation seemed to have drained him of the strength and determination which gave him and his family such a good life.

The funeral at the City of London cemetery in Manor Park, where his old teammate Bobby Moore was buried a few years previously, was attended by many of his old friends in the game, including Geoff Hurst, Patsy Holland and Frank Lampard. His family would have been pleased that Rio Ferdinand attended, representing all the youngsters John had coached at West Ham. In one of the day's most poignant moments, the whole squad of Santos FC arrived to pay their respects to their much-loved coach.

Shortly before John's death, Sue received a letter from Wally St Pier, the legendary chief scout at Upton Park, expressing his personal thanks for everything John had done for young players in the area. Trevor Smith, the much-respected sports reporter on the *Ilford Gazette*, sent John a much-appreciated letter of encouragement during his illness. Within a few weeks of his death, a tribute to John appeared in the programme for the Hammers' match against Arsenal in October 2000. This was a real source of comfort to Sue and the girls. But perhaps the most heart-warming tribute to John's memory came from the people of Hainault.

When John was found to have a heart condition his doctors recommended daily walks and he could often be seen strolling round the lake in Hainault Forest, just a few minutes from his home. As a family they loved the forest and would often go for picnics accompanied by their border collie cross, Angus. They enjoyed visiting the ponies, llamas, sheep and goats and especially the rabbits, where the children, much to their delight, could watch and handle the young bunnies. Although they now live on the other side of London, the grandchildren still visit the forest when they are on one of their regular visits to see their grandmother in Hainault.

Dick made many friends while walking in the forest. A particular friend, and Hainault resident for 40 years, was Irishman Paddy, who has many fond memories of walking with John. In their retirement Paddy and John made daily visits to the forest to feed the ducks, geese and swans. With Paddy being Irish and John a Scotsman, they ribbed each other mercilessly. The Irishman would ask John what he did with all the money he earned at football, unaware that the most John ever earned was 40 quid a week, not the hundreds of thousands of pounds pocketed every week by today's top footballers.

After John died the family commissioned a seat dedicated to his memory close by his favourite part of the forest. His ashes were scattered beneath the seat and a memorial oak tree was planted to provide shade for visitors. Today Hammers fans can visit the forest and pay their respects to one of their former greats, or if that is too much trouble they can view the memorial seat on the Hainault Forest website.

John Dick, an adopted East Londoner and Essex man, commanded huge respect throughout professional football, in youth football across London and in his own community. He was a model professional and great example to young players both at West Ham and Brentford. In many respects he lived an honourable life and his popularity was well deserved. It was fitting that in 1958 John should score West Ham's first goal in Division One, following decades in lower League obscurity. Dick remains the third-most prolific goalscorer in Hammers' history and how they could do with his kind today. But the most fitting memorial to one of the very best characters ever to wear the claret and blue is that written on the seat in Hainault Forest:

'JOHN DICK 1930–2000: in loving memory of a dear husband,
dad, granddad and brother.'

It has been a real privilege to recall the life of an exceptional pioneer.

Malcolm 'Muzzie' Musgrove

Ted Fenton's team of the late 1950s and early '60s played the kind of football that established the club's reputation as the academy of the English game, even if Ron Greenwood's side was more successful. The groundwork for this success had been laid by the men of the post-war generation. One of these was the exceptional winger and provider of many of John Dick's goals, Malcolm 'Muzzie' Musgrove. Our next pioneer is another whose career overlapped the old and the new. When we look at Muzzie's career it raises the important question of what kind of football club are West Ham destined to be.

Are the Hammers a natural top-flight team or an over-achieving Championship outfit? The answer to this sensitive question is – somewhere between the two. The Hammers appear to be perpetually struggling against relegation in the top flight, or bombing along at the top of the Championship (or the old Division Two), six points clear of their nearest rivals. On rare occasions the club bumps along in the Premier League happy with mid-table mediocrity. The best of all seasons for the fans is to be free of relegation and enjoy a good Cup run, with the team playing the kind of exquisite attacking football for which West Ham were once famous. Sadly, this happy state of affairs is experienced rarely and not

for a very long time. Malcolm Musgrove experienced the up and downs of being a West Ham player more than most.

Ted Fenton knew a good player when he saw one and Musgrove was very good. The West Ham manager signed the young Geordie from the north-east club Lynemouth Colliery. He knew about the promising left-winger because Lynemouth had been adopted by West Ham as a nursery club – one of the directors at the north-east club was from East Ham. But it is also likely that one of Fenton's many contacts in the game spotted Muzzie playing for the RAF in his national service days. Musgrove was one of the last generation of professional footballers to be called-up for national service, a fate that eluded Bobby Moore, born a few years later. Luckily for West Ham, the youngster escaped the attentions of Sunderland and joined the East London club in 1953, where he stayed for nearly 10 seasons.

Malcolm Musgrove was born in Lynemouth on 8 July 1933, but spent most of his life away from the north east. His football took him to London, the USA and south-west England, where he finally retired. Essentially an outside-left, Musgrove was in reality a goalscoring midfielder. He was quick, tricky and direct and laid on masses of goals for John Dick and Vic Keeble in the 1957–58 promotion season. Muzzie proved to be one of Fenton's most astute signings.

Immediately at home in his new surroundings, the winger soon settled at Upton Park and made his debut against Brentford in February 1954. He thrived on the thrilling ideas of Cantwell and Allison which were always buzzing around the training ground. He joined the club in one of the most exciting periods in its history and quickly became a fully paid-up member of the Cassetari's café crew. Muzzie loved being part of a group of intelligent and visionary West Ham players who were to have such an enormous influence on the development of the English game. Musgrove was at the heart of this innovative, slightly mad bunch of professionals.

The winger's arrival at Upton Park was well timed, as Fenton began to put together a team capable of achieving promotion from the old Second Division. When Vic Keeble arrived in 1957 to complement John Dick's goalscoring feats, Fenton knew his team was ready.

Musgrove, like many of the promotion-winning side, played under both Fenton and Ron Greenwood. Both managers encouraged entertaining football and cherished fast and skilful wingers. As a club West Ham has a long tradition of exciting wingers going back as far as the great Jimmy Ruffell in the 1930s. If you combine speedy wing play with strong and direct forwards like Dick, Keeble and Geoff Hurst, all natural goalscorers, you have a golden combination. And so it proved, with promotion in 1958 and the glory years of the mid-1960s, when Greenwood turned to Redknapp and Sissons.

There are countless examples of the classic West Ham ploy of Muzzie tearing down the wing to cross from the by-line for Dick or Keeble to score. John Dick knew how much he depended for his goals on the opportunities created for him by the exciting winger. But Musgrove was no one-trick pony. Time and again he danced his way down the centre of the pitch into the penalty area, ignoring the pleas from his forwards, as he slotted home goal after goal, scoring 89 in 301 League and Cup games for the Hammers.

Musgrove had a purple scoring patch in the first three years back in Division One, notching 20, 18 and 14 goals in successive seasons. Good enough for an England call-up for the Irons' flying winger, but disappointingly the selectors ignored Musgrove's claims,

Muzzie goes close against Leeds United 1958–59.

opting instead for the exceptional skills of Blackpool's Stanley Matthews. In any other period, Muzzie's prolific goalscoring and ability to play on the wing or come inside to stiffen the midfield, would have earned him at least 20 caps.

Three games in particular illustrate Musgrove's worth to West Ham, when his outstanding wing play and eye for a goal proved decisive. The first was against Aston Villa in the first season back in the top flight. The Hammers made a promising start to this historic year. They had beaten Portsmouth 2–0 at Fratton Park in their first match, with a goal each from Dick and Keeble. With Allison, Bond, Cantwell, Brown also in the side, the home fans were entitled to look to the new campaign with optimism. On the following Monday night a capacity crowd of over 37,000 crammed into the Boleyn to see their heroes overcome Wolverhampton Wanderers 2–0, with another goal from Dick and a second from Johnny Smith. In the 1960s there were few grounds in football which could match floodlit matches at Upton Park and on that particular evening the atmosphere was spine-tingling.

Two wins in their first two games in Division One and the Boleyn was in Hammers heaven. The following Saturday, the club entertained Aston Villa at Upton Park in a match which has entered Hammers history. Malcolm Musgrove was at his superb best as he ran the Villa defence ragged from his nominal position out on the left wing. Muzzie switched from left to right and occupied long periods in the inside-left position – the Midlanders' defence was helpless against his pace, guile and deft passing. It was no contest. The Hammers ran in SEVEN goals that afternoon – two each from Dick and Keeble, one from Billy Lansdowne and, not content with laying on most of the goals and tearing the Villa defence to ribbons, Muzzie completed the scoring with two of his own. This was an outstanding West Ham side at the top of their game and Musgrove, one of their best players, was simply superb. The home fans who saw the display will never forget it. That day Muzzie was just unplayable.

Of course, the bubble was bound to burst as the Hammers settled into the season. A draw with Wolves at Molineux and an unexpected defeat at Luton dampened spirits a little, but expectations remained high for the visit of the mighty Manchester United. For lots of different reasons this game appears with some frequency in these pages. The match had everything – the drama surrounding Bobby Moore's debut, the anticipation of the Upton Park faithful seeing their side up against the very best in Bobby Charlton and Denis Law and the opportunity for Dick and Keeble to pit their considerable strength against one of the best defences in the land.

In what the authors of the *Essential History of West Ham United* describe as a 'never-to-be forgotten encounter', the Irons overcame their illustrious opponents 3–2, with Dick, Smith and Musgrove scoring for the home side. Again, at the heart of the very best

Musgrove off-target this time in the same match against Leeds.

Hammers football that day was the marvellous Muzzie. The Geordie winger was in the form of his life and that season finally secured the respect and affection of the often critical North Bank.

On a Wednesday evening in late August 1961, 50,000 excited fans squeezed into White Hart Lane to witness the early season derby match between two great London rivals. The Hammers travelled in hope. They had drawn at home with Manchester United in the first game of the season and it was exciting time for the East London club. They had a new manager in Ron Greenwood, a dazzling new set of floodlights at the Boleyn, a brand new roof over the North Bank and a new goalkeeper in Lawrie Leslie. Things were definitely looking up for the Hammers and how the fans must have looked forward to the clash with table-topping Tottenham.

The home side were clear favourites to win and their own lively winger, Terry Dyson, put the home side ahead midway through the first half. But this Hammers side were not easily intimidated and their refusal to cave in before their illustrious neighbours paid off when, five minutes before the interval, Phil Woosnam crashed a 30-yard shot past the disbelieving Bill Brown in the Spurs goal. Musgrove was revelling in the occasion and regularly tormented Tottenham's usually unflappable right-back, Peter Baker. Ten minutes into the second half, Muzzie again slipped past the hapless Baker and thundered a long-range shot into the top corner to put his side 2–1 ahead. But Spurs were a great double-winning side and not in the mood to lose at home to their East London rivals. Dyson scored a second and his side's equaliser late in the second half and the game finished in a 2–2 draw. Man of the Match Malcolm Musgrove had enjoyed one of his greatest games for West Ham at the home of the double-winning Tottenham Hotspur.

Ron Greenwood's appointment as manager in April 1961 signalled the end of the wonderful team of the late 1950s. The former Arsenal coach and manager of the England Under-23 side had his own ideas on the game, one of which was to encourage young players. The influential Noel Cantwell was gone and Malcolm Allison's illness finished his playing career. John Dick and Vic Keeble were coming to the ends of their playing careers and Greenwood clearly saw Musgrove in that same category. Young players like Moore, Peters, John Sissons, Johnny Smith and Harry Redknapp were showing promise and were impatient for first-team experience. But, arguably the most important decision Greenwood made in his early years at the club was to sign the Crystal Palace centre-forward, Johnny 'Budgie' Byrne. Influenced by the great Hungarian team, Greenwood saw Byrne as a deep-lying centre-forward in the manner of Hidegkuti, and in our own time, Lionel Messi of Barcelona. The club had entered a new, exciting period in its history and the Ted Fenton era was being slowly dismantled.

With Greenwood's appointment, Musgrove's great days at West Ham were numbered, despite his outstanding form in the early 1960s. In December 1962 Muzzie, like many West

Looking dangerous against Chelsea.

Ham players coming to the ends of their playing careers, left Upton Park for Leyton Orient. He joined the O's for a fee of £11,000 and later became coach at Brisbane Road under fellow ex-Hammer Dave Sexton. In four seasons at his new club he made 83 appearances, scoring by his high standards, a modest 14 goals.

In the year he left West Ham, Muzzie was elected chairman of the Professional Footballers' Association (PFA), the clearest indication of the respect the former Hammer enjoyed in the game. Musgrove had some strong characters on his management committee, including former colleagues Noel Cantwell and Phil Woosnam, while Maurice Setters, Nobby Lawton and Bobby Charlton were all distinguished figures in the game. Secretary Cliff Lloyd was determined to raise the union's profile and recognised Musgrove as one of the new breed of player-coaches influenced by England manager Walter Winterbottom and the young Ron Greenwood. But leading the players' union was not just about new coaching and training innovations, exciting as these were. Musgrove and Lloyd had to steer the PFA through some of the most difficult years in its history.

In 1963 the George Eastham case sent shockwaves through professional football. The case legitimised a player's right to move clubs, although it did not mean an end to the archaic transfer system. Following the judgement, League clubs and the PFA came to an agreement by which the 'retain and transfer' element of players' contracts was abolished and a more player-sensitive scheme introduced. A tribunal was set up consisting of an independent chairman, a representative from the Football League and one from the PFA. If club and player could not agree on terms, the tribunal would decide on the offending clauses and any subsequent transfer fee. Crucially, a player continued to receive full wages during the course of the dispute. This eliminated the hardships of the old system at a stroke.

A consequence of the new rules was that clubs were more inclined to meet players halfway, whereas previously they had no reason to concede to any player's demands. These new initiatives did not provide total player freedom, but according to the PFA, the contracts were now a 'combination of what was written and real life'. The Eastham case paved the way for the kind of player-power the top players enjoy today and Malcolm Musgrove was at the centre of this turning point for professional footballers. Partly thanks to Musgrove, the old 19th-century wage-slave mentality was now a thing of the past, although old attitudes are hard to shift. Multi-millionaire footballers of today continue to refer to their manager as the gaffer.

Despite the Eastham victory players did not have everything their own way in the 1960s. In 1964 the Football League unilaterally decided to axe the players' Provident Fund. The fund provided a lifeline to many low-paid, injury-hit players and their families facing unemployment. In its place the League introduced a costly insurance scheme. The PFA were incensed by the timing of the League's bombshell. In the same year the pools promoters had more than doubled their payments to the League. Later in 1965 and without consultation, the FA decided to end the £4,000 lump sum payment to the players' injury insurance scheme, agreed as part of the 1956 TV deal. Musgrove and the PFA were in no mood to be bullied by the FA and immediately placed a ban on its members appearing in televised Cup matches. Under severe pressure the FA improved their offer. The PFA had won. The far-sighted Muzzie and Cliff Lloyd insisted that the FA's new TV money should be used to set up education projects for young players.

Not all the PFA's business in the '60s was about improving players' contracts, welfare and wages. In 1964 the *Sunday People* alleged that three Sheffield Wednesday players – England centre-half Peter Swan, Tony Kay and David Layne – had accepted illegal payments to 'fix' a League match against Ipswich on 1 December 1962. All three players were tried and found guilty and handed prison sentences for taking bribes to lose matches. Despite their good work in support of players and their families, the PFA refused all requests to provide for the players' dependants while Swan, Kay and Layne were in prison. The match-fixing scandal sent shock waves through the game and was an issue that Musgrove and the PFA could have done without, at a time when they were fighting hard to improve the situation of their members. This was a perfect case of professional footballers well and truly shooting themselves in the foot, and not for the last time.

In spite of his weighty responsibilities at the PFA, Muzzie remained heavily involved with the game at club level. After leaving the Orient in 1965, he linked up with his old friend Frank O'Farrell at Leicester City, where he stayed for three seasons, during which time City won the Second Division Championship. When O'Farrell was attracted to the huge challenge that is managing Manchester United, he took his old friend with him. The Old Trafford adventure never really worked for the ex-Hammers and they both left United after a year, probably hardened by the experience. In those days football management was an extremely precarious occupation without the huge compensation packages available today. Muzzie walked away from Old Trafford with a miserly six weeks' wages, not much to support a growing family.

Musgrove had gained invaluable experience as a number-two, but was desperate to run his own team and quickly accepted the offer of the vacant manager's job at far-away Torquay United, although he very nearly joined Bob Stokoe at Sunderland. Muzzie had worked with the extrovert Geordie at Charlton but declined the offer and opted instead for the delights of the sunny English Riviera. Malcolm and Jean loved Devon and quickly put down roots in the area. The Gulls and West Ham have enjoyed a close relationship for many years with Bill Kitchener, Tony Scott, John Bond, O'Farrell and Musgrove all finding themselves on the South Devon coast either as players, coaches or managers. The Plainmoor job was one of the most difficult in the Football League and the new manager struggled with small gates and limited means, but stayed for four seasons. The highest position the Gulls achieved in Musgrove's spell as manager was ninth – a creditable achievement given the resources at his disposal. In the 1970s, Torquay trained on the wind-blown vastness of Newton Abbot on the edge of Dartmoor, where they still train to this day.

Like many ex-professionals of the time, Muzzie tried his hand in America, firstly with Connecticut Bicentennials to be with his old boss Ron Greenwood, before swapping the east coast for the industrial setting of Chicago. At the windy city he was offered a coaching post with Chicago Sting, whose cosmopolitan playing staff included Americans, Scots, a Yugoslav, Germans, two Haitians and a young Dutchman named Dick Advocaat. The latter's radical training methods and tactical innovations were largely responsible for Holland's success in the 1994 World Cup finals, held, of course, in the United States. Musgrove's son Martin remembers meeting the great Pele when Chicago played Cosmos in a giant stadium in front of 70,000 intrigued New Yorkers. From Torquay to Chicago was a huge leap and Muzzie began to miss the blood and thunder of English football.

Back in England, he returned to the south-west. Muzzie had retrained as a physiotherapist and enjoyed a spell as physio-coach with Exeter City, but when the Exeter job ended in 1984, Muzzie took up an offer to become head physiotherapist for the Qatar

FA. He enjoyed the challenge of helping to establish the game in the Arab state and accompanied the national side to the Asian games and the Under-16 team to the junior World Cup in China. To date Muzzie's extraordinary post-playing career had taken him to Leicester, Manchester, Torquay, Chicago and the Middle East, but by this time he knew he wanted to return to the red soil and cream teas of South Devon.

Returning from the Gulf in 1984 he was offered a job as reserve-team manager, coach and physio under Dave Smith at Plymouth Argyle. West Ham colleague Ken Brown later took over the Argyle manager's job from Smith and Muzzie enjoyed five happy years at Home Park alongside his old teammate. On leaving Plymouth, another of the West Ham café football think-tank, John Bond, asked Muzzie to join him at Shrewsbury Town as club physio. He remained at Gay Meadow until the late 1990s, helping the Shrews to the Third Division Championship in 1993.

Musgrove finally retired from professional football in 1998 and returned to his beloved Devon, where he is still fondly remembered. Muzzie and Jean had a close family in Torquay with children David, Martin and Allison and their two grandchildren living in close proximity. Malcolm and Jean's two sons and their families still live in South Devon. Martin was a decent footballer and remembers playing for Torquay as a youngster. In a match against Port Vale under the eye of his manager, the formidable Bruce Rioch, Muzzie junior had the unenviable task of marking the former England international Jimmy Greenhoff. Martin also had spells at Exeter and West Ham before embarking on a successful career in his first love, sailing. Older brother David lives in Torquay, close to Plainmoor. He enjoyed many years playing local football and cricket and keeps a watchful eye on the programmes, photographs, letters and other memorabilia that make up his dad's extensive archive.

Sadly, Muzzie contacted Alzheimer's disease soon after he retired and died in a Paignton nursing home on 14 September 2007, aged 74. West Ham United had lost one of their all-time greats and a gifted pioneer and the English game had lost one of its most committed, intelligent and influential figures. But Musgrove would want to be remembered most as an exciting outside-left who could electrify Upton Park with his pacy, direct style and exceptional feats of goalscoring. He was much appreciated by the fans as the following three tributes show:

> *I am very saddened to hear of the passing of Malcolm Musgrove, what an icon he was to West Ham, a top-class player and a lynchpin in the club. A greatly respected man. I am sure that he will be in the great team in the sky.*

> *I never saw him play but he was one of my grandad's all-time favourite players. He was one of the best players in the 1950s. I'm sure he will be taking his place on the wing in the Hammers Heaven XI.*

*We were lucky enough to have the Musgroves as next door neighbours in
Barkingside. Malcolm took me to a game one season. He was a gentleman,
a 'proper' professional footballer. I was lucky enough to know a wonderful
player and a wonderful man.*

Muzzie's son, David, regularly accompanied his dad on scouting trips throughout the
country, often in deserted stadiums looking for a bargain buy or loan signing to take back
to Devon. On these trips Malcolm would introduce the soccer-mad youngster to football
legends like Bobby Robson and Bill Shankly. David remembers how these famous men of
football showed the greatest respect to his dad, both as a player and coach. Muzzie was held
in such regard that his name could open most doors in professional football.

The family are extremely proud of Muzzie's achievements, but as David suggests, his
dad may have been too nice to be a top manager. Professional footballers of the 1950s often
struggled financially when they finished playing. Some became managers and coaches and
some, like Dave Whelan in the north-west, set up successful businesses. Muzzie spent his
post-playing days working as a physiotherapist and coach with his ex-West Ham
colleagues Dave Sexton, Frank O'Farrell, Ken Brown and John Bond, before retiring to his
beloved Devon. Within a few months Muzzie began to show symptoms of early
Alzheimer's and was soon engulfed by the disease he suffered for nine years.

Conscious of his status in football, Jean and the family decided to try to organise a
testimonial match. They wrote to West Ham and received a curt response saying 'we are
unable to commit to additional matches at this time'. Jean Musgrove was deeply upset by
the rejection. Muzzie had served West Ham with real distinction for nearly nine years and
he had narrowly missed out on a testimonial at Upton Park, because he left to join Leyton
Orient just short of the required nine years. There is no sentiment in professional football.

Undeterred by West Ham's disappointing reply, Jean contacted Muzzie's last club,
Shrewsbury Town, who agreed to stage a testimonial match and dinner. The family
employed an agent to organise the event. He turned out to be a forerunner of the shady
characters who control most of the movement of players in today's Premier League. The
agent failed to recruit a major speaker, provided no opposition, neither did he sell any
tickets. At the last minute Muzzie's son Martin stepped in and took responsibility for his
dad's testimonial.

He contacted his dad's old friend Alan Ball, who was the manager of Portsmouth at the
time. Pompey were involved in a relegation battle and Ball promised Martin he would do
his best to get to Shrewsbury for the post-match dinner. Ball was as good as his word. He
turned up for the dinner, gave a moving and entertaining speech and drove back to
Portsmouth that night. England's World Cup hero refused to take a penny for making the
day-long return trip. With the main speaker confirmed and with just days to go, Martin

still had no opposition for the match. To the rescue came Nottingham Forest manager Dave Bassett. Forest were locked in a race for promotion at the time, desperate to get into the Premier League. Despite this Bassett brought his full squad to Gay Meadow. The miserable weather kept the attendance down to a few thousand, but the post-match dinner at the town's Lord Hill Hotel was a great success. The testimonial raised a few thousand pounds, but nothing compared to what might have been raised by a good crowd at Upton Park.

More successful was a testimonial dinner held in London for the old Hammers hero. Jack Charlton, 'a lovely man', was the main speaker and again refused any kind of payment. The testimonial events at Shrewsbury and in London raised a total of about £20,000 – a desultory amount to a man who had given so much to professional football. When you consider that Muzzie's salary as a full-time coach in the early 1980s would have been about £18,000 at most, professional football for players of his era was not a lucrative career choice.

Despite leaving the game with little reward for 45 years' service, Muzzie never complained. His widow Jean, now in her 80s, remains in touch with many of her husband's colleagues from his West Ham days, including Susan Dick, Yvonne Lyall and Janet Bond, while Ken Brown keeps in regular contact. Muzzie's family and all West Ham supporters are rightly proud of his contribution to the success of the great West Ham side of the late 1950s. Malcolm Musgrove was one of the very best of the vintage Hammers.

Phil Woosnam: Welsh wizard

Another of the great players at West Ham in the early 1960s was Welshman, Phil Woosnam. Like Mal Musgrove, Woosnam was a member of the generation that graced Upton Park prior to the glory years of 1964 and 1965. West Ham was the perfect club for the forward-thinking Woosnam and he flourished in the hothouse football atmosphere at the Boleyn. The Welshman responded to the encouragement of Cantwell and Allison and the tactical intelligence of Ron Greenwood.

Phillip Abraham Woosnam was born in Caersws, Wales on 22 December 1932. He joined the Hammers from Leyton Orient in 1959 and stayed until 1962, making 138 appearances in which he scored 26 goals. His time at the club was brief compared with some of the other vintage Hammers, but Woosnam's influence on the team and its playing style should not be underestimated. The inside-forward was certainly one of the most highly educated and intelligent players to play for West Ham. More than any other player, Woosnam illustrates just how much the professional game had changed since the days of our first pioneer, Charlie Dove.

It is difficult to imagine two more different characters than the university-educated, much-travelled Woosnam and Dove, a young docker from the poverty-stricken backstreets of West Ham. Despite the extremes of background Woosnam and Dove share the same lineage – they just represent the club in different stages of its history.

Phil Woosnam showed promise as a youngster and was selected to represent Montgomery Schoolboys at the age of 15 and later gained youth international honours with Wales. He played club football for Wrexham and Aberystwyth Town and captained Bangor University, where he was a scholarship boy. He represented the Welsh Universities before embarking on his national service in 1950. He joined the Royal Artillery as a second lieutenant and was soon selected to play for the army alongside such luminaries as Maurice Setters, Eddie Coleman and the great Duncan Edwards, all of whom played for Manchester United.

In many ways Woosnam's football career stands out from his contemporaries, all of whom would have signed for a professional club at the end of their national service. Following his two years in the army, Woosnam decided that teaching would provide a more interesting career than professional football and probably a more secure one. Like many young Welsh teachers at the time, Woosnam decided to begin his career in East London and was appointed teacher of physics at Leyton County High School for Boys, just

a few miles from Upton Park. Never one for the easy option, it was typical of Woosnam that he chose to study a very difficult science subject, rather than a safer option like PE studies or sports science.

While working as a teacher in a tough East London environment, Woosnam continued to play senior amateur football, firstly with Sutton United before enjoying a spell with Middlesex Wanderers. In 1955, he was voted amateur footballer of the year and made his senior international debut for Wales against Scotland four years later. Woosnam won a total of eight Welsh amateur caps, the first against England in 1951. The brilliant young Welshman enjoyed one of the most distinguished amateur football careers in the post-war period.

Professional football was soon to come calling on this most skilful of inside-forwards, already known in the game as the 'Welsh Wizard'. It was just a question of whether he could resist the advances of professional clubs and give up his teaching career. When his local club, Leyton Orient, offered the young teacher an attractive contract, Woosnam felt he could no longer turn his back on professional football. But the ever cautious young Welshman only joined the Orient on the understanding that he could continue to teach part-time. His wonderful touch, the range of his passing and his tactical awareness enabled Woosnam to dominate games from midfield. He settled into the professional game quickly and in his first season was selected to represent a London XI against Lausanne and was selected by the Welsh selectors for his first full international.

At the age of 26, the Wizard decided to fully commit to his football career. In November 1958 he gave up his teaching job, left the Orient and signed full-time professional forms for West Ham. The highly rated inside-forward had his best years ahead, one of the reasons why the Hammers were prepared to pay Orient £30,000 for his services. Woosnam may have hesitated about giving up his teaching post, but he could not refuse the opportunity to see how far his football could take him. He made his debut against Arsenal in that November and went on to make 153 League and Cup appearances for the club, scoring a total of 29 goals. While at Upton Park he added 15 international caps to the one he gained at Leyton Orient. The inspirational midfield general was also selected to represent the Football League, a good indication of his new standing in the game. At this point in his career the Welshman knew he had made the correct decision to leave teaching and embark on a career in professional football.

West Ham's new star inside-forward proved a tremendous acquisition. The spiky-haired Woosnam quickly established his authority in the Hammers' midfield, where he directed play with his ease on the ball and immaculate distribution. He set the tone for West Ham's style for the whole of the 1960s and perhaps only Trevor Brooking and Alan Devonshire have come close to matching the Welsh wonder's wizardry in the Hammers midfield. Two examples should be sufficient to illustrate Phil Woosnam's capabilities.

On 31 January 1959, midway through the Hammers' first season back in the top division, the club welcomed Nottingham Forest to Upton Park. The match turned out to be a goal bonanza for the fans and the Irons' best performance of the season. All eight goals were special, but sadly there were no cameras at Upton Park that day to witness this extraordinary match. Both teams were committed to attacking football whether they were playing at home or away.

In many ways the match was a vindication of manager Ted Fenton's passionate advocacy of an attacking style based on speedy wingers, skilful midfield players and direct, goalscoring forwards. Fenton had also built a solid defence to support his more creative players. Bond,

Cantwell, Malcolm and Ken Brown were a sound combination, apart from the odd game when John Bond convinced himself he was an outside-right, rather than a competent full-back. John Smith, Mike Grice and Phil Woosnam made up the midfield in the Forest match, ably supported by the mercurial Malcolm Musgrove out on the left. With Dick and Keeble providing the goals, Fenton's Hammers were a real force to be reckoned with in the top flight.

Forest, under manager Billy Walker, were in mid-table that January, but players like Stewart Imlach, Roy Dwight and John Quigley could turn a game with one piece of dazzling skill. Forest had a reputation for attacking football which could result in both heavy defeats and stunning victories. Imlach's son Gary published a book entitled *My Father*, a compelling biography about his dad's life in football. The book contains a photograph of the winger carrying a tray of tea on the train back from Wembley, following Forest's FA Cup Final triumph over Luton Town later that year. What is striking about the photograph is not the celebratory tray of tea, but the size of the huge pipe held in Imlach's teeth.

The Forest forward was certainly on form that winter Saturday at the Boleyn, in front of a raucous crowd of 26,676. The Hammers fans were silenced when, as early as the 10th minute, Forest took the lead. Imlach slipped the ball to Quigley who skipped through a sleepy home defence to guide the ball effortlessly past Ernie Gregory. Despite going behind the North Bank were in relaxed mood – they were well used to their team being 0–1 after 10 minutes and still are. The crowd's patience was rewarded a few minutes later when Dick equalised. New signing Woosnam's defence-splitting pass let in the Scot, who smashed the ball into the top left corner of the net with his weaker right foot.

In unstoppable form, Dick scored again 10 minutes later, again with his right foot. With his back to goal, the Hammers' number-10 turned and crashed a volley past Thomson in the Forest goal. The second goal electrified the Boleyn crowd as their team surged forward in search of a third. But Forest were in no mood to surrender and equalised minutes before half-time when Tommy Wilson rose to head Imlach's pin-point cross past Gregory. A stunned, if excited crowd watched the teams go in for the break two apiece. The half-time Bovril would have warmed the cockles on a bitterly cold day – the football had certainly raised the spirits.

If the spectacular first period was a four-goal thriller, the second half saw the players step up the action in a breathtaking display of attacking football by both sides. Phil Woosnam was beginning to dominate midfield as he did in every one of his four seasons at the club. Urging his team on, Woosnam moved further up the field into the heart of the Forest defence. His dazzling contribution to the match reached a high point on the hour when he controlled Ken Brown's through-ball and struck a trademark dipping volley over Thomson. The North Bank began to relax and enjoy themselves as victory seemed a formality. But they had reckoned without Forest's ability to conjure up goals from nowhere. We will let Martin Godleman (2008) describe the next piece of drama in this enthralling game:

'Roy Dwight, gathering a loose ball out of defence, ran two-thirds of the field. It took him past Ken Brown, Andy Malcolm, captain Noel Cantwell, and finally the 'keeper Gregory before he fired the ball into the corner of the net to make the score 3–3.'

Roy Dwight was to play a decisive role in Forest's FA Cup Final win later that season. He was quite a player, scoring an impressive 27 goals in 53 games for the Nottingham club. Dwight was certainly no stranger to fame. His nephew was one of the biggest celebrities of them all, none other than the rock star and former Watford chairman, Elton John.

Could the Hammers respond to Dwight's moment of genius? Enter Vic Keeble. Dick and Keeble had already scored 28 times between them that season and it was the goal-hungry Geordie who finally swung the game back in favour of the home side. Keeble's match-winner came just two minutes after Dwight had silenced the crowd with his dazzling goal. In the 85th minute, the Hammers' centre-forward settled the game and the frazzled nerves of the North Bank when he latched on to Andy Malcolm's through-ball and in typical Keeble style, charged down the middle and cracked the ball past the helpless Forest 'keeper. It was the type of goal that would become the trademark of Keeble's successor, the great Geoff Hurst.

The Hammers had won a momentous match 5–3 and at the heart of all their best moments was Phil Woosnam. He seemed to be everywhere as his accurate passing took the game away from Forest. He also took time out from his midfield duties to score a stunning goal. It was one of West Ham's best performances back in the top flight, in a season when they achieved the second-highest finish in their history. Man of the Match Woosnam had signalled his arrival at the club in the best possible way and his performance must have gladdened the heart of his manager, the soon to be departed Ted Fenton.

Woosnam made such an impression on his new club that Fenton awarded the Welshman the club captaincy, following the departure of Noel Cantwell to Manchester United. He thrived on the extra responsibility and if anything the captaincy took the ever-confident Welshman to a higher level. Two seasons after the epic encounter at Upton Park with Forest, the Hammers were full of confidence following a promising start to the season. The team included John Lyall, a youthful Bobby Moore and crucially centre-forward Dave Dunmore, bought from Tottenham the previous season. Keeble was gone, along with Cantwell, John Smith and Ernie Gregory. Dunmore proved an adequate replacement for Keeble and the match against Arsenal was, in many ways, a career high point for the goalscoring Londoner.

It would have been a huge disappointment to manager George Swindon that season to see his team just a few places behind the Hammers in the Division One table. Within minutes of the kick-off the Gunners gifted West Ham a goal, which Dunmore gleefully accepted. In the 30th minute Woosnam, who was enjoying the freedom of Upton Park, linked up with John Dick and released a perfect through-ball to Dunmore, who made no mistake from 10 yards for his second goal of the half. 'Bubbles' resounded around the ground as the Hammers went in for the break two goals ahead.

Fenton's inspired decision to use Bobby Moore alongside Woosnam in midfield paid off as the unlikely pair began to dictate the play. Godleman described Woosnam's performance that day: 'Welsh wizard Woosnam was on top form with his mazy runs and dizzy dribbling to confound the Arsenal defence.'

John Dick scored the third after the break when he rounded the Gunners' outstanding goalkeeper, Jack Kelsey. A few minutes later the match's outstanding performer, Phil Woosnam, scored with a low drive through a crowded penalty area. Popular defender Andy Malcolm scored the Hammers' fifth when he turned in a Derek Woodley corner. It was Malcolm's only goal in his long and distinguished career. A few minutes later the lively Dunmore endeared himself to the supporters when he confidently converted a delicious Woosnam through-ball. Arsenal had been humiliated and rarely can 'Bubbles' have sounded as sweet and loud as it did on that November day in 1960. The celebrations in the Boleyn Castle and the Black Horse in Plaistow were just about to begin in earnest. Victories such as these are rare for Hammers fans and they saluted their new hero, Phil Woosnam.

These matches against Nottingham Forest and Arsenal announced Woosnam's arrival as a West Ham great. The 'sublimely gifted' inside-forward had stamped his authority on the playing staff and his wonderfully inventive football set the standard for the next two generations of West Ham players. He had won the Third Division Championship in 1956 with Leyton Orient, but even the rare skills of the world-class Welshman failed to inspire the Hammers to the trophy their fans dreamt about when they won promotion in 1958.

Inevitably, West Ham's record signing became the subject of transfer speculation as his reputation began to spread. Woosnam was ambitious and wanted to win trophies. In 1962 he left the Hammers for Villa Park after four tremendous seasons in the East End. It was an odd choice, as Villa were no more likely than the Hammers to lift the Division One Championship. The more likely explanation for the £27,000 move was the appointment of Ron Greenwood as manager and the arrival at the club of 'Budgie' Byrne, as well as the emergence of Ronnie Boyce and Eddie Bovington. Woosnam left West Ham just before the club finally made the big time and as a result missed out on the glorious years of 1964 and 1965. Had he stayed the Hammers would have been even stronger for his presence in their greatest ever team.

During Woosnam's four seasons at the club, the Hammers enjoyed two top 10 Division One finishes, which is its own kind of success for a club like West Ham, with moderate ambitions. As captain he set high standards for the team, both on the pitch and in the way in which players conducted themselves as professionals. His successor as skipper, Bobby Moore, would have had a more difficult job without Woosnam as his predecessor. In his time at Upton Park the Welshman added 15 full international caps to the one he had gained at the Orient.

Woosnam made 106 appearances for Aston Villa, scoring 24 goals and gaining a further two international caps. He was extremely popular with the Holte End, despite being the first player in the Football League to wear gloves on cold playing days. Villa centre-forward Tony Hateley thrived on the constant supply of defence-splitting passes supplied by the needle-sharp Welshman. Woosnam clearly enjoyed his partnership with Hateley as he helped himself to 20 goals in his last season at Villa Park.

The ex-Leyton High School teacher came to professional football later than his teammates, but quickly hit his stride and within a few games looked the best player at Upton Park by some distance. He retired from the English game after six splendid seasons in Division One. In 1967 Woosnam made a life-changing decision to join Atlanta Chiefs in the US as player-coach. It was an inspired choice. Highly intelligent and extremely capable, Woosnam stood out among his fellow professionals trying to make their mark in retirement as managers and coaches. He impressed his employers at Atlanta and became an influential figure in the emerging North American Soccer League.

In January 1969 Woosnam was appointed commissioner of the NASL, bringing over Villa teammate Vic Crowe as his assistant. Woosnam loved the States and his affection was returned in full when he was offered the prestigious job of coach to the USA World Cup side in 1970. In 1982 he managed the FIFA World XI as part of his vision for the US to host the World Cup. After leading the unsuccessful 1986 bid, in 1994 Woosnam's quest to bring the World Cup to the USA finally succeeded. It is highly unlikely the US would have been awarded the FIFA World Cup without the dedicated and accomplished efforts of Phil Woosnam. During his tenure as NASL commissioner, Woosnam oversaw unprecedented growth in football in the US. In recognition of his contribution to American soccer, the former Hammer was later inducted into the National Soccer Hall of Fame. He continues to live in his adopted country.

Ironically, Woosnam almost never went to America. He revealed in 1984:

> I wanted to continue my playing career in Division One and one week after agreeing to join Atlanta Chiefs, Tommy Docherty asked me to join him at Chelsea. I hadn't signed anything with Atlanta, but I had given them my word and I stuck to it. But more than once I moaned, 'Why didn't you come in for me earlier?'.

Chelsea's loss was America's gain. Woosnam distinguished himself in the US, but older West Ham fans will prefer to remember the talented Welshman dictating play in West Ham's midfield in the late 1950s and early '60s. There is no question that the cerebral Welshman had a tremendous influence on Bobby Moore's gloriously successful side. For that reason alone he fully deserves to be regarded as a true West Ham pioneer.

John Lyall: man of dignity

How West Ham fans must look back to the golden days of the 1980s when, under the leadership of the saintly John Lyall, West Ham were one of the top three sides in the country. They beat Arsenal in the 1980 FA Cup Final and were well placed in the top flight for most of the decade. Only the fourth manager at the club in over 80 years, Lyall represented the very best traditions of West Ham United. These habits and traditions were pioneered by founder Arnold Hills and his manager Syd King. The torch was then picked up and carried by Charlie Paynter, Ted Fenton, Ron Greenwood and finally, John Lyall.

Some might think it odd to regard the Essex man as an early pioneer. However, he deserves the status for two reasons. Firstly, as a young man he played with the great names of the 1950s and if it were not for a career-ending injury, he might have developed into a real Hammers legend. Secondly, in his time as a coach at the Boleyn, Lyall had a decisive influence on the club's admired playing style. He was part of the '50s generation, yet was a thoroughly modern manager.

John Angus Lyall was born in Ilford, Essex on 24 February 1940. His mother Catherine was from the Isle of Lewis and his father, James, hailed from Kirriemuir in north-west Scotland, a birthplace Lyall shared with Sir James Barrie of *Peter Pan* fame. Kirriemuir is set in the rural vastness of the Angus Glens where young John might have acquired his lifelong devotion to fishing. John's dad, son of a jute weaver, was the second oldest of eight children, while his mother, one of six, was in service. His parents, who had moved to England separately, met and married in London. Like many East End folk, John's parents moved out to leafy Ilford in search of better schools and a more pleasant environment.

In Ilford, the Lyalls rented a flat above a shop close to the Ilford Palais, where West Ham players used to enjoy their Saturday nights during the 1960s. One of the neighbours was the respected football journalist and TV presenter, Peter Lorenzo. In those days Lorenzo, who wrote the notes for the 1965 European Cup-Winners' Cup programme, was honing his skills at the *Ilford Recorder*. John Lyall remembered kicking a ball against Lorenzo's wall for hours on end. The budding reporter and TV presenter was patient with the noisy youngster and the pair later became great friends.

Young John regularly came home from the park after an evening kick-about with his mates covered from head to foot in mud. On such occasions his mother would plunge him into a tin bath at the back of the house, where he would sit until he was allowed in for his tea. His mother was old school and extremely proud of her son. According to John, Mrs Lyall even used to wash and iron his bootlaces and on one occasion in the early '50s, bought young John a brand new pair of 'Arthur Rowe' boots. The brand was fitting as Rowe was responsible for Spurs' famous push and run style, the basis of the adult Lyall's own football philosophy.

Like many of us, John and his mates spent their summer evenings and school holidays playing football in local Valentine's Park, where Trevor Bailey, Keith Fletcher, Graham Gooch and later Nasser Hussain entertained the locals during the Essex cricket festival. The youngster was happy to play football morning, noon and night. He attended Parkhill Primary, the same school as Trevor Brooking. Like Brooking after him, Lyall passed the 11+ which meant a place at the prestigious Ilford County High. His teachers quickly recognised his sporting promise and John was soon selected to play football for both his school and the Ilford District side.

Following a recommendation from schoolteacher and former Hammer John Cartwright, Ted Fenton and Wally St Pier watched the young full-back playing for Ilford Schoolboys against Walthamstow Boys at the George White ground in Billet Road. They liked what they saw. Forest Gate-born Fenton persuaded Lyall's parents that professional football was a worthwhile career. John's parents were not convinced that it was a suitable vocation for a grammar school-educated Ilford lad. Brought up on the virtues of integrity, responsibility and hard work, the Lyalls were keen for their son to complete his education before even considering a future on the risky road of professional football.

To his credit, Ted Fenton listened to John's parents, who were reassured when West Ham offered the youngster a job in the club's offices. This would not only supplement his income, but would provide John with some important on-the-job training. Fenton's persuasive manner won over the Lyalls and John was able to sign his contract. The new apprentice would have been more than happy with his generous starting wage of £4 a week. In the club's offices John was fortunate to work closely with secretary Frank Cearns and his assistant, Pauline Moss, who was succeeded by that great club servant, Eddie Chapman. The experience would have been invaluable. As Geoff Hurst said later about John, 'he knew the club from top to bottom'.

Happy with Fenton's offer, Lyall's parents agreed John should leave school and he signed for West Ham at the age of 15. As John was an 'A' stream pupil, the Lyalls were required to pay Ilford High School a £10 leaving fee, a sizeable sum at the time. In the end it was a small price to pay to launch such a wonderful career. The young full-back was confident he had made the right decision and could not have been happier as he took his first tentative steps on his new life as a professional footballer.

Encouraged by his family, he made good progress. John was a member of the West Ham side which lost 8–2 on aggregate to Manchester United in the FA Youth Final. When he was selected for England Youth against Luxembourg in 1957, a bright future seemed assured. But the Luxembourg match, in which Jimmy Greaves scored four goals, proved to be the only significant international honour in Lyall's short playing career. When he finally made his first-team debut in 1960, the young left-back showed his true potential. In a League match against Chelsea, Lyall came head-to-head against the dangerous England winger, Peter Brabrook. To his manager's delight, he kept the England man quiet for most of the game and the Hammers won the match 4–2, thanks largely to an unlikely hat-trick from stand-in centre-forward, John Bond. Lyall later said that along with Bryan Douglas and Cliff Jones, Brabrook was among the most difficult opponents he ever faced.

The young full-back had impressed the 29,000 inside Upton Park on his debut, but had to wait some time before he was assured of a regular place in the side. A strong-tackling full-back, Lyall made 21 appearances in 1960–61, in what he later described as, 'my only good season as a player'. Ted Fenton took the young defender under his wing and the youngster responded to his manager's encouragement. Lyall later described Fenton as, 'an excellent trainer…an innovator who tried to vary training routines'.

But serious injury severely disrupted young Lyall's progress. Frustratingly, John spent the next three seasons in and out of the side, mostly due to recurrent cruciate knee problems. In 1964, following two major operations, the troublesome knee began to deteriorate and was finally diagnosed as inoperable. Having played just 35 games for the club, Lyall was forced to retire and his playing career was over at the tender age of 23. It was a consolation to Lyall that he had the opportunity to play in West Ham's defence alongside the young Bobby Moore. The two young footballers had grown up together and become great friends. For Lyall, Moore was 'imperious, aloof, commanding, composed and a hard trainer'. Moore would have been devastated by Lyall's enforced retirement, as was his new manager, Ron Greenwood.

In many ways this was a difficult time for the Lyall family. John's promising career in professional football was threatened with injury. At that time his parents must have wondered whether they had made the right decision. But John was a positive character throughout his life and was determined to secure a future in the game. He had also found real happiness in his private life. John and Yvonne had been at the same primary school together but never really became friends. They would meet every morning at the same Ilford bus stop, but, as John admitted later, he just could not bring himself to talk to her. Eventually, he plucked up courage by showing her a letter from the FA inviting him to play for England Youth – not that Yvonne was particularly impressed by John's wonderful news. His opening line – 'I'm playing for England tonight' – did not mean much to Yvonne, who was not a great football fan.

Like Tina Moore, Yvonne was a bright Essex girl who attended Clark's College in Ilford, before leaving to take up a job in the London Stock Exchange. Yvonne was one of three girls. Their father was a local builder who found peace and quiet when he retired to Holland-on-Sea out on the Essex coast. Dad was very strict with the girls, but Yvonne talks about him with great affection. She remembers spending the whole of one Saturday taking in a pair of slacks until they resembled fashionable Teddy girl trousers, only for dad to declare, 'you no need think you are going out in those', before throwing them in the dustbin. Yvonne's mum was from Walthamstow and one of nine children, a particularly large family, even by East London standards.

John and Yvonne became engaged on John's birthday in February 1958. They married in May 1961 and moved out to the then quiet Essex village of Abridge, where they paid just £2,775 for their first house together. Like many professional footballers, John had a summer job to supplement his modest wages. He worked as a plasterer off-season, while Yvonne stayed at home typing letters, often until late at night. The couple were careful with money and saved enough to buy their first car, a Morris Traveller. However, John continued to take the short bus journey to Grange Farm for training, leaving the car at home with Yvonne.

The Lyalls were a strong and resourceful young couple. Many young professionals would have been completely devastated by having their career cut short at such a young age. But Lyall showed great courage in the way he rebuilt his life. Such strength of character would stand him in good stead in his years as manager at West Ham and later Ipswich. During this most difficult time, West Ham showed what a great club they were back in the '60s. Everyone at Upton Park fully supported their injured young full-back, providing John with what would now be called a portfolio of jobs. In his autobiography (1989), Lyall recalls missing a game due to his father's illness, only to find at the end of the week that Ted Fenton paid him the full wage of £38, instead of the expected £14. The gesture showed how the club respected their unfortunate young full-back.

Unable to play or train, John filled his week working as a wages clerk, doing a bit of coaching at Stepney School (where he worked with a very young Trevor Brooking) and running the Hammers youth team. The keen and enthusiastic Lyall responded well to the responsibility and impressed his employers with his commitment and hard work. He was also granted a testimonial by the club in 1964, which raised the princely sum of £3,797. Cantwell, Dick, Musgrove, Woosnam and Terry Venables all played in the match, which was held on the Monday evening prior to the FA Cup Final against Preston. Later Greenwood used Lyall's injury to motivate his players in his team talk against Preston, while John kept himself busy organising the players' pool.

John learned a great deal from working with club trainer Bill Robinson and fully embraced the Cassetari café culture. Like Fenton, John was a keen cricketer as a youngster and the pair played regularly for Clayhall CC. He loved nothing more than to train with great club cricketers like Frank Rist, who played with Fenton for many years at Colchester

United. Like Syd Puddefoot, Bobby Moore and Geoff Hurst, Lyall caught the eye of Essex secretary Doug Insole playing for the Ilford district team and was invited to play for the county's Club & Ground side on a number of occasions.

The club were so impressed by their new part-time youth coach that, in 1967, they offered John the job on a full-time basis. He spent the next few years learning his trade under the expert tutelage of Ron Greenwood, whom he succeeded in September 1974. According to Yvonne Lyall, John idolised Greenwood, who could do no wrong in the young man's eyes. Shortly after his appointment as successor to Ted Fenton, Greenwood, sensing the Lyalls were extremely concerned about their future, quietly assured Yvonne, 'don't worry, we will look after you'. The new manager was as good as his word as he undertook the role of John's friend and mentor.

Lyall blossomed as a coach under Greenwood, contributing to his guru's tactical ideas like the famous near-post cross, richly exploited by Geoff Hurst in the 1966 World Cup. Martin Peters' signature drifting role behind Hurst and Clyde Best, forged on the training ground at Chadwell Heath by Greenwood and Lyall, brought the England midfield star a hatful of goals. In 1971 Greenwood recognised his prodigy's contribution to the club's progress and promoted Lyall to assistant manager. Within three years the star apprentice had succeeded his mentor as West Ham manager, who as the saying goes, 'moved upstairs'.

Following Greenwood's elevation to the post of director of football at Upton Park in 1974 and eventually to the England job, Lyall was formally appointed full-time manager. The new boss exceeded all expectations. Building on Greenwood's fine work, Lyall enjoyed 708 games in charge at West Ham. His record speaks for itself – two FA Cups, the Final of the European Cup-Winners' Cup, the Final of the League Cup and the Division Two Championship by a whacking 13 points. In 1985–86 he took West Ham to their highest ever League finish in the top flight.

Lyall was his own man and built his own team. He was a shrewd judge of footballers and in Phil Parkes and Ray Stewart he acquired two players of the very highest quality. Exciting European nights at the Boleyn, Wembley Cup Finals, promotion and three top 10 League finishes is a superb return by the Hammers' modest standards. No wonder the Ilford man was so popular at Upton Park. The club had handled the succession from Greenwood to Lyall superbly.

John's achievements at Upton Park did not go unnoticed and life may have turned out very differently had he not held fast to the moral standards that ruled his professional life. He had overcome the trauma of a potentially crippling knee injury which ended his playing career at the age of 23. Rather than lose himself in self-pity, John became one of the most successful managers of his generation. It was probably only a matter of time before the inevitable approach came.

One morning in June 1984, Yvonne took a call in the old farmhouse from their close friend, the journalist Dennis Signy. John was always happy to speak to an old friend, but this was no ordinary social call. Signy was very close to Jim Gregory, the chairman of Queen's Park Rangers, one of the most successful clubs at that time. Lyall knew that the QPR manager, Terry Venables, had recently accepted a fabulous offer to join Barcelona, but was completely shocked when Signy asked him if he would be prepared to talk to Gregory about the new managerial vacancy at Loftus Road.

West Ham had consolidated their position in Division One, finishing in the top 10 in the first three seasons following promotion. Lyall was ambitious to challenge the top clubs and had no wish to leave Upton Park. He was aware he still had one year left on his contract. The call from Signy threw Lyall into a state of shock, but he felt he had to listen to Gregory. He told Signy that QPR should take the official route and formally approach West Ham. After a long discussion with his manager, the Hammers' chairman, Mr Len Cearns, reluctantly gave QPR permission to speak to John.

Lyall had come to know and respect Jim Gregory through the transfers of Phil Parkes and Paul Goddard. He also knew that the longest-serving chairman in the Football League had rebuilt QPR from top to bottom and had proved his ambition for his club by signing England midfield star, Tony Currie. Gregory had real ambitions. What impressed Lyall was that the QPR chairman had successfully managed the difficult job of rebuilding Loftus Road while at the same time maintaining high playing standards – something that West Ham failed to do in the 1990s. Gregory was determined for QPR to be able to compete with top clubs like Liverpool, Everton and Nottingham Forest.

A meeting was arranged and John arrived at Gregory's house and the QPR chairman offered him the job on the spot. If he accepted the offer, John would be £200,000 a year better off and in the same pay bracket as top managers Brian Clough and Ron Atkinson. Gregory made Lyall's decision even harder by offering a five-year contract, plus a new Jaguar and the house with a lake that John had long coveted. The QPR chairman piled on the pressure. John could bring his own staff and have total freedom on all playing matters, including new signings. Back at Upton Park, John worked with Eddie Bailey, Mick McGiven, Ronnie Boyce and Tony Carr. He decided he would take McGiven and Bailey, arguing that Carr and Boyce should stay with their beloved West Ham.

Lyall was now in a real dilemma. He discussed the offer at length with Yvonne, who John knew had missed out on a normal family life. The QPR job would give the family financial security and allow John to retire early. They would be made for life. West Ham had always treated him wonderfully and until Gregory's intervention he had never thought about leaving the club he had served so loyally since the mid-1950s. But this time Lyall let his head rule his heart and accepted QPR's proposal. He was torn, but John put his family first.

Then came the blow from which Lyall never fully recovered. The West Ham board refused to let him go. He had to stay and serve out his contract. Later we learn that Cearns demanded £150,000 in compensation from QPR and briefly threatened illegal approach proceedings. John was devastated, but refused to become a commodity in an auction and eventually, with clenched teeth, he reluctantly turned down Gregory's generous offer. Lyall had been at West Ham for 29 years and was the longest-serving manager in Division One, behind Lawrie McMenemy. Frustrated, QPR turned to Alan Mullery and when that did not work out, appointed coach Frank Sibley as stand-in manager. There were later rumours that John would go to Spurs, before they appointed Peter Shreeves. But, in the end, following some bitter wrangling with chairman Cearns, Lyall signed a four-year contract with West Ham and the QPR episode was over.

During this period of managerial uncertainty, the team's form suffered. But once matters were settled they soon improved and enjoyed a good run in the FA Cup, before losing in the sixth round to a Norman Whiteside-inspired Manchester United. Lyall's team was weakened by the retirement of Trevor Brooking and a serious knee injury to Alan Devonshire. The emergence of the elegant Alan Dickens and the young Paul Allen bolstered the midfield. The side was further strengthened by the young and prolific Tony Cottee, Paul Goddard from QPR and the uncompromising Scottish international full-back, Ray Stewart. With Frank McAvennie and Mark Ward added to the side, Lyall was ready for an assault on the League title. Despite his disappointment over the QPR job, John continued to work tirelessly for the Hammers. He was the energy behind the new gymnasium at Chadwell Heath, as he sought to improve the club's outmoded training facilities.

But John Lyall never forgot the way he was treated by the West Ham board over the Gregory affair and gradually distanced himself from the club's owners. He no longer spent time with board members after matches, preferring the company of his players and friends in the press. As Yvonne recently observed, distancing himself from the board did not help John in 1989, when he needed help most. But he knew that the QPR offer was a lost opportunity.

Life goes on and Lyall got on with the job. Despite his quietly-spoken and gentlemanly demeanour, John Lyall was no pushover. He introduced some much-needed steel to the team that was lacking in the Greenwood era. But with players of the quality of Alvin Martin, Goddard and David Cross, Lyall had no need to ditch the club's proud tradition of playing exciting, pulse-raising, attacking football.

Lyall continued to show he cared about the Hammers and despite the QPR rumours, the Upton Park faithful adored him. He rebuilt the decent Bonds, Brooking and Lampard side into one of the best ever seen at Upton Park. John Lyall's 'boys of '86' are the stuff of Hammers legend. For the record the team included Phil Parkes, Ray Stewart, Tony Gale,

Neil Orr, George Parris, Steve Walford, Alan Dickens, Alan Devonshire, Mark Ward, Frank McAvennie, Tony Cottee, and skipper, Alvin Martin. Cottee and McAvennie scored 46 goals between them and Lyall's side won 26 out of their 42 games – the same number as the teams ahead of them, Everton and Liverpool.

Lyall had bounced back from his disappointments. His team of 1985–86 enjoyed one of the most impressive seasons in the club's history, finishing third behind Liverpool and Everton. However, this proved to be the high point as the Hammers fell away the following season, finishing in 15th place in Division One. The fans were despairing and it would have been deeply frustrating for Lyall to see Everton and Liverpool again finish in the top two places that season.

The team of 1986 was a close-knit group of players who responded to their manager's coaching methods and his subtle man management. But once again West Ham proved their credentials as a selling club, when both parts of the goalscoring machine of McAvennie and Cottee were shipped out, the latter for a record British transfer fee. Although he returned to Upton Park for a second spell, the Hammers missed Cottee's goals. In 1988 Lyall brought Arsenal's Liam Brady to the Boleyn to inject some much-needed experience into the midfield. But the elegant Irish veteran failed to save the Hammers from relegation and the club returned to its second home in Division Two – a rare moment of failure in Lyall's long career.

Through the 1980s, with John an established manager, the Lyall family began to prosper. They sold their Abridge home of 23 years and moved to Stanford Rivers, just outside the little Essex town of Ongar, where they acquired the handsome Old Rectory in Stanford Rivers. Their only son, Murray, was born and Yvonne was happy with her friends and family around her. John's professional life was going from strength to strength and the family saw no reason to move from their lovely Essex home. That was, until West Ham dropped their bombshell.

Up until 1989, with just five managers throughout most of their history, West Ham had resisted the temptation of sacking their manager at the earliest opportunity. But under the pressures of the modern game the inevitable happened. One Friday morning in the June following the relegation season, Yvonne took a call at their Ongar home from chairman Len Cearns. John was out and was asked to contact his chairman the following Monday, after Cearns had returned from his weekend at the family's country retreat at Aldeburgh. On the Monday morning Lyall was summoned to Cearns' luxury Chigwell villa and brutally sacked on the spot. John had been busy tying up the loose ends of the players' contracts for the following season, while looking forward to a much-needed break with his family. Cearns was well prepared and presented John with a deal. The club was offering a testimonial match and a lump sum. Lyall told his chairman what he could do with his deal – 'If you think the fans are going to pay for my pension out of their own pockets, you've

A smiling John Lyall at Upton Park.

got another think coming,' was his angry response. 'I am keeping the car, just in case you were going to ask for it back,' Lyall told his chairman, waving the keys of the club Jaguar in his face, 'and you can write that in your deal.'

When Yvonne returned home on Monday afternoon she spotted John's car in the driveway. 'Hello,' she said, 'lovely to see you home so early.' John replied, 'I've been sacked Von. I think I'll spend the afternoon cleaning those gutters.' Mick McGiven collected John's personal possessions from the ground and the most successful manager in West Ham's history became an unemployment statistic.

The fans were horrified – West Ham just did not behave like this, we are a family club. The club issued a terse 70-word statement announcing they had sacked the man who had served the club as player, coach and manager for 34 years. The dependable Lyall was deeply shocked by the club's crass behaviour and later wrote in his autobiography, 'You tend to look at other factors…success in the FA Cup…loyalty…long service…I couldn't say I noticed much sympathy, reluctance or any other emotion as he terminated my 34 years at the club. There was no personal acknowledgement or thanks from Mr Len.'

Lyall was awarded an *ex gratia* payment of £100,000 and left in what must have been very difficult personal circumstances. He was extremely popular at Upton Park and at the training ground. Not just with the players, but the car park attendants, ground staff and even the postman. He never forgot his roots and ensured that everybody visiting Chadwell Heath got a warm welcome and a cup of tea.

Lyall took a five-month break which he spent working on his house and garden. John was accomplished at DIY and loved nothing more than fixing things around the house. Although he was always a positive person and must have been bitterly disappointed, he retained a sense of perspective. When he first became a manager, he had told Yvonne he intended to retire when he was 55 – no lifelong Sir Alex Ferguson-type commitment for John Lyall. The now ex-West Ham manager knew that he owed Yvonne a long retirement. He was aware that, although professional football had given the family a comfortable and interesting life, for long periods Yvonne was alone at home. John was only too aware of the time pressures on football managers – the after-match media circus, the player needing a consoling word, foreign travel and so on. John never once told Yvonne what time he would be home from work, because he knew some club matters would make him late. Neither did Yvonne go to matches – 'I wouldn't go to work with him if he worked in a bank', was her reasoning. Fortunately, the Lyalls' marriage was an unusually strong one and able to withstand the pressures of modern professional football. Others were not so lucky.

During this period of enforced rest, John did some scouting for Bobby Robson's England side and accepted a part-time coaching job at Tottenham with his old friend Terry Venables. Then later that year, completely out of the blue, the Ipswich chairman, John Cobbold, called John at home and offered him the manager's job at Portman Road. He discussed the offer at length with Yvonne, who knew if John took the job it would mean selling the Old Rectory at Abridge, where they were close to friends and family. Ipswich Town was a well-supported family club and had been in the Cobbold family for generations. If John accepted the Ipswich offer he would join a distinguished list of Ipswich managers, including Sir Alf Ramsey and Sir Bobby Robson. He also knew that the Cobbolds were a very well-respected Suffolk family. It was the perfect job for John Lyall.

John accepted the Ipswich offer and the couple sold the Old Rectory and bought a beautiful farmhouse up the A12 near Colchester. John Lyall was the new Ipswich manager. The old West Ham boss finally built the lake he had always wanted and John and Yvonne were able to enjoy many happy hours fishing together deep in the tranquillity of the Suffolk countryside, their peace occasionally disrupted by the grandchildren pleading for John to join them in a lively kick-about. The Lyalls' son Murray, whose family had also decamped to Suffolk, was a carpenter by trade and is now a successful construction manager. With John's enthusiastic help he lovingly restored the old farm and its grounds. The move to Suffolk was a great success, although Yvonne missed the friends she had made at their old house in Essex.

John enjoyed a few successful years as manager at Portman Road. The club won promotion to the newly-formed Premier League in 1992 and John enjoyed a good relationship with the fans and the board of directors. He kept to his philosophy of playing open, attacking football that he had acquired under Ted Fenton and Ron Greenwood. I do not expect John gave West Ham a moment's thought when he went about his work at Ipswich – he was far too professional to harbour regrets. He thoroughly enjoyed his time with his new club, but was determined to keep his promise to retire from professional football at the age of 55. With Ipswich struggling in the top flight on their shoestring budget, John agreed to become director of football, leaving Mick McGiven to run the day-to-day affairs of the club. In December 1994 John kept his promise to Yvonne and retired to his Suffolk home, never to return to professional football. John was now able to repay the debt he owed to his loyal family. After 40 years of long hours, weeks away from home and constant media attention, John Lyall was finished with the game he loved so much. He had simply had enough.

The couple had some wonderful memories of their time in football. Yvonne recently recalled that John always enjoyed a very good relationship with the press. Among his personal friends were Vic Railton, Reg Drury, Bernard Joy and Peter Lorenzo – all very distinguished football journalists. They trusted John and knew that if there was a story they would be the first to hear. Yvonne remembers Bernard Joy's special invitation dinner parties with great affection. It was an honour to be invited to Joy's soirèes in the company of Bill Nicholson, Jimmy Hill, Alex Stock and Sir Stanley Rous and their wives, where Chatham House rules always applied. Yvonne recalls how the Nicholsons lived all their married life in their house in White Hart Lane where Bill had an allotment. How things have changed!

The Lyalls enjoyed 10 years of peaceful retirement together, fishing and working on their farm. With grandchildren Scott, Charlie and Sam on their doorstep to keep John fit and active, the couple were enjoying their well-earned rest, until tragedy struck. John and Yvonne had spent the morning shopping and the afternoon pottering in the garden with Murray and their grandsons. That evening Yvonne decided to go up early, leaving John downstairs watching football in his favourite chair. Yvonne was suddenly disturbed by what she has described as a 'terrible noise'. Thinking intruders had entered the house, she rushed downstairs only to find John collapsed in his chair. Yvonne did all she could and the paramedics arrived within a few minutes. They worked furiously to save John's life, but to no avail. Like his father before him, John had suffered a major heart attack and died within minutes.

Yvonne had the awful task of breaking the tragic news to Murray, his wife Samantha and the boys. They took it badly. The boys were inconsolable and were kept away from school for days. Murray took two months' leave and threw himself into organising the funeral and memorial service, taking care of his mother and dealing with all the complex and upsetting legal business which follows the sudden death of a parent. Yvonne could not go back into the house and stayed with Murray and his family for a few weeks before she felt able to return.

The news of John's death spread quickly across the world of football. Murray and Samantha were desperate to contact the rest of the family before they heard the terrible news on the radio or television. Members of John's great West Ham team of the 1980s called to offer their condolences, as did all John's old friends in the game. West Ham fans travelled up to Ipswich to drape claret and blue shirts on the entrance gates at Portman Road, while down in the East End of London, Hammers fans paid their own quiet tributes at Upton Park. Yvonne has kept the claret and blue shirts, many carrying heart-felt messages, left at the Portman Road gates as a reminder of the great affection in which her husband was held at both clubs.

The family were overwhelmed by the response to John's death. When Ron Greenwood died in February 2006, just two months before John, his family decided on a very quiet, family service. But Yvonne felt she could not exclude ex-players and colleagues who desperately wanted to pay their respects to their great friend. The family agreed on a cremation, followed two months later by a memorial service at St Mary-le-Tower in

Ipswich. Among those who attended the funeral were Trevor Brooking, Ray Stewart, Patsy Holland – who placed a letter in the coffin – and Sir Alex Ferguson. Ferguson spoke at the service, which must have meant a great deal to the family. Mark Ward, the Hammers' former winger, sent flowers from his prison cell, while Terry Venables and Billy Bonds proved reliable sources of comfort for the family. John's ashes were placed in the local church at Tattingstone, a short walk from the Lyall home.

Yvonne continues to receive regular calls from Billy Bonds and Phil Parkes, while David Cross and Chris Kiwomya send flowers, every year on the anniversary of John's death, to the little Suffolk church. She is also comforted by the knowledge that the likes of Alan Devonshire and Patsy Holland are only a telephone call away.

Yvonne and her family still live at their Suffolk farm and keep in regular contact with old friends from West Ham and Ipswich, including Jean Musgrove, Susan Dick and Vic Keeble. One of Yvonne's closest friends is Pat Godbolt, who worked with nine managers in her time as the secretary at Ipswich Town. But for Yvonne and the family, the loss of John remains extremely hard to bear. Christmas and anniversaries have a particular poignancy. The Lyalls were a close-knit family. John, Yvonne, Murray, Samantha and the kids decamped to Center Parcs for Christmas every year after John retired and kept going for four years after he died. The close proximity of her grandchildren must be a great source of comfort to Yvonne. Young Charlie, in particular, is a great help around the grounds, driving the tractor and generally keeping things under control.

The Lyalls grew up on the East London and Essex border in the 1950s and retained many of the traditional family values of the period. For years the couple attended an evening class in Bury St Edmunds – a 60-mile round trip from their home in Tattingstone. John learnt upholstery, while Yvonne sat at the other end of the room learning to make curtains. John was the only man in the class, a source of great delight to his female classmates. The couple spent many of their winter evenings in the workshop at the top of the Suffolk house, Von running up curtains and John upholstering one of the many chairs now scattered around the home. It is unlikely that today's high profile managers, under constant media glare, would have either the time or inclination to attend an evening class in upholstery, or anything else.

On Friday 9 May 2008, the Lyall family organised a testimonial dinner at Upton Park to honour the memories and achievements of West Ham's two greatest managers, Ron Greenwood and John Lyall. Between them Ron and John ran West Ham from 1961 to 1989, although John had been at the club since 1955. The pair had a father and son relationship and together created the famous 'West Ham way'. The event was attended by players, colleagues and friends and raised a considerable sum for charity. The money went to the Alzheimer's Society and Lawford Junior Football Club in Suffolk where John's grandsons play their football.

John Lyall's death created a hole at the heart of West Ham that has never been filled. A minute's silence was held in his honour before the FA Cup semi-final against Middlesbrough. The fans, who understood what he achieved at the club, sang 'John Lyall's claret and blue army' throughout the 60 seconds. It was entirely appropriate that the fans broke the silence. The West Ham players paid their own tribute to the club's most successful manager that day, winning 1–0 to reach the FA Cup Final for the first time since Lyall's team beat Arsenal in 1980.

The *Guardian*'s Julie Welch wrote this moving tribute:

> *The former West Ham United and Ipswich Town manager John Lyall, who has died of a heart attack aged 66, was an affable man, an almost complete contrast to the brooding, preening, haunted characters in charge of teams today. His death comes two months after that of his mentor Ron Greenwood (obituary, February 10), whom he succeeded as manager in 1974.*

West Ham fans will always remember John Lyall for his integrity, leadership and inspirational coaching. His death was truly the end of an era. On 5 December 2007 a blue plaque was erected at the Boleyn by the Heritage Foundation in memory of Lyall's contribution to the history of this great old East London club. The plaque is placed on the left-hand side of the main entrance to the ground in Green Street. To the right of the entrance are memorial plaques for Ron Greenwood and Bobby Moore. Two years later, after an unseemly delay, West Ham at last provided their own fitting tribute to their former manager when they renamed the main gates at Upton Park the John Lyall Gates.

In an emotional unveiling ceremony attended by many of Lyall's players, including Sir Trevor Brooking, Ray Stewart, Alan Devonshire, Tony Cottee and many others, the most moving tribute came from Lyall's son Murray, who admitted: 'Dad didn't like a fuss and would probably be squirming a bit with all this attention on him, but also deep down, very proud as all of us are. It was an emotional but fantastic day.'

There is no question that West Ham took their time to provide a permanent tribute to John Lyall, despite continual pressure from friends and family. Tony Cottee and Frank Lampard Snr, among others, helped to convince the club that they should show some respect to their tradition. David Gold and David Sullivan, the new owners, are West Ham fans and will understand the way the fans feel about their club and the achievements of its pioneers. It is very disappointing then to learn of the club's recent treatment of the Lyall family and one of John's former colleagues, physiotherapist Rob Jenkins.

The club decided to withdraw the privileges awarded to the Lyall and Greenwood families, a crass and thoughtless decision. This tactless act is well documented in the fanzine *EX*. Editor Tony McDonald writes, 'Both families had received complimentary directors' box tickets but, following the takeover by David Sullivan and David Gold – who have made great play of their credentials as West Ham fans – last season, that privilege was downgraded to a pair of season tickets.' (*EX* magazine No. 56)

In a further example of insensitivity the club failed to inform the families of their decision. McDonald explains: 'The families only learned that these too had been taken away when calling the club in early August to ask what the arrangements would be for the new season.'

Murray Lyall responded to this act of corporate callousness with commendable restraint. 'I fully appreciate the financial plight of the club and can understand the reasoning why the season tickets have been withdrawn…but what I do find unacceptable is that no one in authority had the decency to contact us and explain.'

Murray's wife Samantha called the club four times prior to the 2010–11 season, before the operations director finally broke the bad news that the season tickets had been withdrawn with immediate effect. In a further act of insensitivity, Samantha was offered tickets at a reduced price. In effect the decision meant that John Lyall's son and grandson were regarded as just another couple of fans and not the family of one of the most respected and successful managers in West Ham's long history.

We also know that Murray Lyall received a telephone call from the club asking if he would like to pay £175 for corporate hospitality tickets, for an event to be held in the lounge named after his father. As Tony McDonald wrote in his article entitled *What Have We Become* – 'you couldn't make it up could you?'

Yvonne Lyall expressed her own thoughts to *EX* magazine. 'After my husband's 34 years' loyal service to the club in a playing, coaching and managerial capacity, I feel my family should have been shown greater respect and understanding given our tragic loss four years ago and the legacy he left behind.'

Yvonne was more forthright when I spoke to her recently about the club charging Murray for corporate entertainment events in the John Lyall Lounge. 'What an insult', was her emotional reply.

Ron Greenwood and John Lyall were East End royalty. West Ham's behaviour towards their families was inexcusable. Did owners Gold and Sullivan sanction such insensitive policy-making? Probably not. It is more likely the decision was taken by one of the new corporate club functionaries who know about balance sheets, but nothing about the club's traditions or its history. Of course, Gold and Sullivan and CEO Karren Brady should have made it their business to know. After all, the club trades on its name as a family club, a reputation created by the likes of Greenwood, Lyall and Rob Jenkins.

Fans will insist that the Lyall Gates are taken down and re-erected at the new Olympic Stadium to ensure John's memory endures. They will be encouraged to have read in the *Sun* newspaper that Ms Brady agrees: 'West Ham fans will be able to pass through the John Lyall Gates as they approach the new stadium.'

A blue plaque dedicated to the memory of John Lyall at Upton Park.

Brian Clough once said, 'what the hell do directors know about football?'. It is to be hoped that the regrettable business over West Ham providing a fitting tribute to their great manager is now settled and in the process the club has learned something about the value of its traditions and heritage.

It is not difficult to assess John Lyall's contribution to the history of West Ham United. With grace and dignity he created one of the most respected teams in Europe. Younger supporters can only look back in wonder at his achievements. With Ron Greenwood and Bobby Moore, John Lyall created a brand that today's so-called business gurus can only dream about.

Let us leave the last word on the great man to three legends of football.

Club legend, Tony Gale, wrote: 'John was a man of strong morals, both on and off the pitch and I don't know of any player who had a bad word to say about him.' (West Ham official programme, 28 April 2006)

Sir Trevor Brooking described his old manager as a 'modest man and unbelievable coach' and Sir Bobby Robson said of his old friend, 'He (is) a very knowledgeable and well-informed manager and one of the best readers of the game that I know.'

John Lyall would have made old Arnold Hills a very proud man.

Two old favourites...

Football is all about personal opinions and I am sure every Hammers fan could come up with a different set of favourite players. But most would agree those featured here are the very best West Ham players up to 1960. Of course, some very good players and servants of the club have inevitably been left on the cutting room floor. John Bond, now sadly very ill, Mike Grice and Andy Malcolm are just a few of the old names that could have easily been included.

Non-playing staff have also made a contribution to Hammers' history in the early days. Legendary chief scout Wally St Pier, who unearthed some rare East London football diamonds and Tony Carr, who remains in charge of the renowned West Ham academy, have become as celebrated at Upton Park as many of the great players mentioned in this book. But there are two vintage Hammers that do deserve more than a simple name-check.

Tom Robinson was born in Poplar in 1849 and when Arnold Hills decided to set up his own works football team, Robinson was taken on as coach. The local man had previously worked for Castle Swifts and was a well-known figure in East End sporting circles. At the Memorial Grounds he trained a whole range of local athletes, including cyclists, boxers and footballers. He could be regularly seen in his uniform of cloth cap and roll-neck sweater leading training runs along the Beckton Road. But Tom was no diehard traditionalist. On the Monday following a match, he would take the players for a brisk walk to loosen aching joints – what modern coaches would today call a warm-down.

Ironworks training took place on Tuesday and Thursday nights in a gas-lit room at Trinity Church School in the Barking Road. As with most trainers at the time, Robinson led his players through a set of army physical training exercises using punchballs and weights to strengthen the upper body. Little time was spent on working with the ball, a tradition that continued at the club until the late 1950s, when Malcolm Allison took it upon himself to introduce some much-needed modern training techniques. Despite his strict discipline and backbreaking training regime, Robinson was popular with the players and often took them back to his Benledi Street home for a hearty, full English breakfast.

In 1898, Robinson lost his job as the Ironmakers' trainer to Jack Ratcliffe. But he had physical education in his blood and continued to work with young athletes in the area. In 1904, Syd King realised he had made a mistake in releasing the Poplar man and invited Tom to join the newly-established West Ham United as their principal trainer. Robinson served the club for a further eight years before he retired in 1912.

Tom Robinson moved effortlessly from Castle Swifts, who he joined in the 1880s, to Thames Ironworks and finally West Ham United. Old Arnold Hills had the greatest respect for Robinson's commitment to local young people. With his characteristic drooping moustache, he was a pioneer for the hundreds of East London enthusiasts who followed the wonderful example set by the club's first serious coach.

The Hammers showed their appreciation for their long-serving trainer by granting old Tom a testimonial match at Upton Park against West London rivals Queen's Park Rangers. It was a fitting tribute.

Harry Hooper was born in Pittingham, County Durham on 14 June 1933 and showed early promise as a lively winger for his local club, Hilton Colliery. Hooper was brought to West Ham as a 17-year-old by his father Harry Snr, who in 1950 had been appointed first-team coach at Upton Park. Young Hooper went on to make 119 appearances, scoring a total of 39 goals. The young outside-right made his debut for the Hammers against Burnley on 3 February 1951. The team that day included Malcolm Allison, Jimmy Andrews, Ernie Gregory and Frank O'Farrell. He was in exulted West Ham company, but Hooper was a confident youngster and in his first season at the club played in 11 games and scored a modest three goals. He certainly played well enough to impress his watching manager, Ted Fenton. But Hooper had to wait until the 1953–54 season to secure a regular place in the side. By this time the outside-right had become a fans' favourite with his pace and wonderful close control. How the Hammers fans love a good winger. Blows & Hogg wrote that, 'Harry Hooper…who patrolled down the right touchline displaying sublime skills and inventiveness which hadn't been seen at Upton Park since the pre-war days…'

Hooper made a difference to the West Ham side. In the 1954–55 season the Hammers finished eighth in Division One, with Harry finishing the season as second-top scorer with 13 League and Cup goals. But by far his best season for the club was 1955–56. In a team which had now included John Bond, Ken Brown and Malcolm Musgrove, Hooper scored 15 goals in 30 League games. His reputation as a winger who could destroy the best defences was growing and he soon caught the eye of the England selectors. Hooper became the first Hammer to be selected for the England Under-23 side when he appeared in the match against Italy at Stamford Bridge. The Hammers winger scored twice in England's 5-2 victory and his performance earned him a place in the England B team. He played six times for the B side between 1954 and 1957 and was selected as a reserve for England's squad for the 1954 World Cup in Switzerland. Unfortunately, some say unfairly, he was one of the five players left on standby by Walter Winterbottom. Although he played twice for the Football League representative side and once for a London XI, Hooper never won a full international cap. Like Malcolm Musgrove, Harry had to compete for his England place with the likes of Stanley Matthews and Tom Finney.

Hooper's outstanding performances at Upton Park were bound to attract the attention of bigger clubs. And few were bigger or more famous than Wolverhampton Wanderers. The West Ham fans were desperate to keep their most exciting player, who delighted the Chicken Run with his dazzling runs towards the North Bank. However, Fenton always had an eye for business and Hooper was dispatched to Wolves for a record fee for a winger of £25,000. Hooper's move to the Black Country in 1956 caused almost as much uproar among the fans as Puddefoot's sale to Falkirk back in the 1930s. They accused the club of lacking ambition and acting as a breeding ground for the top clubs. Hooper later revealed that he had not wanted the move and would have been perfectly happy to stay at the Boleyn where his career was developing very nicely:

> *The truth is I never wanted to leave West Ham. I explained to Ted [Fenton] that I didn't want to go but he said there was nothing he could do – the club needed the money because the school in Castle Street wanted their land back, which was then serving as the main entrance to the ground on Green Street. The money received from Wolves paid for the current main entrance which was completed in time for the club's promotion in 1958.*
> (Blows and Hogg, 2000)

Hooper's reluctance to leave Upton Park may have contributed to his disappointing form at Molineux, despite being the club's leading scorer in his first season. An impressive 19 goals in 39 League games, in a forward line that included England star forward, Johnny Hancocks, Jimmy Mullen and Peter Broadbent, was no mean achievement for the ex-Hammers flyer. Wolves manager Stan Cullis was effusive in his praise: 'Hooper was fast, direct, able to play on either wing and was both accurate and powerful in his use of the ball with either foot. In short, he was an ideal winger.'

But he began to struggle at his new club and Cullis eventually sold Hooper to local rivals Birmingham City, for a fee of £20,000. Despite appreciating Hooper's ability, his new manager, a strict disciplinarian, was not impressed by the former Chicken Run idol's reluctance to settle at Wolves. Cullis argued that, 'At Molineux, Hooper found it extremely difficult to adapt himself to our style. He played several outstanding games for us but there was no doubt that he did not carry out our tactical principles to the extent I considered was essential.'

For West Ham fans, the Wolves manager's words were simply code for 'Cullis failed to get the best out of the best winger in the country'. But Hooper was far happier at St Andrew's where he stayed for three seasons, scoring 34 goals in 105 games and gaining a runners'-up medal in the 1960 Fairs Cup. In September 1960 Harry left Birmingham and returned to his native north-east with Sunderland, this time for a fee of £18,000. The winger, despite inevitably slowing down late in his career, still commanded a decent price. He left Sunderland in 1962 and spent a few season in non-League football ending up at Heanor Town, his last club before he finally retired from the game.

Harry Hooper returned to Upton Park recently and talked fondly of his time at West Ham. He was certainly a favourite of the fans as one of them testified when the flying winger was sold to Wolves: 'I remember almost crying when we sold Hooper, who was my favourite player.'

Tom Robinson and Harry Hooper, along with the Hammers pioneers featured in this book, represent the very best of this great football club. It is the fervent wish of every Irons follower that the club should continue to adhere to its traditions, including developing local young players and playing exciting, attacking football. These things are the very essence of West Ham United.

Last thoughts...

The reputation of the original West Ham academy of football took over 100 years to build. The present guardians of West Ham United need to respect and protect this tradition, not fritter away West Ham's lifeblood on the altar of business. Without its special values West Ham is just another football club, probably languishing in the lower divisions rather than sitting proudly in the top half of the Premier League where it belongs. The 2010–11 season was one one of the most wretched in living memory.

On 15 May 2011 Hammers' fans travelled to Wigan's DW Stadium for the penultimate game of the season, more in hope than expectation. They had seen their team lose five of their previous six matches, a depressing run which left them rooted at the foot of the table. Under manager Avram Grant, the Irons had been in the bottom three all season after losing their first four games. The Wigan match began with the travelling Hammers fans in fine voice with 'Bubbles' drowning out the home support. The home side were themselves deep in the relegation mire and their fans were understandably nervous. The away supporters' passionate loyalty was rewarded when Demba Ba put the Irons ahead in the 15th minute. When he scored again in the 26th minute, they began to dream of an unlikely great escape. But the Irons' shambles of a defence destroyed the dream in minutes. Wigan scored three times in the second half, dashing the claret and blue travelling army's faint hopes of three points and another season in the Premier League. By 5.00pm that day West Ham were relegated.

Grant took the club down in his first season at the club. His appointment was a mistake, with little thought given to the Israeli's less than impressive managerial record. As Valon Behrami said, 'The players loved Zola and were deeply shocked when he left, and they didn't want Grant.'

Club chairman David Gold admitted the board had made a mistake in appointing Avram Grant. The new regime may have business acumen and understand how to make money, but they are learning that running a Premier League outfit like West Ham, with its fiercely loyal supporters, is not like selling popular magazines – it is a hundred times more complicated.

Grant was sacked in the tunnel shortly after the final whistle at the Wigan match. He probably deserved it, but the manner of his dismissal says a great deal about the way the business of professional football is conducted. CEO Karren Brady did a fine job in securing the Olympic Stadium, but failed to keep the Hammers in the Premiership. The move to

Stratford, something the fans should delight in, has become an embarrassment. 'Olympic Stadium…you're having a laugh' will ring round every Championship ground in the 2011–12 season and beyond.

Hammers fans will hope that the board will learn from the hasty dismissals of Gianfranco Zola and Steve Clarke, Grant's appointment and the botched attempt to secure Martin O'Neill as Grant's replacement. In fairness to Gold and Sullivan, they inherited a business in financial meltdown and have invested millions of pounds of their own money into the club. They cannot continue to do this indefinitely and relegation will renew speculation about the club's future.

On 1 June 2011 West Ham announced that Sam Allardyce had been appointed the club's new manager. It is a good appointment. Allardyce is not in the cerebral tradition of Greenwood and Lyall, nor is he a ducker and diver in the Fenton and Redknapp mode. He is highly professional, extremely thorough and well versed in modern coaching methods. Allardyce is also an excellent motivator and knows what it takes to get West Ham back into the Premier League. He has appointed Kevin Nolan, the club's excellent new summer signing from Newcastle, as his captain. The fans will give Grant's successor a cautious welcome, but undoubtedly feel a tinge of excitement. They will get behind their team as ever – the fans are the one constant factor in the whole sorry mess.

In reality, West Ham United fans have enjoyed just five periods of success in the history of their club – five outstanding teams in over 100 years. Syd King's team of the 1920s, Ted Fenton's promotion-winning side of the late 1950s, Ron Greenwood's triumphant team of the mid-1960s, and John Lyall's 'boys of '86'. The fans have also have witnessed long barren periods, like 2010–11, when it was difficult to see where the next win was coming from. Few clubs have experienced such extreme emotions – so many highs and so many lows. The fans will fervently hope Sam Allardyce will help them turn the corner.

With the club's finances in such a ruinous state, the new manager will need every ounce of his considerable experience if the Hammers are to regain their Premiership place over the next few seasons. The intolerable scenes at the club's 2011 end of season dinner illustrate how far standards have fallen at West Ham since the great days of Greenwood, Moore and Lyall. There is a football club to save. Gold, Sullivan, Brady and their staff have a colossal challenge confronting them.

The Championship is an opportunity to retreat from the demands of the Premier League and for the new manager to rebuild. Clubs like West Ham can only hope for mid-table comfort in the top flight and will always lose more matches than they win. The fans will stay positive in their new surroundings and not panic. They will hope West Ham's new manager and his board show similar resolve. The proud and distinguished traditions created by the early pioneers must not be squandered through lack of imagination or resolve.